FOUR VIEWS ON THE HISTORICAL ADAM

Books in the Counterpoints Series

Church Life

Exploring the Worship Spectrum: Six Views

Evaluating the Church Growth Movement: Five Views

Remarriage after Divorce in Today's Church: Three Views

Two Views on Women in Ministry

Understanding Four Views on Baptism

Understanding Four Views on the Lord's Supper

Who Runs the Church? Four Views on Church Government

Exploring Theology

Are Miraculous Gifts for Today? Four Views

Five Views on Apologetics

Five Views on Biblical Inerrancy

Five Views on Law and Gospel

Five Views on Sanctification

Four Views on Christian Spirituality

Four Views on Divine Providence

Four Views on Eternal Security

Four Views on Hell

Four Views on Moving Beyond the Bible to Theology

Four Views on Salvation in a Pluralistic World

Four Views on the Book of Revelation

Four Views on the Spectrum of Evangelicalism

How Jewish Is Christianity? Two Views on the Messianic Movement

Show Them No Mercy: Four Views on God and Canaanite Genocide

Three Views on Creation and Evolution

Three Views on Eastern Orthodoxy and Evangelicalism

Three Views on the Millennium and Beyond

Three Views on the New Testament Use of the Old Testament

Three Views on the Rapture

Two Views on Women in Ministry

FOUR VIEWS ON THE HISTORICAL ADAM

Denis O. Lamoureux

John H. Walton

C. John Collins

William D. Barrick

Gregory A. Boyd

Philip G. Ryken

Matthew Barrett and Ardel B. Caneday, general editors
Stanley N. Gundry, series editor

We want to hear from you. Please send your comments about this book to us in care of zreview@zondervan.com. Thank you.

ZONDERVAN

Four Views on the Historical Adam
Copyright © 2013 by Matthew Barrett and Ardel B. Caneday

This title is also available as a Zondervan ebook. Visit www.zondervan.com/ebooks.

Requests for information should be addressed to:

Zondervan, *Grand Rapids, Michigan* 49530

Library of Congress Cataloging-in-Publication Data

　　Four views on the historical Adam / Matthew Barrett and Ardel B. Caneday, general editors ; Denis O. Lamoureux, John H. Walton, C. John Collins, William D. Barrick ; Gregory A. Boyd, and Philip G. Ryken, pastoral reflection contributors ; Stanley Gundry, series editor.
　　　　p. cm. — (Counterpoints: Bible and theology)
　　ISBN 978-0-310-49927-5 (softcover)
　　1. Adam (Biblical figure) 2. Evangelicalism. 3. Reformed Church — Doctrines. I. Barrett, Matthew Michael, 1982- editor of compilation.
BS580.A4F68 2013
222'.11092 — dc23　　　　　　　　　　　　　　　　　　　　　　　　2013015377

Cover design: *Tammy Johnson*
Interior design: *Matthew Van Zomeren*

Printed in the United States of America

---

13 14 15 16 17 /DCI/ 20 19 18 17 16 15 14 13 12 11 10 9 8 7 6 5 4 3 2 1

CONTENTS

ABOUT THE EDITORS AND CONTRIBUTORS

Matthew Barrett (PhD, The Southern Baptist Theological Seminary) is Assistant Professor of Christian Studies at California Baptist University as well as the founder and executive editor of *Credo Magazine*. He is the author of several books, including *Salvation by Grace: The Case for Effectual Calling and Regeneration*.

Ardel B. Caneday (PhD, Trinity Evangelical Divinity School) is Professor of New Testament and Greek at the University of Northwestern—St. Paul in the Department of Biblical and Theological Studies, where he has taught for more than twenty years. He is the coauthor of *The Race Set Before Us: A Biblical Theology of Perseverance and Assurance*.

Denis O. Lamoureux (PhD, University of St Michael's College; PhD, DDS, University of Alberta) is Associate Professor of Science and Religion at St. Joseph's College in the University of Alberta, the first tenure-track position in Canada dedicated to teaching and research on the relationship between scientific discovery and Christian faith. He is the author of *Evolutionary Creation: A Christian Approach to Evolution*; *I Love Jesus and I Accept Evolution*; and *Darwinism Defeated? The Johnson-Lamoureux Debate on Biological Origins*.

John H. Walton (PhD, Hebrew Union College) is Professor of Old Testament at Wheaton College Graduate School. He is the author or coauthor of several books, including *Chronological and Background Charts of the Old Testament*; *Ancient Israelite Literature in Its Cultural Context*; *Covenant: God's Purpose, God's Plan*; *The IVP Bible Background Commentary: Old Testament*; and *A Survey of the Old Testament*.

C. John Collins (PhD, University of Liverpool) is Professor of Old Testament at Covenant Theological Seminary. Chair of the Old Testament translation committee for the English Standard Version, he is the author of *Genesis 1–4: A Linguistic, Literary, and Theological Commentary*; *The God of Miracles: An Exegetical Examination of God's Action in the World*;

Science and Faith: Friends or Foes? and *Did Adam and Eve Really Exist? Who They Were and Why You Should Care.*

William D. Barrick (ThD, Grace Theological Seminary) is Professor of Old Testament at The Master's Seminary. Previously an exegetical consultant for Bible translation projects in six languages with the Association of Baptists for World Evangelism, he has written or contributed to 24 books, including *Coming to Grips with Genesis* and a commentary on Genesis for Logos Bible Software. He has also written more than 120 periodical articles and book reviews.

Gregory A. Boyd (PhD, Princeton Theological Seminary) is senior pastor at Woodland Hills Church in St. Paul, Minnesota. Previously a professor of theology at Bethel University, he is the author of many books, including *Letters from a Skeptic; Repenting of Religion; Myth of a Christian Nation; God at War;* and *Satan and the Problem of Evil.*

Philip G. Ryken (PhD, University of Oxford) is President of Wheaton College in Wheaton, Illinois, and former senior minister of Tenth Presbyterian Church in Philadelphia. Several of his more than 30 books authored include *Loving the Way Jesus Loves* and expository commentaries on Exodus, Jeremiah, Luke, and other books of the Bible.

ABBREVIATIONS

ANE	Ancient Near East
AYBS	Anchor Yale Bible Series
BTCB	Brazos Theological Commentary on the Bible
CAD	*The Assyrian Dictionary of the Oriental Institute of the University of Chicago* Edited by E. Reiner et al. Chicago: University of Chicago Press, 1956–2011.
CANE	Civilization of the Ancient Near East
CBQMS	Catholic Biblical Quarterly Monograph Series
COS	*The Context of Scripture.* Edited by W. W. Hallo and K. L. Younger. 3 vols. Leiden: Brill, 1997.
GTJ	*Grace Theological Journal*
HCSB	Holman Christian Standard Bible
ICC	International Critical Commentary
ITC	International Theological Commentary
JANES	*Journal of the Ancient Near Eastern Society*
JSOT	*Journal for the Study of the Old Testament*
JSOTSup	Journal for the Study of the Old Testament Supplement Series
JTS	*Journal of Theological Studies*
LBI	Library of Biblical Interpretation
NAC	New American Commentary
NCBC	New Cambridge Bible Commentary
NET	New English Translation of the Bible
NICOT	New International Commentary on the Old Testament
NIVAC	NIV Application Commentary
NLT	New Living Translation of the Bible
NRSV	New Revised Standard Version of the Bible
OED	*Oxford English Dictionary*
SBJT	*Southern Baptist Journal of Theology*
SPCK	Society for Promoting Christian Knowledge
Sup	Supplement / Supplement Series

TDOT   *Theological Dictionary of the Old Testament.* Edited by G. T. Botterweck, H. Ringgren, and H.-J. Fabry. 15 vols. English ed. Grand Rapids: Eerdmans, 1974–2006.

THOTC   Two Horizons Old Testament Commentary

VT   *Vetus Testamentum*

VTSup   Vetus Testamentum Supplement Series

WBC   Word Biblical Commentary

WTJ   *Westminster Theological Journal*

ZIBBC   Zondervan Illustrated Bible Backgrounds Commentary

BIBLE VERSIONS

ADAM, TO BE OR NOT TO BE?

MATTHEW BARRETT AND ARDEL B. CANEDAY

The title of this book, *Four Views on the Historical Adam*, implies the presence of conflict among Christians. Who likes discord? No one relishes it. But in this present age is disagreement not inevitable? When we face controversy, one crucial factor is how we behave in what we have to say and how we respond to others with whom we disagree. The contemporary notion concerning public discourse that anyone who openly and plainly expresses disagreements with others engages in hate-speech is hardly a new concept. The apostle Paul, no stranger to conflict, recognized how controversy renders relationships tenuous when he inquired of the Galatians, "Have I now become your enemy by telling you the truth?" (Gal. 4:16).

Therefore, at the outset of this book it is fitting to ponder J. Gresham Machen's observations on controversy in the church:

> Our preaching, we are told, ought to be positive and not negative; we ought to present the truth, but ought not to attack error; we ought to avoid controversy and always seek peace....
>
> With regard to such a program, it may be said at least that if we hold to it we might just as well close up our New Testaments; for the New Testament is a controversial book almost from beginning to end. That is of course true with regard to the Epistles of Paul. They, at least, are full of argument and controversy—no question, certainly, can be raised about that. Even the hymn to Christian love in the thirteenth chapter of I Corinthians is an integral part of a great controversial passage with regard to a false use of the spiritual

gifts. That glorious hymn never would have been written if Paul had been averse to controversy and had sought peace at any price.[1]

Machen intimately knew alienation that comes with controversy.[2] But like the biblical authors, Machen understood that as important as peace and unity are, genuine peace and unity are never acquired at the cost of truth.

The point Machen makes concerning how controversy gave birth to much of the New Testament, especially the letters, can be extended to the creeds of the church. Throughout history, as significant theological disagreements have emerged, they have constrained the church to clarify beliefs that distinguish Christian beliefs from erroneous beliefs. Painful as conflict has been for the church, the convening of councils — beginning with the Jerusalem Council during the days of the apostles — to engage competing beliefs and to formulate expression of the common faith has been necessary. Wisdom constrains us to be grateful for Christians preceding us whose close and careful devotion to quests for truth brought about the great creeds that Christians universally confess.

Thus, when conflict emerges among Christians, our quest for truth must not avoid conflict but face it, even if this makes us uncomfortable. With this perspective in mind, we invite readers to engage each contributor of this book who gives expression to one of four perspectives on the historicity of Adam, a current point of dispute among evangelicals. The beliefs articulated by the four scholars conflict with one another at significant points, even though they all hold other important beliefs in common. We offer this respectful conversation among scholars, who present four distinct views followed by two pastors who offer divergent responses, to encourage thoughtful conversation on the issue of Adam's historicity, governed by belief that seeks to understand and thus to speak truth.

Some Historical Reflections

More than a century ago, even though various theories of evolution were already being considered among Christians, the publication of Charles Darwin's *On the Origin of the Species* in 1859 began to compel some

---

1. J. Gresham Machen, *Machen's Notes on Galatians*, ed. John H. Skilton (Philadelphia: P&R Publishing, 1973), 6.
2. See D. G. Hart, *Defending the Faith: J. Gresham Machen and the Crisis of Conservative Protestantism in Modern America* (Phillipsburg, NJ: P&R Publishing, 2003).

evangelicals to give those theories greater attention. Consequently, many within Protestant churches and institutions began to embrace the theory of evolution.

The Christian view of creation that Darwinism rivaled was not monolithic, even if the popular belief among Christians was that God created the cosmos approximately 4,000 years before the coming of the Christ. This belief preceded the publication of *The Annals of the World* by James Ussher, Archbishop of Armagh, who attempted to identify the time of creation's beginning with precision.[3] For example, both leading church Reformers Martin Luther and John Calvin believed that creation was not yet 6,000 years old and that God created all things within six twenty-four-hour days.[4] Calvin is thoroughly conversant with Augustine, agreeing with him at several points, but also rejecting his belief that God created all things instantaneously.[5]

However, in 1876 Thomas Huxley declared that the teaching of Darwin's theory of evolution was as assuredly verified scientifically as was Copernicus's theory of heliocentricity.[6] A majority of scientists had come to accept evolution, and increasing numbers of Christian leaders, such as James McCosh, president of Princeton College (1868–88), also embraced it.[7] The editor of a religious weekly publication in 1880 estimated that a fourth and perhaps even half the ministers in major evangelical denominations had abandoned belief in the historical Adam.[8]

Nevertheless, others resisted the trend by holding to the historicity of Adam and Eve while regarding humanity's antiquity a nontheological issue. Growing numbers of evangelicals did not agree with the Reformers' view concerning the nature and length of the six days of

---

3. James Ussher, *The Annals of the World* (London: E. Tyler for F. Crook and G. Bedell, 1658).

4. See Martin Luther, *Luther's Works: Lectures on Genesis*, ed. and trans. Jaroslav Pelikan (St. Louis: Concordia Publishing House, 1958), 3, 5–6. See also John Calvin, *Institutes of the Christian Religion*, trans. F. L. Battles (Philadelphia: Westminster, 1960), 1.14.1.

5. With reference to Augustine's teaching that God instantaneously created all things, see Calvin, *Institutes*, 1.14.2.

6. Ronald Numbers, *Darwinism Comes to America* (Cambridge, MA: Harvard University Press, 1999), 44.

7. See Fred G. Zaspel, "B. B. Warfield on Creation and Evolution," *Themelios* 35.2 (2010): 202. See also idem, "Princeton and Evolution," *The Confessional Presbyterian* 8 (2012): 93.

8. See Ronald Numbers, *The Creationists: The Evolution of Scientific Creationism* (Berkeley: University of California Press, 1992), 3.

creation, while at the same time they accepted the creation accounts of Genesis 1–2 as authoritative concerning the historicity of Adam and Eve, whether they believed God's act of creation was recent or ancient.[9] For example, B. B. Warfield, who as a youth had embraced Darwin's theory of evolution but later came to reject it,[10] states,

> The question of the antiquity of man has of itself no theological significance. It is to theology, as such, a matter of entire indifference how long man has existed on earth. It is only because of the contrast which has been drawn between the short period which seems to be allotted to human history in the Biblical narrative, and the tremendously long period which certain schools of scientific speculation have assigned to the duration of human life on earth, that theology has become interested in the topic at all.[11]

Warfield differs from many Christians today who, since the resurgence of six-day-young-earth creationism in the mid-twentieth century, find theological significance as to when God created all things. Yet, even though Warfield regarded the antiquity of humanity as of little theological concern, he viewed the origin and historicity of Adam differently. As he writes:

> The question of the unity of the human race differs from the question of its antiquity in that it is of indubitable theological importance. It is not merely that the Bible certainly teaches it, while, as we have sought to show, it has no teaching upon the antiquity of the race. It is also the postulate of the entire body of the Bible's teaching — of its doctrine of Sin and Redemption alike: so that the whole structure of the Bible's teaching, including all that we know as its doctrine of salvation, rests on it and implicates it.[12]

---

9. See B. B. Warfield, "Calvin's Doctrine of the Creation," *Princeton Theological Review* (1915): 190–255.

10. On the relationship between Warfield and McCosh, see Zaspel, "Princeton and Evolution," 95. Cf. Zaspel, "B. B. Warfield on Creation and Evolution," 198–211.

11. B. B. Warfield, "On the Antiquity and the Unity of the Human Race," *Princeton Theological Review*, 9.1 (1911): 1–2; idem, "On the Antiquity and the Unity of the Human Race," *Studies in Theology* (1932; Grand Rapids: Baker, 1981), 235–36.

12. Ibid., *Princeton Theological Review*, 18–19; *Studies in Theology*, 252.

Though not all, many Protestants, especially evangelicals, viewed evolutionary scientists' claims concerning human origins as challenging Scripture's authority and truthfulness, even the Christian gospel itself. This was one of several ideas that prompted Christian leaders in the early years of the last century to take measures to counter diverse movements they believed were subverting the Christian faith.

The Fundamentals: A Testimony to the Truth, edited by A. C. Dixon and R. A. Torrey and published from 1910 to 1915, consisted of ninety essays in twelve volumes that affirmed the evangelical faith over against higher criticism, liberalism, socialism, modernism, and naturalistic Darwinism. Concerning evolution, contributors to these volumes could be found on both sides, some believing evolution to be inconsistent with Scripture, while others concluded that "limited forms of evolution might have been used by God in creation."[13] For example, in his chapter, "The Doctrinal Value of the First Chapters of Genesis," Dyson Hague writes, "Man was created, not evolved. That is, he did not come from protoplasmic mud-mass, or sea ooze bathybian, or by descent from fish or frog, or horse, or ape; but at once, direct, full made, did man come forth from God."[14]

And in case Adam and Eve's historicity was in question, Hague goes on to affirm,

> Adam was not a myth, or an ethnic name. He was a veritable man, made by God; not an evolutionary development from some hairy anthropoid in some imaginary continent of Lemuria. The Bible knows but one species of man, one primitive pair. This is confirmed by the Lord Jesus Christ in Matt. 19:4. It is re-affirmed by Paul in Acts 17:26 ... Rom. 5:12; 1 Cor. 15:21, 47, 49. Nor is there any ground for supposing that the word Adam is used in a collective sense, and thus leave room for the hypotheses of the evolutionary development of a large number of human pairs.... So closely does the apostle link the fall of Adam and the death of Christ, that without Adam's fall the science of theology is evacuated of its most

---

13. George M. Marsden, *Fundamentalism and American Culture*, 2nd ed. (Oxford: Oxford University Press, 2006), 122.

14. Dyson Hague, "The Doctrinal Value of the First Chapters of Genesis," in *The Fundamentals*, vol. 1, edited by R. A. Torrey and A. C. Dixon (reprint, Grand Rapids: Baker, 2003), 280.

salient feature, the atonement. If the first Adam was not made a living soul and fell, there was no reason for the work of the Second Man, the Lord from heaven. The rejection of the Genesis story as a myth tends to the rejection of the Gospel of salvation. One of the chief cornerstones of the Christian doctrine is removed, if the historical reality of Adam and Eve is abandoned, for the fall will ever remain as the starting point of special revelation, of salvation by grace, and of the seed of personal regeneration. In it lies the germ of the entire apostolic Gospel.[15]

However, as George Marsden observes, other contributors such as James Orr and George Frederick Wright conceded that the days of "creation might have been very long, allowing for the possibility of some evolutionary development."[16] Nevertheless, these men "argued strongly against Darwinian claims that evolution could explain the origins of life or the uniqueness of humans."[17] As Orr says, he is only open to "later evolutionary theory" that is a "revolt against Darwinianism." He concludes, "Certainly there would be contradiction if Darwinian theory had its way and we had to conceive of man as a slow, gradual ascent from the bestial stage, but I am convinced ... that genuine science teaches no such doctrine."[18] Marsden notes that "mediating positions" like Orr's were common during this time period as "battle lines were not yet firmly fixed against every sort of biological evolutionism."[19]

Moreover, even among those who did reject evolution, not all of them affirmed a young-earth view. Instead, some sought to accommodate their understanding of Genesis 1–2 to the concept of a much older earth than previously accepted. For example, the 1917 edition of the *Scofield Reference Bible* advocated the Gap Theory, which had been developed a hundred years earlier by Thomas Chalmers. Along with variations of the Day-Age theory, it became popular.

---

15. Hague, "The Doctrinal Value of the First Chapters of Genesis," in vol. 1 of *The Fundamentals*, 282–283, 285.

16. Marsden, *Fundamentalism and American Culture*, 280.

17. Ibid.

18. James Orr, "The Early Narratives of Genesis," in *The Fundamentals*, vol. 1, 239. See also James Orr, "Science and Christian Faith," in *The Fundamentals*, vol. 1, 345–47.

19. Marsden, *Fundamentalism and American Culture*, 122.

The Scopes Trial of 1925, which proved to be an embarrassment for evangelicals despite legal victory for the anti-evolution side, demonstrates that many evangelicals, including leaders who identified themselves as "fundamentalists," held to what is called today an Old-Earth Creation view.[20] This was true of William Jennings Bryan, who argued for the prosecution, and of William B. Riley who, as founder and chief spokesman of the World Christian Fundamentals Association (WCFA), called on Bryan to act as co-counsel for the WCFA during the trial in Dayton, Tennessee.[21] Both Bryan and Riley advocated forms of a Day-Age Theory.[22]

While evangelicals and fundamentalists embraced views that accommodated an old earth, others — such as Seventh-Day Adventists, for example — held that the earth is young, as they interpreted the geological data with reference to the flood of Genesis 6. Not until after publication of *The Genesis Flood* by John Whitcomb and Henry Morris in 1961 did evangelicals and fundamentalists in large measures again embrace a young-earth creation view.[23] Interestingly, the conservative evangelical publisher Moody Press declined to publish *The Genesis Flood* because it was concerned that "firm insistence on six literal days could offend their constituency."[24] This decision suggests how revolutionary six-day-young-earth creationism was in the middle of the last century.[25]

On Thanksgiving Day 1959, at the Darwin Centennial Celebration in Chicago, Sir Julian Huxley, grandson of Thomas Huxley, announced in his address, "The Evolutionary Vision," that religion itself is subject to the laws of evolution and would eventually evolve itself out of existence. His obituary for the "dinosaur" of religion, particularly Christianity,

20. For a detailed history of the trial, see Edward J. Larson, *Summer for the Gods: The Scopes Trial and America's Continuing Debate over Science and Religion* (New York: Basic Books, 1997).

21. William Vance Trollinger Jr., *God's Empire: William Bell Riley and Midwestern Fundamentalism* (Madison: University of Wisconsin Press, 1990), 33.

22. Numbers claims, "William Jennings Bryan, the much misunderstood leader of the post–World War I antievolution crusade, not only read the Mosaic 'days' as geological 'ages' but allowed for the possibility of organic evolution — so long as it did not impinge on the supernatural origin of Adam and Eve" (*The Creationists*, 13).

23. Zaspel, "Princeton and Evolution," 92.

24. Instead, in 1961 the book was published by another Christian publisher: John C. Whitcomb Jr. and Henry M. Morris, *The Genesis Flood: The Biblical Record and Its Scientific Implications* (Philadelphia: Presbyterian & Reformed Publishing, 1961). In 2011 the publisher released a fiftieth-anniversary version of that book.

25. Zaspel, "Princeton and Evolution," 92.

turned out to be premature. Shortly thereafter, *The Genesis Flood* began to ignite a resurgence of belief among evangelicals in six-day-young-earth creation, which annoyed and embarrassed not just atheists and irreligionists, but many fellow evangelicals as well.

The Debate Behind the Debate

Since the mid-twentieth century, debate over the age and origin of the universe has continued within evangelicalism. Evangelicals have remained confident that God exists and is the Creator of our universe. But as to how he created the universe and how long he took to do so, there is much disagreement. In his recent book, *Mapping the Origins Debate*, Gerald Rau outlines six contemporary models.[26]

First, there is *Naturalistic Evolution*, which is highly dependent on philosophical naturalism. This first view falls outside the bounds of evangelicalism because it excludes belief in a Creator. Instead, natural causes explain all things. Evolution is *the* method of explaining the origin of the universe, including how humans came to exist. Atheism is the worldview that governs its advocates such as Richard Dawkins, Daniel Dennett, Stephen Jay Gould (although he was agnostic), Edward O. Wilson, Ernst Mayr, and Eugenie Scott. If Thomas H. Huxley was "Darwin's bulldog" in the nineteenth century, this role has been inherited in the twentieth and twenty-first centuries by men like Dawkins and Dennet who believe religion is a poison to society, ignoring the reality of science (by which they mean "evolution").

A second model is *Nonteleological Evolution*, the view that, while the supernatural may exist, it does not intervene after the universe comes into existence. In prior centuries this view was known as "deism." Today, those who hold this view may not appreciate such a label. Liberal Protestantism, Process theology, Buddhism, Hinduism, and New Age theology are all, in their own ways, variations of this view. Some of its most famous supporters include Christian de Duve, Ian Barbour, and John Haught. This view affirms evolution and shares many similarities with naturalistic evolution because even though a supernatural being may have jump started the process, the universe, as it evolved, did not

---

26. Gerald Rau, *Mapping the Origins Debate: Six Models of the Beginning of Everything* (Downers Grove, IL: InterVarsity Press, 2012), see especially 31–56.

originate or progress with an intended *telos*, or plan, in view. Therefore, the randomness that characterizes evolution in philosophical naturalism is preserved, as is the attempt to explain everything from naturalistic causes. In short, this view is best described as a form of theistic evolution, one that is not limited to Christian perspectives.

Third, there is *Planned Evolution*. As the label suggests, this differs from the previous view in that it affirms purpose. God did have a *telos* in view from the beginning. Therefore, while evolution is again affirmed, it is teleological in nature. Advocates of this view tend to be monotheists, some Jewish or Islamic, but most identify with Christianity. Typically, advocates attempt to reconcile Genesis with evolution, some by viewing Genesis as an "ancient drama" whose author(s) held to an ancient, primitive cosmology. Various interpretations are given of Adam and Eve. Typically, they are seen as a group of people or as names (symbols) used to refer to humanity as a whole, but not as a single pair from whom all of humanity originates. Rau identifies several advocates of this view, including Howard Van Till and Kenneth Miller as well as Francis Collins and the BioLogos Foundation. Like the previous view, this is another version of theistic evolution. Although purpose is involved, God typically does not intercede in the process of evolution. Rather, natural causes are an adequate explanation.

A fourth model is *Directed Evolution*, differing slightly from Planned Evolution. For our purposes, one significant difference is that directed evolutionists are more likely to see Adam and Eve as historical persons, even the parents of all humanity. Furthermore, not only is God the Creator, but he intervenes, or more specifically, "directs" the cosmos on a continual basis. But again, evolution is the method and means by which the universe originates. Rau suggests that advocates might include Henry Schaefer, Deborah Haarsma, Loren Haarsma, and Michael Behe.

The last two views, Planned Evolution and Directed Evolution, are both categorized by Rau as "non-concordist," meaning they do not attempt to align the Bible and modern science. Similarly, the days in Genesis are not seen as "sequential, but tell us something about God's relation to the world."[27] Interpretations of the days of creation include various views:

---

27. Ibid., 206.

1. *The Framework view*: "In the beginning, the earth was form-less and void, so God gave form and filled the void. The framework tells us what happened, but nothing about the length or order of the creative acts."

2. *The Analogical Day view*: "God creates for six days and rests for one, analogous to our six days of work and one of rest."

3. *The Cosmic Temple view*: "God establishes the whole earth as his temple and takes up his residence there on day seven, similar to stories of the establishment of the temple in other ancient literature. Thus he gives creation function, rather than creating the form."[28]

By way of contrast, the last two views that follow (old-earth and young-earth creationism) are labeled by Rau as "concordist," and each affirms six successive days of creation.

A fifth model is *Old-Earth Creationism* (OEC). With this view we now move from evolutionary-based models to creation-based models. Advocates of these two creation models (old-earth and young-earth) believe God created directly rather than through an evolutionary process. This first model receives its distinctiveness in how it explains the age of the earth. While rejecting evolution, this model still sees the earth as very old (billions of years). Yet the old age of the earth can be harmonized with the six days of Genesis, even though "day" is interpreted to account for long eons of time (more on this shortly). Genesis 1 is viewed as compatible with scientific discovery, properly interpreted. Rau observes, "OEC sometimes chooses to interpret the Bible in the light of scientific evidence, but other times chooses to interpret science in light of the Bible." For example, it

accepts the standard geological chronology that the earth is billions of years old, by taking the term *day* in Genesis 1 to mean an unspecified period of time. On the other hand, adherence to the idea that God created in distinct phases (days) leads to the interpretation of periods of rapid appearance of species in the fossil record as creative events.[29]

---

28. Ibid., 206–7.
29. Ibid., 49.

Advocates of old-earth creationism are many, but some stand out, including Hugh Ross and Reason to Believe as well as Stephen Meyer and the Discovery Institute Center for Science and Culture.

Sixth is *Young-Earth Creationism* (YEC), sometimes referred to as "scientific creation" or "creationism." For advocates of this view, Scripture is always to be given priority over science, so that where science draws conclusions that disagree with Genesis 1–2, science is to be rejected. This view earns its distinctiveness in several ways. First, it rejects evolution (especially naturalistic evolution) as contrary to Scripture, particularly Genesis 1–2. Also, while it agrees with old-earth creationism that there are six successive days in Genesis 1–2, it disagrees that there is room in the text for long periods of time. Rather, "day" in Genesis 1–2 is a twenty-four-hour period. Additionally, the earth is young, perhaps not much older than six thousand years. This view sees Adam and Eve as historical persons as well as the first persons from whom all of humanity derives. Some more influential advocates include Ken Ham and Answers in Genesis, Jonathan Sarfati and Creation Ministries International, John D. Morris and the Institute for Creation Research, Walt Brown and the Center for Scientific Creation, Paul Nelson and John Mark Reynolds of the Discovery Institute, as well as other individuals such as Steven Austin, Jerry Bergman, D. Russell Humphreys, Michael Oard, John Sanford, and Kurt Wise.

As mentioned, these last two views, old-earth and young-earth creationism, affirm six successive days of creation. However, there are various interpretations of these six days. Rau lists four:

1. *The Gap view* (held among old-earth advocates): "There is a gap between the original creation in Genesis 1:1 and the recreation of the world in six days after it 'became' without form and void in Genesis 1:2. Fossils are part of the old creation. (Now rare)"

2. *The Intermittent Day view* (held among old-earth advocates): "Each day of creation was twenty-four hours long, but separated by long periods in which there was no creative work. (Now rare)"

3. *The Progressive or Day-Age Creation view* (held among old-earth advocates): "Each day was a long period of time. The luminaries were created in day one but only became visible in day four, perhaps due to clearing of the atmosphere."

4. *The Twenty-Four-Hour Day view* (held by young-earth advocates): "Each day was twenty-four hours long. This is usually
connected in modern YEC with flood geology (fossils bearing
strata were laid down in the global flood) and mature creation
(apparent age)."[30]

While these categories and labels are not exhaustive, they do capture
most views. However, there is a movement that does not fit neatly into
just one category, and that is Intelligent Design (ID), usually credited to
Charles Thaxton, Walter Bradley, and Roger Olsen (all of whom were old-
earth creationists) and their 1984 book, *The Mystery of Life's Origin*. Phillip
Johnson's 1991 work is perhaps more well-known, *Darwin on Trial*, where
he argues that Darwinists and neo-Darwinists come to their conclusions,
not because of the evidence for evolution but rather because they have
accepted the philosophical worldview of naturalism, which assumes that
only natural causes can account for human origins.[31] A number of scholars
have joined the ID movement from diverse backgrounds, including the
fields of science, philosophy, law, mathematics, and theology.[32]

Today ID has found a home in the Discovery Institute Center for
Science and Culture and is defended by scholars such as Michael Behe,
who created a stir with his 1996 book, *Darwin's Black Box: The Biochemical Challenge to Evolution*. There he argues for "irreducible complexity,"
the belief that the cosmos is made up of complex systems, each with a
makeup involving certain active parts that must be in place prior to the
entire system operating, something that can only be accounted for if a
Creator previously imposed design, structure, and configuration (e.g.,
DNA, the flagellum).[33] Some other notable scholars who have joined
in the ID movement are Stephen C. Meyer, William A. Dembski, Paul
Nelson, Jonathan Wells, and C. John Collins.[34]

ID's uniqueness is that it seeks to develop, as Stephen Meyer states,
an "evidence-based scientific theory about life's origins that challenges

---

30. Ibid., 207–8.

31. Phillip E. Johnson, *Darwin on Trial* (Downers Grove, IL: InterVarsity Press, 1991).

32. Interestingly, even some non-Christians have argued against evolution using a design
argument. Consider Australian molecular biologist Michael Denton and his book *Evolution:
A Theory in Crisis* (Chevy Chase, MD: Adler & Adler, 1986).

33. Michael J. Behe, *Darwin's Black Box: The Biochemical Challenge to Evolution* (New York:
Free Press, 1996).

34. Also consider Paul Chien, Guillermo Gonzalez, Dean Kenyon, Charles Thaxton,
David Berlinkski, David DeWolf, and Thomas Woodward.

strictly materialistic views of evolution."[35] In other words, it seeks to argue empirically and non-religiously for design in nature and thus a Designer (Creator). As Rau explains, this does not necessarily mean a total rejection of evolutionary processes.[36] ID advocates range from directed evolutionists to old-earth and young-earth creationists, though not all proponents of those views also uphold ID.

Why devote so much space to outlining these diverse views of origins? The reason is that it truly is the *debate behind the debate*.[37] In other words, while this book focuses on the historicity of Adam, readers will doubtless notice that each contributor also addresses the origins debate. Why? Because how one understands the days of Genesis, evolutionary theory, and even the age of the earth to a certain extent will impact, in one way or another, what one believes about Adam and Eve. While not every view outlined above is represented in this book, the contributors do represent the major positions, and in this debate over Adam their interpretation of Genesis 1–2 is evident, and at times even a pivotal factor in how they believe Adam is to be understood.

Adam, to Be or Not to Be?

Whether he intended it or not, Francis Collins's establishment of the BioLogos Foundation helped to spur a new round of vigorous disagreement about human origins among evangelicals. His high profile as longtime head of the Human Genome Project provided Collins significant influence when, as a confessing evangelical, he launched BioLogos on its mission: "To help communicate the harmony of faith and science to the modern Church," with his view of science including an acceptance of evolution.[38] As he states:

> I find theistic evolution, or BioLogos, to be by far the most scientif-
> ically consistent and spiritually satisfying of the alternatives. This
> position will not go out of style or be disproven by future scientific

35. Stephen C. Meyer, *Signature in the Cell: DNA and the Evidence for Intelligent Design* (New York: Harper One, 2009).

36. Rau, *Mapping the Origins Debate*, 53.

37. For one example of the origins debate, see J. P. Moreland and John Mark Reynolds, eds., *Three Views on Creation and Evolution* (Grand Rapids: Zondervan, 1999). Young-earth creationism is represented by Paul Nelson and Reynolds, old-earth (progressive) creationism by Robert C. Newman, and theistic evolution by Howard J. Van Till.

38. See the statement at http://biologos.org.

discoveries. It is intellectually rigorous, it provides answers to many otherwise puzzling questions, and it allows science and faith to fortify each other like two unshakable pillars, holding up a building called Truth.[39]

Collins and other theistic evolutionists (some preferring the label "evolutionary creationists") question the notion that the Genesis account requires belief in Adam's historicity. In *The Language of God* Collins queries,

> But what about the Garden of Eden? Is the description of Adam's creation from the dust of the earth, and the subsequent creation of Eve from one of Adam's ribs, so powerfully described in Genesis 2, a symbolic allegory of the entrance of the human soul into a previously soulless animal kingdom, or is this intended as literal history?[40]

In his more recent book, *The Language of Science and Faith*, coauthored with Karl Giberson (author of *Saving Darwin: How to Be a Christian and Believe in Evolution*), Collins says that when it comes to how God created us — specifically Adam and Eve — neither "science nor the Bible answers that question." As Collins and Giberson conclude,

> Based on what we know today about both science and the ancient world of the Hebrews, it is simply not reasonable to try to turn the brief comments [of Genesis] into a biologically accurate description of how humans originated. One point is that the Genesis account does not tell us how God created — only that God did create and that human beings are a part of God's plan and not an accident.[41]

We would be remiss not to mention another well-known theistic evolutionist who does not hold to a historical Adam, Peter Enns. An affiliate professor of biblical studies at Eastern University and a past contributor to BioLogos, Enns is author of *The Evolution of Adam*. He

---

39. Francis Collins, *The Language of God: A Scientist Presents Evidence for Belief* (New York: Free Press, 2006), 209–10.

40. Ibid., 206–7.

41. Karl W. Giberson and Francis S. Collins, *The Language of Science and Faith* (Downers Grove, IL: InterVarsity Press, 2011), 206.

acknowledges that a historical Adam has been the traditional Christian view but concludes that "[t]o appeal to this older consensus as a way of keeping the challenge of evolution at bay is not a viable option for readers today."[42] Enns instead argues that "the special creation of the first Adam as described in the Bible is not literally historical."[43] Enns has been at the forefront of the discussion over Adam in part because of his contention that the apostle Paul should be viewed as a first-century man who incorrectly believed in Adam's historicity, but only because Paul did not have access to current archaeological and scientific knowledge.

Enns and Francis Collins, as well as the opposing response from those who affirm a historical Adam, have done much to frame public discourse on the topic. The first view in this book, presented by Denis O. Lamoureux, agrees with Enns and Collins in rejecting a historical Adam, though Lamoureux's perspective is not identical to that of either of them. The other three views presented in this book uphold a historical Adam in one way or another. Each contributor offers his own distinctive view, differing from one another not only in regard to how they view Scripture's accounts concerning creation in light of evolutionary science, but especially with regard to how they view Adam. Nevertheless, all agree on the central importance of resolving the question of Adam's historicity adequately.

It is to this central question that we now turn.

A Preview of *Four Views on the Historical Adam*

In addressing the debate over a historical Adam, each contributor has been asked to present the case for his position, supporting his view from the Scriptures as well as addressing any extrabiblical material (e.g., Ancient Near Eastern literature, evolutionary theory) that might be relevant to the topic. In defending their positions, we have asked them to answer three key questions:

1. *What is the biblical case for your viewpoint, and how do you reconcile it with passages and potential interpretations that seem to counter it?* In responding to this question, each contributor was

---

42. Peter Enns, *The Evolution of Adam: What the Bible Does and Doesn't Say about Human Origins* (Grand Rapids: Brazos Press, 2012), xvi..
43. Ibid.

asked to explain his overarching hermeneutic as well as the specific hermeneutic he employs when interpreting the first chapters of Genesis, including New Testament references to those chapters. In doing so, it was necessary for each contributor to speak to how evolution should or should not affect his hermeneutical approach to Genesis 1–2, especially when it comes to the historicity of Adam.

2. *In what ways is your view more theologically consistent and coherent than other views?* Each contributor was asked to relate his view of Adam to his view of revelation (special and general), Scripture (specifically the doctrine of inerrancy), creation, redemption in Christ, and any other relevant theological matter. Therefore, while the bulk of each chapter focuses on details surrounding the origins debate, at various points each contributor draws out implications of his view for corresponding theological issues.

3. *What are the implications your view has for the spiritual life and public witness of the church and individual believers, and how is your view a healthier alternative for both?* In this final question we get to the big picture surrounding the debate. Each contributor devotes some attention to the particular "problems" his view solves for a personal understanding of the Bible, the integration of faith and science, the gospel of Jesus Christ, and the church's witness to Christ in the public square.

Answering these questions are four scholars who have devoted themselves to the issue at hand. While it is not possible to represent every position in this Counterpoints book, we are confident that these scholars represent the four major positions that evangelicals today must evaluate. Following are brief introductory summaries of these four views without supporting argumentation.

1. *No Historical Adam: Evolutionary Creation View*, by Denis Lamoureux, Associate Professor of Science and Religion at St. Joseph's College in the University of Alberta, and author of *Evolutionary Creation: A Christian Approach to Evolution.*[44]

---

44. Denis Lamoureux, *Evolutionary Creation: A Christian Approach to Evolution* (Eugene, OR: Wipf & Stock, 2008).

Lamoureux argues that while Christians in the past affirmed a historical Adam, the evidence for evolution precludes such belief today. Rather, God created the universe through the natural process of evolution, and humanity's existence also results from evolutionary development. Evolutionary genetics and the fossil record indicate that humans "share with chimpanzees a last common ancestor that existed around six million years ago" and that we descended not from one couple (Adam and Eve), but from a group of around 10,000. While Lamoureux acknowledges that some scholars have tried to incorporate a historical Adam with an evolutionary view (e.g., Bruce Waltke, Darrel Falk, Denis Alexander), he argues that such an attempt is misguided because it seeks to combine modern science with ancient science, the latter of which God accommodated as an incidental vessel through which he communicated inerrant spiritual truths.

Specifically, Lamoureux rejects scientific concordism, the idea that God chose to reveal through the Scriptures certain scientific facts and that modern science, properly understood, can be aligned with the Bible. To the contrary, he says, the authors of Scripture had an ancient perception of the world, apparent in their belief in a three-tiered universe, their view of the "firmament," and elsewhere. When it comes to humanity's biological origins, the biblical authors likewise had a primordial understanding. They held to "*de novo* creation," the belief that God created man and everything else directly, immediately, and completely, that is, fully mature.

Lamoureux argues that Adam did not exist, but that this fact does not damage the core and essential beliefs of the Christian faith. Although the biblical authors affirmed an ancient view of the world and man's biological origins (e.g., Paul's view of Adam in Romans 5:12–19), this in no way should erode our confidence in Scripture. Adam is not a historical person, but another example of an incidental vessel through which Scripture conveys inerrant spiritual truths. While Adam is not historical, the Second Adam, Christ Jesus, is a historical person who died for our sins.

2. *A Historical Adam: Archetypal Creation View*, by John Walton, Professor of Old Testament at Wheaton College. Walton is the author of numerous books, including *The Lost World of Genesis: Ancient Cosmology and the Origins Debate*.[45]

In contrast to Lamoureux, Walton believes that Adam was a historical person. However, his historicity is not where Scripture places its emphasis. Rather, Scripture's primary concern is to speak of Adam and Eve as archetypal representatives of humanity. Walton argues that not only do Old and New Testament passages support his view, but also evidence from Ancient Near Eastern literature strongly buttresses his claim.

Nowhere is this archetypal emphasis more evident than in Genesis 2. The author is *not* concerned with the material formation of Adam and Eve as biological beings. Rather, the author is concerned with the function of mankind. Consequently, the purpose and intent of Genesis 2 is *not* to make a statement about our biological origins, nor about the biological origins of Adam and Eve. Evangelicals are misguided if they pit the Bible over against modern science when it comes to the issue of human origins.

Therefore, Walton makes space for the possibility that Adam and Eve, though historical persons, may not be the first humans who came into existence or the parents of all humankind.

While Walton acknowledges that evolution can be used in wrong ways (e.g., to argue for a purposeless, godless process), he believes that there is nothing inherently troubling with evolution "guided purposefully by an infinitely powerful and sovereign God." While Walton does not take a stance on evolution, rejecting it or accepting it, his model allows for the incorporation of evolution.

Additionally, the theological points Scripture makes in appealing to Adam (sin, death, second Adam, etc.) do not rest upon the belief that Adam and Eve are historically the first

45. John H. Walton, *The Lost World of Genesis: Ancient Cosmology and the Origins Debate* (Downers Grove, IL: IVP Academic, 2009).

and only persons or the parents of mankind. Their parenthood is to be viewed archetypally, not materially. Walton emphasizes that Scripture's inerrancy applies to explicit claims and affirmations of the text; since the Bible makes no scientific claims about our material human origins, inerrancy is not brought into question by various views on origins. One should not apply inerrancy, he argues, to claims the text does not make.

3. *A Historical Adam: Old-Earth Creation View*, by C. John Collins, Professor of Old Testament at Covenant Theological Seminary. Collins is the author of *Did Adam and Eve Really Exist? Who They Were and Why You Should Care* and *Science and Faith: Friends or Foes?*[46]

Collins argues that Adam and Eve were real, actual, historical persons. A historical Adam and Eve make the best sense not only of the story line of Scripture, but also of our human experience as sinners, children of Adam, in need of redemption through the second Adam, Jesus Christ.

Collins takes Genesis 2 as describing historical persons, whom God created as those made in his own image. Genesis 2 sets the stage for the entire biblical story line and worldview, and Collins believes the biblical authors were aware of this. They were narrating salvation-history, specifically God's "great works of creation and redemption," and not merely a catalog of timeless truths. Sin came into the world through Adam, and the entire Old Testament is the story of how God enters into a covenant relationship with his people precisely because they have been estranged from him due to sin. God is on a mission, therefore, to rescue sinners, and he does so ultimately through the death and resurrection of the second Adam, Jesus Christ.

Collins also believes the New Testament authors affirmed a historical and biblical story line beginning with Adam. Christ himself believed in a historical Adam, according to Collins, and Paul compares and contrasts our death in Adam

46. C. John Collins, *Did Adam and Eve Really Exist? Who They Were and Why You Should Care* (Wheaton, IL: Crossway, 2011); idem, *Science and Faith: Friends or Foes?* (Wheaton, IL: Crossway, 2003).

to our life in Christ. Collins, therefore, concludes that the story line of Scripture demonstrates that (1) humankind is one family, originating from one pair of ancestors (Adam and Eve), (2) God created Adam and Eve supernaturally, and (3) Adam and Eve, the "headwaters" of humankind, brought sin into the world. Apart from this biblical narrative, which features a historical pair, the story line of Scripture makes little sense, as does our human experience as sinners, children of Adam, in need of redemption.

Collins's affirmation of an old earth sets his belief in a historical Adam apart from the next contributor, Bill Barrick (young-earth creationist). Collins reads Genesis 1–2 in such a way that would not preclude some evolutionary processes or long intervals of time elapsing in the biblical days of creation. Moreover, Collins entertains the possibility that Adam and Eve, though the headwaters of the human race that follows, may not have been the only pair of humans in the beginning. So while Adam is a historical person, he may not have been the only person, but perhaps was the chieftain of his tribe. Nevertheless, while willing to affirm an old earth, Collins remains critical of theistic evolution, at least in its strongest forms, because he believes it fails to account for the uniqueness of human beings, as those made in the image of God, something that goes beyond mere natural processes.

Collins upholds inerrancy but argues that a literalistic view of, for instance, twenty-four-hour days in Genesis 1 is not necessitated by a careful and accurate reading of Scripture.

4. *A Historical Adam: Young-Earth Creation View*, by William D. Barrick, Professor of Old Testament at The Master's Seminary. Barrick contributed to the book *Coming to Grips with Genesis: Biblical Authority and the Age of the Earth*, is the Old Testament editor of the Evangelical Exegetical Commentary series, and is the author of the Genesis commentary in that forthcoming series.[47]

---

47. Terry Mortenson and Thane H. Ury, eds., *Coming to Grips with Genesis: Biblical Authority and the Age of the Earth* (Green Forest, AR: New Leaf Publishing, 2008).

Barrick makes a case from Scripture for Adam as a historical person and as the originating head of humankind. Adam is not primarily an archetype (Walton) nor a product of biological evolution (Lamoureux). Rather, he is the first person, supernaturally created by God, and the father of all mankind. Barrick argues that such a view is apparent not only in Genesis 1–2 but throughout the New Testament as well, especially in the writings of Paul.

Moreover, like Collins, Barrick believes numerous biblical doctrines follow from and are dependent on a historical Adam. Perhaps most important is the gospel itself. Appealing to Paul's argumentation in Romans 5:12–19, among other texts, Barrick stresses that without a historical Adam—and consequently a historical fall into sin—there is no need for a historical second Adam, namely, Christ Jesus, to undo Adam's sin and its consequences for Adam's children. Barrick contends that the arguments made against a historical Adam today are similar to those used by theological liberals of a past era to argue against Christ's historical resurrection.

Barrick argues that a historical Adam is foundational to a plethora of other doctrines as well, including a biblical understanding of God's creative activity, the history of the human race, the nature of mankind as made in God's image, the origin and nature of sin (e.g., original sin), the existence and nature of death, the reality of salvation from sin, the historical events recorded in Genesis, and Scripture's authority, inspiration, and inerrancy.

Barrick affirms a historical Adam within the bounds of a young-earth perspective, a view he believes Scripture strongly supports. In other words, the days of creation are twenty-four hour days. Therefore, Barrick rejects not only theistic evolution (Lamoureux), but also old-earth creationism (Collins). He concludes that a historical Adam and a young-earth perspective are integral to one another.

Concerning the relationship between faith and science, Barrick argues that because Scripture is inspired by God and therefore inerrant, the author of Genesis (Moses),

superintended by the Holy Spirit, wrote an accurate, historical narrative of the days of creation. Accordingly, Moses,
Jesus, and Paul did not adopt a mistaken view of the cosmos,
but their assertions and assumptions written in Scripture,
properly interpreted and understood, are correct and without
error. Furthermore, Barrick affirms that the author of Genesis intended to record the material creation of the world, not
just an archetypal representation of humanity's origins, and
that Genesis is always to be given priority over ANE stories.
The same principle applies to science: Where the claims and
theories of modern science (i.e., evolution) contradict what the
Bible says, one is to side with Scripture, for it alone is inspired
by God and therefore inerrant and authoritative.

While these very brief summaries highlight the main tenets of each
view, not only is there far more to be said, but how each contributor
argues his case, bringing the evidence to bear on the issue, calls for careful attention from readers. But first, a most important question must
be asked.

What Impact Does This Debate Have on the Christian Faith?

Too often in debates of this nature we fail to take the next step. While
we may rise to the highest levels of intellectual debate, we easily neglect
that which is most important, namely, applying the debate concerning Adam's historicity to the Christian life. Doing so is not easy. Nevertheless, it does allow us to see which views are able to be applied
consistently and which views impact Christian living either positively
or negatively. Therefore, at the end of this book we have included two
pastoral reflections, by two scholars who have much experience in the
church, Gregory Boyd and Philip Ryken, to represent two different
stances on the debate and its impact on the Christian faith.

Gregory Boyd, who taught at Bethel University for sixteen years,
is senior pastor of Woodland Hills Church in St. Paul, Minnesota. As
the title of his chapter indicates, Boyd argues that our faith is secure
whether or not there was a historical Adam. On the other side is Philip
Ryken, who had been pastor at Tenth Presbyterian Church in Philadelphia since 1995 until being appointed president of Wheaton College

in 2010. In his chapter Ryken argues, opposite of Boyd, that without a real, historical Adam we cannot rightly understand the world or our Christian faith.

Both Boyd and Ryken enter the discussion having read the contributors' chapters and responses to one another. Their purpose is to write from the perspective of a pastor-theologian, not regurgitating all of the details that were covered in the four chapters of the book, but instead looking at the big picture and how this issue changes (or doesn't change) the Christian faith and the church. In doing so, they seek to address questions such as:

- Does Adam's existence or nonexistence affect the rest of the Christian faith and those doctrines Christians have historically affirmed throughout the centuries?
- Does Adam's existence or nonexistence shape a Christian worldview, especially the biblical story line from creation, fall, and redemption, to new creation?
- Does Adam's existence or nonexistence have an impact on the gospel, or how the gospel is preached and applied, specifically in the church?
- Does Adam's existence or nonexistence have influence on how we live the Christian life and "do church" as the body of Christ?
- Does Adam's existence or nonexistence make a difference in our evangelical witness to a watching world?
- What is at stake in this debate for evangelicals in the church today?

How Important Will This Debate Be for Evangelicalism?

In his chronicling of the historical Adam controversy, Richard Ostling asks the probing question, "Is the Adam and Eve question destined to become a groundbreaking science-and-Scripture dispute, a 21st-century equivalent of the once disturbing proof that the Earth orbits the sun?" He answers,

> The potential is certainly there: the emerging science could be seen to challenge not only what Genesis records about the creation of humanity but the specie's unique status as bearing the "image of God," Christian doctrine on original sin and the Fall, the genealogy

of Jesus in the Gospel of Luke, and, perhaps most significantly, Paul's teaching that links the historical Adam with redemption through Christ (Rom. 5:12–19; 1 Cor. 15:20–23, 42–49; and his speech in Acts 17).[48]

For the traditional view, original sin, the image of God, redemption in Christ, and the reliability and inerrancy of Scripture, as well as how biblical history itself is to be understood, are all connected to Adam's existence as the father and representative of the human race. Therefore, to reinterpret Adam is not without serious consequences.[49]

According to many theistic evolutionists, however, to continue reading Genesis 1–3 as recording actual history with Adam and Eve as the first human pair is a serious blunder, for it means that we have put our heads in the sand, ignoring the scientific evidence for human biological evolution. Therefore, theistic evolutionists conclude that the integrity of our faith is at stake in the Adam debate. To reject evolution is to reject science and intellectual honesty.

So who is right? Is Adam a historical person or not? And what is at stake in such a debate? We invite you to explore the answers to these questions in the chapters that follow.

---

48. Richerd N. Ostling, "The Search for the Historical Adam," *Christianity Today* 55, no. 6 (June 2011): 24.

49. For example, see D. A. Carson, "Adam in the Epistles of Paul," in *In the Beginning: A Symposium on the Bible and Creation*, ed. N. M. de S. Cameron (Glasgow: The Biblical Creation Society, 1980), 41; R. Albert Mohler Jr., "False Start? The Controversy over Adam and Eve Heats Up" (August 22, 2011), http://www.albertmohler.com/2011/08/22/false-start-the-controversy-over-adam-and-eve-heats-up/.

NO HISTORICAL ADAM:
EVOLUTIONARY CREATION VIEW

DENIS O. LAMOUREUX

Christians throughout history have steadfastly believed that Adam was a real person. Yet in light of the evolutionary sciences, some evangelical Christians are questioning his existence. This chapter embraces evolutionary creation—the belief that the Father, Son, and Holy Spirit created the universe and life, including humans, through an ordained, sustained, and intelligent design-reflecting natural process. Similar to the way that the Lord used embryological mechanisms to create each of us in our mother's womb, He also employed evolutionary processes to create humanity. This chapter rejects the assumption that God revealed scientific facts in the Bible thousands of years before their discovery by modern science. Instead, Holy Scripture features an ancient understanding of the physical world (e.g., the 3-tier universe with a flat earth). The Word of God also has an ancient conceptualization of biological origins, which asserts that living organizations were created quickly and completely into fully mature forms. The apostle Paul's references to Adam are rooted in this ancient biology. The chapter concludes that the biblical figure Adam is a vital, but incidental, ancient vessel that transports inerrant spiritual truths: only humans are created in the Image of God, only humans have fallen into sin, and our Creator judges us for our sinfulness.

Introduction

In the last chapter of *Evolutionary Creation: A Christian Approach to Evolution* (2008), I began with a provocative claim: "My central conclusion in this book is clear: Adam never existed, and this fact has no impact whatsoever on the foundational beliefs of Christianity."[1] Needless to say, such a view of human origins is rarely heard within evangelical circles. If you are offended by my position on Adam, I apologize. My intention is not to upset any brother or sister in Christ. Rather, my hope and prayer is that we can open a conversation on human origins and ask how we are to read passages dealing with Adam in the Word of God. Some might be surprised to learn that my goal is not to win people over to my view.[2] Instead, I simply want evangelicals to be aware that there are born-again Christians who love the Lord Jesus and who do not believe there ever was a first man named "Adam."

My calling as a Christian is driven by an unquenchable fire in my heart of hearts. It is a pastoral concern. Evangelical students attending public universities are leaving the church in alarming numbers.[3] You might know a few, maybe someone in your family. One reason for this exodus is science, biological evolution in particular.[4] So here is all that I am asking: I want young men and women to know that there is a Christian view of origins that accepts evolution and recognizes that our faith does not rest on the existence of Adam. Should they become convinced that humans evolved, they will be equipped never to lose a step in their Christian walk, because our faith is based *only* on Jesus Christ, His sacrifice on the Cross, and His bodily resurrection from the dead—and not on a historical Adam.

---

1. Denis O. Lamoureux, *Evolutionary Creation: A Christian Approach to Evolution* (Eugene, OR: Wipf and Stock, 2008), 367. Hereafter cited as *EC*. Implicit in my conclusion is the issue of what constitutes "the foundational beliefs of Christianity." Many say the historicity of Adam is foundational, but this I challenge.

2. I find constructivist pedagogy is an effective way to teach origins. See the final exam questions for my online science-religion course: www.ualberta.ca/~dlamoure/final.pdf.

3. One survey indicates that roughly half of evangelical Christians entering a university leave the church after graduation. Steve Henderson, "A Question of Price *versus* Cost," *Christianity Today* (March 2006), 86.

4. In "Six Reasons Young Christians Leave Church" the Barna Group notes, "One of the reasons young adults feel disconnected from church or from faith is the tension they feel between Christianity and science.... One-quarter embrace the perception that 'Christianity is anti-science' (25%). And nearly the same proportion (23%) said they have 'been turned off by the creation-versus-evolution debate'" (No author, 28 Sept. 2011), at: http://www.barna.org/teens-next-gen-articles/528-six-reasons-young-christians-leave-church. See also Karl W. Giberson, "Creationists Drive Young People Out of the Church" (19 Nov. 2011), at http://www.huffingtonpost.com/karl-giberson-phd/creationists-and-young-christians_b_1096839.html.

It is important to point out that I am not the only evangelical questioning the historicity of Adam. A landmark issue of *Christianity Today* in June 2011 featured a cover with a Neanderthal-looking male and the title "The Search for the Historical Adam." The cover commented, "Some scholars believe that genome science [i.e., genetics] casts doubt on the existence of the first man and first woman. Others say that the integrity of the faith requires it." Notably, the article not only assumed the universe is old, but that biological evolution is true. The debate is whether there really was an individual who corresponds to the biblical figure Adam. This *CT* article is evidence that the historicity of Adam is not a settled issue. And the fact that I am included in this book, published by the leading evangelical publisher, Zondervan, is more proof this is the case.

My Faith and My Science

A few years ago I was invited by an evangelical seminary to deliver a lecture on human origins. Just before entering the auditorium, I overheard a man complain, "Well, how can Lamoureux be a Christian? He doesn't believe in Adam, so there's no way he believes in Jesus and the Bible." Right then and there, I knew this was going to be a tough audience! So I think it is necessary to share a bit about my personal testimony and my understanding of biological evolution.

First and foremost, I am a thoroughly committed and unapologetic evangelical theologian trained to the PhD level. I'm a born-again Christian. By God's grace and in answer to my mother's prayers, I accepted Jesus Christ as my Lord and Savior in 1980 while serving as a United Nations peacekeeper on the island of Cyprus. It was through reading the gospel of John that the Holy Spirit convicted me of my sins and shameful lifestyle. If I had to pick a conversion day, it was on Good Friday that the Father revealed to me His unfathomable love for humanity. He sent His Son Jesus to die for us on the Cross. Think about that. The Creator of the world loves us so much that He willingly died for us. So I went to Cyprus to be a peacekeeper, and I met the Prince of Peace! I also believe that the Bible is the Holy Spirit–inspired Word of God. In my morning devotions I drink deeply from Scripture for my spiritual nourishment. The day I wrote this paragraph, I read the first six chapters of the wonderful book of Hebrews. Additionally, I believe in miracles and have experienced numerous signs and wonders. I also embrace intelligent design, because I believe it is consistent with what Scripture teaches about God being the designer of the universe.[5] When I look at nature, I see that the beauty, complexity, and functionality "declare the glory of God" (Ps. 19:1). And for the last thirty-two years I have enjoyed fellowship in Baptist, Pentecostal, and Alliance churches.

Second, I am a thoroughly committed and unapologetic evolutionary biologist, also trained to the PhD level. I find that the evidence for evolution is *overwhelming*. Every science that deals with origins fits tightly together and comes to only one conclusion: the universe and life evolved. I have experienced the fruitfulness and predictability of the theory of evolution. Every time a new fossil is discovered, it always fits exactly where it should. I have yet to see evidence that falsifies biological evolution. In fact, evolution is the easiest theory to disprove. Find just one human tooth near the bottom of the geological record and you could destroy evolutionary science. That's no exaggeration, but I wouldn't hold my breath waiting for it to happen. I also recognize the explanatory power of evolutionary theory. As many have said, biology makes sense in the light of evolution. Although my career focuses on the relationship between science and religion, at the University of Alberta I have the privilege of collaborating with one of the world's foremost paleontology groups.

It is important to add that for a good part of my life I have struggled with the relationship between Christianity and evolution. As a freshman university student in 1972, I lost my boyhood faith because of one introductory course on evolutionary biology. By my senior year, I became an atheist. So yes, it is completely reasonable for Christians to be worried about the destructive impact of evolution on faith.

Upon returning from Cyprus, I began to fellowship at an evangelical church and soon met some young-earth creationists. They convinced me that evolution was Satan's primary weapon for attacking the faith of university students. These anti-evolutionists also introduced me to

---

5. Regrettably, intelligent design theorists have distorted the biblical notion of design by conflating (blending) it with a god-of-the-gaps view of origins, therefore creating a false dichotomy between design and evolution. See *EC*, 53–104; my debate with Phillip Johnson in *Darwinism Defeated?* (Regent College Publishing, 1999); and my criticism of Michael Behe at www.ualberta.ca/~dlamoure/p_behe.pdf.

so-called "theistic evolution." It was dismissed as a view of origins held by liberal Christians, because they really weren't committed to Jesus and didn't trust the Bible or take God at His word. For me, *true* Christians were young-earth creationists. How convinced was I of this? In 1983 I walked out of first year medical school with the intention of becoming a creation scientist in order to declare war on evolutionists in universities. If that isn't a commitment to young-earth creation, then I don't know what is.[6]

To equip myself for the battle, I went to graduate school for thirteen straight years. Beginning in theology, I discovered what seminarians before me have experienced—that is, biblical interpretation is much more complicated than what we learn in Sunday school. It became evident that when the Holy Spirit inspired the biblical authors, He allowed them to use some of their ancient ideas about nature (i.e., ancient science). In other words, God *accommodated* in the revelatory process and came down to the level of ancient people in order to communicate inerrant, life-changing, spiritual truths.

A professor I will never forget is Dr. Loren Wilkinson at Regent College, one of the best evangelical schools of theology. During his science-religion course, I asked him what he thought about young-earth creation. He responded tersely, "It is error." I can still remember how the word "error" shook my soul. In Wilkinson's closing remarks to the class, he looked at me and said, "Denis, I have a serious concern. Should you ever give up your belief in young-earth creation, would you also give up your faith in Christ?" Ouch!

That wasn't Wilkinson talking. The Holy Spirit was flowing through his words and casting a light on my understanding of Christianity. I mumbled and stumbled and really didn't answer. Deep in my heart of hearts I knew that my relationship with Jesus was more important than any position on origins. And if I may make a bit of a Pauline boast (2 Cor. 11:21–28), I won the Evangelism Prize at Regent. No one should doubt that I am an evangelical Christian.

After seven years of theology, the Holy Spirit challenged me during a morning devotion: "I have called you to study the origins debate, but how much do you really know about evolutionary biology?" Ouch

---

6. See my young-earth creationist article at www.ualberta.ca/~dlamoure/p_yec.jgp.

again! Sometimes the Lord points out things we don't want to hear. I had taken only one first-year university course on evolution. Even more bluntly, the Holy Spirit then admonished, "Since you know so little, if you criticize evolution, you would be bearing false witness ... and that's sinful."[7] Triple ouch!

So in 1991 I entered a PhD program on the evolution of teeth and jaws. I was still a zealous anti-evolutionist, and my plan was to "fly under the radar" and collect scientific evidence to disprove evolution that I would publish after graduation. However, dealing with the fossil evidence firsthand day in and day out, I started to see an evolutionary pattern. After three years of attempting with all my energy to fit the scientific data into an anti-evolutionary theory, I gave up and accepted biological evolution.

I knew immediately that I would be marginalized by the evangelical community. Indeed, that has happened. I have been blocked from teaching at my denominational college and seminary, and evangelical publishers have rejected my book proposals. Nevertheless, I believe we should follow the biblical and scientific evidence no matter where it leads.

So that's a very condensed version of my story.[8] Let me close by underlining that I embrace the time-honored complementary relationship between Scripture and science—the Two Divine Books Model. Together the Book of God's Words and the Book of God's Works offer us a revelation of the Father, Son, and Holy Spirit. In my Christian walk I have held a wide variety of interpretations of both Books. Yet despite all these, my faith has always been set solidly upon the never-changing Rock, our Lord and Savior Jesus. As Hebrews 13:8 states, "Jesus Christ is the same yesterday and today and forever." And I hope you are saying a hardy "Amen!"

Terms and Definitions

Evolutionary creation asserts that the Father, Son, and Holy Spirit created the universe and life, including humans, through an ordained, sustained,

---

7. It is always distressing to hear an evangelical Christian with unbridled confidence declare, "Evolution is a lie because we didn't evolve from chimps or monkeys!" Sadly, our tradition does not even understand the fundamentals of the theory of evolution. No evolutionary biologist today believes we evolved from chimpanzees or monkeys.

8. My full story is online at: www.ualberta.ca/~dlamoure/wl_story.html.

and intelligent design-reflecting evolutionary process. The world did not arise through blind chance, and our existence is not a fluke or mistake. It was the Lord's primary plan from the very beginning to create men and women, and for us to enjoy a loving personal relationship with Him. This Christian approach to evolution vehemently rejects the atheistic interpretation of evolution preached by the notorious Richard Dawkins.[9]

Evolutionary creationists believe that the Creator established and maintains the laws of nature, including the mechanisms of a teleological evolution (Greek *telos* implies "planned, purposeful"). In other words, the evolution of life is a *purpose-driven natural process*.[10] Evolutionary creation also claims that humans descended from pre-human ancestors and that the Image of God and human sin were mysteriously manifested. These Christian evolutionists experience the Father's love and presence in their lives. Through the power of the Holy Spirit, they read the Bible as the living Word of God. And evolutionary creationists enjoy a personal relationship with Jesus who graciously blesses them and answers their prayers.

The term "evolutionary creation" seems like a contradiction in terms. However, the most important word in this category is the noun "creation." Evolutionary creationists are first and foremost creationists. They believe in a Creator and that the world is His creation. The qualifying term is the adjective "evolutionary," which simply indicates the method that the Lord used to make the universe and life. This view of origins is often called "theistic evolution." But that word arrangement places the process of evolution as the primary term and makes our Creator secondary and merely a qualifying adjective. I find such an inversion in priority completely unacceptable.

Another reason for employing the category of evolutionary creation is that it distinguishes evangelical Christians who love Jesus and accept evolution from the evolutionary interpretations of deists (who believe in an impersonal, never-present god-of-the-philosophers) and liberal

---

9. Dawkins seems to believe that insulting Christians is a productive strategy. He claims that I am "an intellectual coward" and "a man with an air of desperation." See www.ualberta. ca/~dlamoure/dawkins.html. For my criticism of Dawkins's famed proclamation that "Darwin made it possible to be an intellectually fulfilled atheist," see my two papers "Darwinian Theological Insights: Toward an Intellectually Fulfilled Christian Theism" at www.ualberta. ca/~dlamoure/p_darwin_1.pdf and www.ualberta.ca/~dlamoure/p_darwin_2.pdf.

10. My terminology was inspired by Rick Warren's book *The Purpose Driven Life* (Grand Rapids: Zondervan, 2002).

Christians (who believe that Jesus was merely an enlightened human who never rose physically from the dead).

To introduce evolutionary creation to my evangelical brothers and sisters, I have found it helpful to draw a parallel between our own creation in our mother's womb and the evolution of all living organisms. I have yet to meet a Christian who believes that while in the womb the Lord came out of heaven and literally attached an arm or a leg to their developing body. Instead, we all believe that embryological development is a natural process that God providentially maintains during pregnancy. As Psalm 139:13–14 proclaims, "You [God] knit me together in my mother's womb. I praise you because I am fearfully and wonderfully made."

Our creation in the womb is proof that the Creator uses physical mechanisms to create life. Similarly, evolutionary creationists believe that biological evolution is an ordained natural process that God has sustained throughout eons of time. It is the Lord's "knitting" process that produces every living organism, each crying out that they are "fearfully and wonderfully made." From my experience in science, embryological development and biological evolution reflect intelligent design and "proclaim the work of his [God's] hands" (Ps. 19:1).

Of course, the burning question every evangelical Christian must be asking is, "How does Lamoureux interpret biblical passages dealing with origins?" I will attempt to offer an answer in this chapter. But at this point it is necessary to reveal my position regarding the historical events in Scripture: *Real history in the Bible begins roughly around Genesis 12 with Abraham.* Like many other evangelical theologians, I view Genesis 1–11 as a unique type of literature (literary genre) that is distinct from the rest of the Bible. So from my perspective, was Abraham a real person? Yes. Was there a King David in the tenth century BC? Yes. Were the Jews deported to Babylon in the sixth century BC? Yes. Was there really a man named Jesus in the first century AD? Yes. Do the Gospels report eyewitness accounts of actual historical events, including the Lord's teaching and miracles, and especially His physical resurrection from the dead? *Absolutely yes!* Even though I do not believe that Adam was historical, I thoroughly believe in the historicity of Jesus and the biblical testimonies of His life.[11]

---

11. See 1 John 1:1–3; 2 Peter 1:16–18; Luke 1:1–4; Acts 1:1–19. Also see Richard Bauckham, *Jesus and the Eyewitnesses* (Grand Rapids: Eerdmans, 2006).

Another term we need to define is "scientific concordism."[12] Most evangelical Christians are not familiar with this category, yet nearly all of them embrace this view of the relationship between science and Scripture. Scientific concordism is the *assumption* that the facts of science align with the Bible. Stated another way, it is the *assumption* that God revealed scientific facts to the biblical writers thousands of years before their discovery by modern scientists. A 2004 survey reveals the extent of this assumption within American evangelicalism. Respondents were asked about the creation of the world in six days (Gen. 1) and the flood of Noah (Gen. 6–9): "Do you think that's literally true, meaning it happened that way word-for-word; or do you think it's meant as a lesson, but not to be taken literally?"[13] Unsurprisingly, 87 percent of American evangelicals believe that the entire world was actually created in six literal days and that there really was a global flood.

Evangelicalism is a scientific concordist Christian tradition. And since nearly all evangelicals read Genesis 1 and Genesis 6–9 literally, they undoubtedly believe that the creation of Adam from the dust of the ground as described in Genesis 2 is also "literally true, meaning it happened that way word-for-word."

Now, I want to emphasize that scientific concordism is a reasonable assumption. After all, God created the world and He inspired the Bible, and to assume an alignment between the Lord's Two Books is a logical expectation. But here are two questions you must ask yourself: (1) Is scientific concordism true? (2) Is it an inerrant feature of the Word of God? Of course, it is well within the power of the Holy Spirit to reveal twenty-first-century scientific facts to biblical authors.[14] Yet, is that what the Lord did in the revelatory process? In my opinion, this is *the central issue* in the origins debate. Purported arguments against evolution are secondary to how we interpret the biblical accounts of origins, especially the creation of humans. So let's turn to the Bible in an attempt to answer this question about the truthfulness of scientific concordism.

---

12. This term usually appears simply as "concordism." See Paul Seely, *Inerrant Wisdom* (Portland, OR: Evangelical Reformed, 1989); Stanley Jaki, *Genesis 1 through the Ages* (London: Thomas Moore Press, 1992).

13. Survey conducted February 6–10, 2004, by International Communications Research (Media, PA) at www.icrsurvey.com/studies/947a1%20Views%20of%20the%20Bible.pdf.

14. Another question is, Why does it have to be *our* twenty-first-century science?

My method will be as follows. In the same way that the Word of God judges our thoughts and remodels our mind (Heb. 4:12; Rom. 12:1–2), I will let evidence *within Scripture itself* evaluate our scientific concordist evangelical tradition — and maybe even reshape our view of how the Holy Spirit revealed through the biblical writers.

Is Scientific Concordism True?

One of the best places to explore whether or not the Bible includes modern scientific facts is to consider passages dealing with the heavens. For example, most Christians are aware that Scripture refers to the daily movement of the sun across the sky. Ecclesiastes 1:5 states, "The sun rises and the sun sets, and hurries back to where it rises." Psalm 19:6 says, "It [the sun] rises at one end of the heavens and makes its circuit to the other."

Of course, evangelicals are quick to explain that these verses use phenomenological language (Greek *phainōmenon* means "appearance"). That is, the "rising" or "setting" of the sun is only a visual effect caused by the rotation of the earth on its axis, giving us the appearance that the sun "moves." But did the inspired writers of Scripture use phenomenological language in the same way that we do today? History offers the answer. The notion that the earth rotates daily, causing the visual phenomenon of the sun to "rise" and "set," was accepted only in the 1600s — thousands of years *after* the Bible was written.[15]

Scripture does use phenomenological language to describe the natural world. There is, however, a subtle and important difference between what the biblical authors saw and believed to be real in nature, and what we see and know to be a fact of science. For ancient people, observation of the natural world was limited to their unaided physical senses, such as the naked eye. Today scientific instruments like telescopes have extended our view of the universe. Consequently, it is essential to understand that statements in Scripture about nature are from an *ancient phenomenological perspective*. What the biblical writers saw with their eyes, they believed to be real, like the literal rising and literal setting of the sun.

---

15. A similar response asserts that the terms "sunrise" and "sunset" are poetic or figurative language. I am often challenged, "Check any newspaper and you find the times for sunrise and sunset, but no one today takes this to mean the sun literally rises or sets." But again, these terms did not become poetic or figurative until after the 1600s.

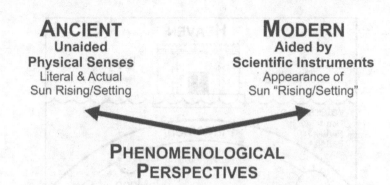

Figure 1. Ancient and Modern Phenomenological Perspectives.

In contrast, today we view the world from a *modern phenomenological perspective*. When we see the sun "rising" and "setting," we know that it is only an appearance or visual effect caused by the rotation of the earth. Figure 1 distinguishes between the ancient and modern phenomenological perspectives.

It is crucial that these two different phenomenological perspectives of nature not be confused and conflated (blended together) when reading Scripture. This is the error most Christians make in attempting to explain biblical passages that deal with the movement of the sun. They read these Scriptures through *their* modern phenomenological perspective, and as a result they force *their* modern scientific ideas *into* the Bible. This common mistake is known as "eisegesis" (Greek *eis* means "in, into"; *ēgeomai*, "to guide"). But everyone agrees that the goal of reading is to practice "exegesis" (*ek*, "out, out of") and to draw out the author's intended meaning. Therefore, we need to respect the Word of God and read it through ancient eyes and an ancient mind-set.[16]

Philippians 2:6–11 is a beloved passage in Scripture. We often sing this hymn in the praise and worship service at my church. It reveals the great mystery that God emptied Himself and descended to become a man in the person of Jesus. The apostle Paul concludes the hymn in verses 9–11:

---

16. John Walton's *Ancient Near Eastern Thought and the Old Testament: Introducing the Conceptual World of the Hebrew Bible* (Grand Rapids: Baker Academic, 2006) is a fine introduction to reading Scripture through an ancient mindset.

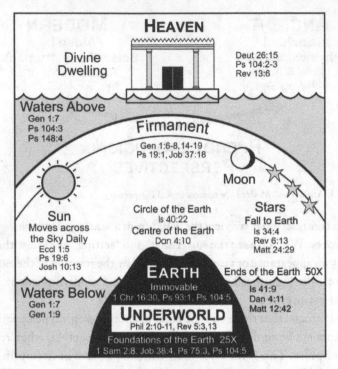

Figure 2. The 3-Tier Universe. Regional geography and the horizon led ancient Near Eastern people to believe the earth was surrounded by a circumferential sea. Travel
in any direction came to a body of water: Mediterranean Sea is west, Black and
Caspian Seas north, Persian Gulf east, and Arabian and Red Seas south.

> Therefore God exalted him [Jesus] to the highest place
>   and gave him the name that is above every name,
> that at the name of Jesus every knee should bow,
>   *in heaven* and *on earth* and *under the earth*,
> and every tongue acknowledge that Jesus Christ is Lord.

When singing this hymn, we do not often think about the phrase
"under the earth." Yet if we examine the original Greek, it is a translation of *katachthoniōn*, which is made up of the preposition *kata* meaning
"down" and the noun *chthonios* referring to the "underworld" or "sub-
terranean world."[17] Therefore, a more accurate translation of verse 10 is

---

17. Regrettably, evangelical Bibles do not fully translate passages referring to the underworld, and it is for this reason that few evangelicals are aware of it. In the Old Testament, the

"at the name of Jesus every knee should bow, [1] in heaven and [2] on earth and [3] in the underworld." In other words, Paul is referring to an ancient understanding of the structure of the cosmos known as the "3-tier universe" and depicted in Figure 2.[18]

So what are we to do with Philippians 2:10? Does this verse weaken our confidence that the Bible is really the Word of God? Or to put it bluntly, as some often ask, "Did God lie in the Bible?" First, let me make something perfectly clear: God does NOT lie! Holy Scripture states that "it is impossible for God to lie" (Heb. 6:18).

Second, let's not lose perspective. Is the purpose of Philippians 2:6–11 to reveal science and the structure of the universe? Most Christians would say "no." This hymn is a revelation of our Lord and Savior Jesus Christ. It delivers foundational spiritual truths of our faith—the mystery of the Incarnation, Jesus' sacrificial death on the Cross, His resurrection and exaltation in heaven, and His lordship over the entire creation. Anyone who embraces these inerrant truths will be born-again.

Third, I suggest that with Philippians 2:10 *we must submit to the very words in the Word of God*—even if we may not like it or fully understand it, or if it challenges our traditional evangelical assumption that scientific concordism is an inerrant feature of the Bible. The Greek word *katachthoniōn* in verse 10 refers to the underworld, and it clearly indicates that Paul accepted the 3-tier universe.[19]

Hebrew *shᵉʾōl* is rendered "grave" and left as a transliteration in footnotes, which is unhelpful to most readers (Num. 16:30; Prov. 5:5; Isa. 14:15). Similarly, the New Testament translates the Greek *hādes* as "depths" or "hell" or offers only the transliteration (Matt. 16:18; Luke 10:15; Rev. 20:14).

18. It is possible that Paul accepted egocentricity (the belief that the earth is spherical and literally at the center of the entire universe). Regardless, neither view aligns with physical reality.

19. Some attempt to write off this reference to the 3-tier universe as "poetic" because it appears in a hymn. However, this argument is based on the popular idea that poetry only deals with figurative language. The proper definition of poetry refers simply to *structured writing*. Poetry is not limited to figurative language because it can refer to physical reality. For example, the psalms are poetically structured, and Psalm 148:3 states, "Praise him [the Lord], sun and moon; praise him, all you shining stars." No one today writes off the existence of the sun, moon, and stars in this verse because it is in a poetic format.

Moreover, real people and real historical events can appear in poetic passages. Psalm 106 refers to Moses (vv. 16, 23, 32) and the crossing of the Red Sea (vv. 7, 9, 22). Christians do not dismiss these verses as merely "poetic" and not corresponding to historical reality. Finally and most importantly, if one writes off the 3-tier universe in Philippians 2 as "poetic" because it appears in a hymn, then this opens the door to writing off the historicity of Jesus in this hymn. I doubt any Christian wants to do that.

Figure 3. The Message-Incident Principle.

Let me propose a concept for interpreting biblical passages such as Philippians 2:10 that deal with the natural world: the Message-Incident Principle in Figure 3.

Most Christians already embrace this notion in some implicit way. We believe that the main purpose of the Bible is to reveal inerrant, life-changing, spiritual truths. When referring to nature, the Holy Spirit in the revelatory process allowed the use of an incidental ancient science. Rather than confusing the biblical writers and their readers with modern scientific concepts, God *accommodated*. This was the best science-of-the-day as conceived from an ancient phenomenological perspective.

Qualifying ancient science as "incidental" does not imply that it is unimportant. The science in Scripture is vital for delivering spiritual truths. It acts like a cup that brings "living water" (John 4:10) to our thirsty souls. The word "incidental" carries the meaning "to happen in connection with something more important." In the case of Philippians 2:10–11, the *Message of Faith* reveals the lordship of Jesus over the entire creation, and the *incidental ancient science* is the 3-tier universe. To repeat, the Holy Spirit did not lie in the Bible. God accommodated and allowed Paul to use his ancient understanding of the structure of the world. And yes, as we shall see later in this chapter, Paul's belief in ancient science has significant implications for his position on the historicity of Adam.

Two of the best biblical passages for exploring the truthfulness of scientific concordism deal with the creation of the heavens in Genesis 1. On the second day of creation,[20]

---

20. In this passage and in the one that follows, I use the TNIV Bible and replace the word *vault* with the more accurate translation *firmament* (as found in the KJV Bible) and replace the word *sky* with *heaven* (also in the KJV). Justification for my decision appears in the next paragraphs.

God said, "Let there be a *firmament* between the waters, to separate water from water." So God made the *firmament* and separated the water under the *firmament* from the water above it. And it was so. God called the *firmament* Heaven (Gen 1:6–8).

On the fourth day of creation,

God said, "Let there be lights in the *firmament* of the heaven to separate the day from the night, and let them serve as signs to mark seasons and days and years, and let them be lights in the *firmament* of the heaven to give light on the earth." And it was so. God made two great lights—the greater light to govern the day and the lesser light to govern the night. He also made the stars. God set them in the *firmament* of the heaven (Gen 1:14–17).

When I first read these passages as a new Christian, I scribbled question marks in the margins of my Bible because I didn't have a clue what they meant. What is a firmament? And what is the water above it? Of course, my problem was that I was reading Scripture through my modern scientific mindset (eisegesis). If I would have *respected* the Bible and tried to view nature through ancient eyes and an ancient mindset (exegesis), then creation days two and four would have made perfect sense. For example, what did the divinely inspired author of Genesis 1 see when he looked up? A huge blue dome. To suggest that there was a sea of water in the heavens being held up by a solid structure was completely reasonable to him. Believing that the sun, moon, and stars were placed in the firmament in front of the heavenly sea is exactly what it looks like from an ancient phenomenological perspective. In fact, this was science-of-the-day in the ancient Near East as seen in Figures 4 and 5.[21]

Some evangelical Christians attempt to argue that the firmament refers to the atmosphere or outer space, and the waters above the firmament to clouds, water vapor, or a pre-flood water canopy.[22] But let's look at the actual Hebrew words in the Word of God and then submit to them. The noun translated four times as "firmament" in Genesis 1:6–8

21. Diagrams redrawn from Othmar Keel, *The Symbolism of the Biblical World* (New York: Seabury Press, 1978), 36, 174.
22. Hugh Ross, *The Genesis Question* (Colorado Springs: NavPress, 1998); John C. Whitcomb and Henry Morris, *The Genesis Flood* (Phillipsburg, NJ: P&R Publishing, 1961).

Figure 4. Egyptian Universe. The firmament (shaded) and stars are the sky goddess Nut. The sun god Re (falcon head) travels in a boat across the heavenly sea and is received by the afterlife god Osiris at the entrance of the underworld (lower right corner). The sun passes through the underworld to rise again in the East. Earth god Geb is reclined; air god Shu is above Geb.

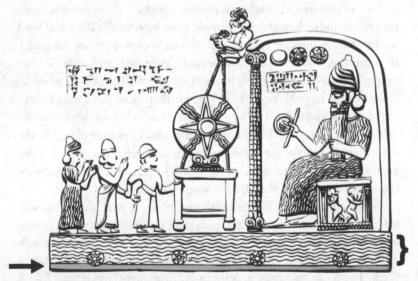

Figure 5. Mesopotamian Heavens. The firmament (shaded; arrow) supports the heavenly sea (bracket) and stars. Sun god Shamash is seated. This structure of the heavens is similar to Psalm 104:2–3, "He [God] stretches out the heavens like a tent and lays the beams of his upper chambers on their waters."

and three times in Genesis 1:14–17 is *rāqîaʿ*. Its root is the verb *rāqaʿ*, which means to flatten and hammer out. This word carries a sense of flattening something solid. For example, Exodus 39:3 and Isaiah 40:19 use *rāqaʿ* for pounding metals into thin sheets; Numbers 16:38 employs the related noun *riqqûaʿ* (a plate) in a similar context. The verb *rāqaʿ* even appears in a passage about the creation of the sky, which is thought to be a solid surface like a metal. Job 37:18 asks, "Can you join [God] in spreading out [*rāqaʿ*] the skies, hard as a mirror of cast bronze?"

The noun translated five times as "water/s" in Genesis 1:6–7 is *mayim*. If the divinely inspired author of Genesis 1 had intended to refer to clouds or water vapor, there are three common Hebrew words he could have used (*ʿēd, ʿānān, nāsî*), but he didn't.[23] Christians who claim that the waters above collapsed during Noah's flood fail to recognize that Scripture states the firmament and heavenly sea were still intact and overhead during King David's day. As Psalm 19:1 states, "The heavens declare the glory of God, and the firmament [*rāqîaʿ*] proclaims the work of his hands." Psalm 148:3–4 asserts, "Praise him [God], sun and moon; praise him, all you shining stars. Praise him, you highest heavens, and you waters [*mayim*] above the skies."

Now what are we to do with these passages in Genesis 1 about the creation of the heavens? The Message-Incident Principle allows us to appreciate that the Holy Spirit accommodated to the level of the ancient Hebrews and used the science-of-their-day in order to reveal the inerrant spiritual truth that God created the visually dominant blue "structure" overhead with the sun, moon, and stars "embedded" in it. This Message of Faith remains steadfast for us today: the Creator made the visual phenomenon of the blue sky and all the heavenly bodies.

There is also another important divine revelation in Genesis 1. You will have noticed in Figures 4 and 5 that the ancient Egyptians and Mesopotamians believed astronomical structures were divine beings. But inspired by the Holy Spirit, the writer of Genesis 1 offers a radical message: the heavens and heavenly bodies are mere creations of the God of the Hebrews. Not only that, but the sun, moon, and stars were to "serve as signs to mark seasons and days and years" (Gen. 1:14 TNIV). Instead of humans bowing down to serve the heavenly bodies, the

---

23. Respectively, Genesis 2:6; 9:13; Jeremiah 10:13.

heavenly bodies were created by God to serve humans. Indeed, this was a liberating message for those enslaved to the idolatry of the heavens.

There are significant implications regarding the ancient science in all these biblical passages about the heavens. First, the structure of the universe found in the Bible does not align with physical reality as we know it through modern science. The sun does not literally move across the sky every day, we do not live in a 3-tier universe, and there is no heavenly sea held up by a solid firmament implanted with the sun, moon, and stars.

Second, and much more challenging to us as Bible-believing Christians, is God's creative action in Genesis 1 with the making of the heavens. The second day of creation begins, "God said, 'Let there be a firmament between the waters, to separate water from water.'" On the fourth day, "God said, 'Let there be lights in the firmament of the heaven.'" Do you see the problem? God's *very words* ("Let there be …") in the Book of God's Words do not align with physical reality in the Book of God's Works. To state this problem more incisively, *Holy Scripture makes statements about how God created the heavens that in fact never happened.* So, to ask the question once more, "Did God lie in the Bible?" Again my answer is "No! The Lord accommodated in the Bible."

Some Christians assume that the concept of accommodation "waters down" the Bible, but this is not true. Let me offer some reasons for divine accommodation. First, it is a corollary of divine revelation. That is, built into the belief that God reveals to us is the fact that the Infinite Holy Creator has to descend to the level of finite sinful creatures in order to communicate with them. The notion of accommodation is also rooted in the Ultimate Act of Divine Revelation—the Incarnation. As Philippians 2:7–8 states, God "humbled himself" and "made himself nothing" in order to become a man in the person of Jesus.

The Lord Himself accommodated in His teaching ministry by using parables. He employed earthly stories (ancient ideas) to deliver inerrant heavenly messages. As Christians we experience divine accommodation personally in our prayer life. Does the Lord not descend to speak to you at your spiritual and intellectual level? And when a five-year-old asks about where babies come from, parents accommodate by coming down to the level of the child. They communicate the central message—a baby is a gift from God—without presenting the incidental details of sex. *Spiritual truths can be revealed without using physical facts.*

To conclude, we can now return to the question posed in the title of this section, "Is scientific concordism true?" My answer is "no." The structure and origin of the universe presented in the Bible do not align with the scientific facts. Yet, this fact does not weaken our belief that Scripture is the Word of God. It only indicates that the Holy Spirit graciously descended to the level of the inspired authors and used the science-of-their-day as an incidental vessel to reveal inerrant Messages of Faith. There are numerous other examples of ancient science in Scripture. If you would like to examine some of these, I have put a book chapter online at www.ualberta.ca/~dlamoure/ancient_science.html.

Genesis 1 and the Creation of Life

Many of you must be wondering, if the astronomy in Genesis 1 is ancient, then is the biology also ancient? Even more challenging is the question of divine creative action. As we noted, the first chapter of the Bible presents God creating a universe with the sun, moon, and stars placed in a firmament that supports a heavenly sea. But since the heavens are not structured in this way, the Creator did not actually make the astronomical world as stated on creation days two and four. Could it be that the creation of living organisms in Genesis 1 is similar in that it is an ancient view of biological origins? And does this mean that God did not actually create life as described on creation days three (plants), five (birds, sea creatures), and six (land animals, humans)?

To explore this possibility, we must attempt to think about living organisms from an ancient phenomenological perspective. When looking at different creatures, what would ancient people have seen? With plants they would have observed that wheat produces seeds that, when planted, only sprout wheat. The seeds from fruit would give rise to trees that always bear the same fruit. With animals they would have seen that hens lay eggs that always hatch chicks, ewes only give birth to lambs, and women are always the mothers of human infants. In the eyes of the ancients, living organisms were *immutable*. That is, they were static and never changed. Biological evolution was not a consideration, because the fossil record and evolutionary genetics had yet to be discovered.

The notion of the immutability of living organisms is clearly present in Genesis 1. That chapter states ten times that plants and animals reproduce "according to its/their kind/s." Christian anti-evolutionists assume that this phrase is biblical evidence against biological evolution.[24] However, they fail to recognize that it reflects an ancient phenomenological perspective of living organisms. The phrase "according to its/their kind/s" is an ancient biological category; more specifically, it reflects an ancient taxonomy.

Recognizing that ancient peoples believed living organisms were immutable, how would they have conceptualized the origin of life? Again, we need to think like them. For example, they would have seen that goats begat goats, which begat goats, which begat goats, etc. In thinking about the origin of goats, they would have reversed this data set of goat begats, and working backwards through time they came to the very logical conclusion that there must have been an original goat or an original pair of goats created by God. This thought process is known as "retrojection" (Latin *retro* means "backward"; *jacere*, "to cast, throw"). It is the very same type of thinking used today in crime-scene investigations; present evidence found at the scene is used to reconstruct events in the past.

Similarly, in reconstructing the period when God created living organisms, the ancients reasonably concluded that each creature must have originated quickly and completely formed. This view of origins is termed "*de novo* creation" (Latin *de* means "from"; *novus* "new"). It appears in most ancient creation accounts and features a divine being who acts through miraculous interventions to make fully formed living organisms (and astronomical structures). *De novo* creation was the origins science-of-the-day of ancient peoples, including the Holy Spirit – inspired author of Genesis 1.

The ancient biology in Genesis 1 has a profound implication. Stated precisely, the creation of life is accommodated through ancient taxonomical categories. Similar to the way that Genesis 1 filters divine creative acts in the origin of the heavens through an ancient astronomy, the Creator forms living organisms in accordance with ancient biological concepts — the immutability of creatures and their *de novo* creation. To state the implication of this ancient biology in Genesis 1 even more incisively, *Holy Scripture makes statements about how God created living organisms that in fact never happened.*

---

24. See Todd Wood and Paul Garner, eds., *Genesis Kinds: Creationism and the Origin of Species* (Eugene, OR: Wipf and Stock, 2009).

So to ask the question once more, "Did God lie in the Bible?" My answer again is a resounding "No! The Lord accommodated in the Bible." The Holy Spirit used the biology-of-the-day as an incidental vessel to reveal inerrant spiritual truths in Genesis 1. In particular, God is the Creator of life, all living organisms are very good, and humans were made in the image of God. Consequently, Genesis 1 does not reveal how God actually created plants, animals, and ... humans.

Genesis 2 and the *De Novo* Creation of Adam

Throughout history Christians have steadfastly believed that the creation of Adam from the dust of the ground in Genesis 2:7 refers to a real historical event. They have also held firmly to the notion that all humans have descended from Adam and that the genealogies in Scripture are evidence for this belief (Gen. 5:3; 1 Chron. 1:1; Luke 3:38). Yet, could it be that the Bible's account concerning the creation of the first man reflects an ancient understanding of human origins? Is it possible that the lists of humans begetting humans in biblical genealogies are similar to the data set of goats begetting goats? And if this is true, then maybe the creation of Adam in Genesis 2 is the result of retrojecting the common experience of humans giving birth to humans, who give birth to humans, etc., backward in time to the *de novo* creation of a first human.

To assist in answering these questions, let's examine the origin of humans in some ancient Near Eastern creation accounts. There are two basic creative mechanisms. One is a natural plant-like sprouting of humans from the earth;[25] the other is an artificial craftsman-like fashioning of people using some earth or other material. Regarding the former, the *Hymn to E'engura* states that "humans broke through the earth's surface like plants."[26] In the Sumerian text *KAR 4*, the gods plant the seeds of humans into the earth and people later "sprout from the ground like barley."[27] And in the *Hymn to the Pickax*, a god strikes

25. It must be remembered that the ancients believed in preformatism (one-seed embryology). Influenced by their experience in farming, they assumed that only males had "seed" with an entire miniature human being inside. *EC*, 138–42.

26. Richard J. Clifford, *Creation Accounts in the Ancient Near East and in the Bible*, CBQMS26 (Washington: Catholic Biblical Association, 1994), 30.

27. Ibid.

the ground with a hoe-like axe "so that the seed from which people grew could sprout from the field."[28] (Interestingly, this sprouting mechanism seems to be the creative process used in Genesis 1:24, where God commands, "Let the land produce living creatures." The Hebrew verb translated "produce" is *yāṣā'* and it is the same verb used in Genesis 1:12: "The land produced vegetation.")

With regard to the craftsman mechanism of making humans, it appears in *Atrahasis* where a goddess mixes clay and the blood of a slain god to fashion seven males and seven females.[29] In *Enki and Ninmah*, an intoxicated divine being uses earth to make imperfect human beings.[30] And in *Gilgamesh*, a pinch of clay is used to create a man.[31] Clearly, these last three examples of the *de novo* creation of humans are similar to Genesis 2:7, where the Lord acts like a craftsman and forms Adam from the dust of the ground.

So what exactly am I saying about Adam? Adam's existence is based ultimately on an ancient conceptualization of human origins: *de novo* creation. To use technical terminology, *Adam is the retrojective conclusion of an ancient taxonomy*. And since ancient science does not align with physical reality, it follows that *Adam never existed*.[32]

I am quite aware of how shocking this idea is to nearly every evangelical Christian. I am sorry if this is upsetting. But consistency argues that if the creation of the heavens in the Bible reflects an ancient astronomy, then we should not be surprised that the Holy Spirit also accommodated in allowing the biblical authors to use the science-of-the-day regarding human origins.

Nor should we be surprised that these divinely inspired writers connected their genealogies back to Adam. Ancient accounts of origins not only present the creation of the universe and life, but also the origin of the community. The ancient Hebrews would have seen the growth of their tribe, and they would have remembered family genealogies and

---

28. Walter Beyerlin, ed., *Near Eastern Religious Texts Relating to the Old Testament* (Philadelphia: Westminster Press, 1978), 75.

29. Clifford, *Creation Accounts*, 74.

30. Ibid., 75.

31. Ibid., 48–49.

32. Obviously, this conclusion challenges the traditional doctrine of original sin. Yet this is unsurprising, since it was formulated by anti-evolutionists and scientific concordists such as church father Augustine (364–430).

important people from their past. It is significant to note that in the book of Genesis the early Hebrews were an oral community, because the first reference to their writing appears in the book of Exodus.[33] Consequently, the limits of human memory would have restricted the number of individuals that they remembered in their genealogies, and this is reflected in the brevity of the first genealogies in Scripture (Gen. 4; 5; 11). So what are these genealogies? Similar to the ancient science in the Bible, they are an ancient understanding of the origin of the Hebrew community conceived from an ancient phenomenological perspective.

But more importantly, Genesis 2 reveals radical spiritual truths. For the nations surrounding the Hebrews, the gods in many of their origins stories create humans in order to free themselves from work. The basic message is that men and women are slaves of the gods. In sharp contrast, Genesis 2 reveals the Message of Faith that the Lord cares for humanity. He meets their physical and psychological needs by offering food and companionship. In this way, the God who loves us is being revealed at this early stage of biblical revelation.

The New Testament and the Historicity of Adam

In nearly every public lecture that I deliver, Christians are quick to challenge me that Jesus and the apostle Paul refer to Adam as a historical person. By appealing to Genesis 1:27 and 2:24, the Lord admonishes in Matthew 19:4–6, "Haven't you read ... that at the beginning the Creator 'made them male and female' and said, 'For this reason a man will leave his father and mother and be united to his wife, and the two will become one flesh.' So they are no longer two, but one flesh. Therefore what God has joined together, let no one separate."

Paul makes the issue more challenging by placing Adam's sin and death alongside God's gifts of salvation and resurrection from the dead through Jesus. In Romans 5:12 and 15 he writes that "sin entered the world through one man, and death through sin, and in this way death came to all people, because all sinned.... For if the many died by the trespass of the one man, how much more did God's grace and the gift that came by the grace of the one man, Jesus Christ, overflow to the

33. Exodus 17:14; 24:4, 34:27–28.

many!" Paul also claims in 1 Corinthians 15:21–22 that "since death came through a man, the resurrection of the dead comes also through a man. For as in Adam all die, so in Christ all will be made alive." What are we to do with these passages that certainly appear to affirm that Adam was a real historical person?

Let us first examine Jesus' admonition in Matthew 19:4–6. The context of this passage is not a debate over the historicity of Adam. Rather, the Lord was responding to a question about divorce. The Pharisees had asked Him, "Is it lawful for a man to divorce his wife for any and every reason?" (v. 3). Jesus' use of Genesis 1:27 and 2:24 is typological. The relationship between Adam and Eve is an archetype (an ideal model) of what God intended marriage to be. (Indeed, this is an inerrant Message of Faith that needs to be heard and obeyed by our generation.) So what was Jesus doing? He was accommodating to the Jewish belief of the day that Adam was a real person. And there are numerous examples of the Lord coming down to the level of His listeners and using the science-of-the-day.

In the mustard seed parable Jesus employed the ancient idea that the mustard seed was "the smallest of all seeds on earth" (Mark 4:31) to reveal a message about the kingdom of God. Of course, most Christians know that orchid seeds are much smaller, and they also know that Jesus did not come to earth to reveal scientific facts about plants! Instead, this parable is prophetic. God's kingdom began with a small number of disciples and has grown into a worldwide faith.

Similarly, in prophesying His death and resurrection, the Lord states, "The hour has come for the Son of Man to be glorified. Very truly I tell you, unless a kernel of wheat falls to the ground and dies, it remains only a single seed. But if it dies, it produces many seeds" (John 12:23–24). Do seeds die before they germinate? No. If they did, they wouldn't germinate. However, doesn't the outer casing of seed look as if it rots just before germination, giving the ancient phenomenological perception that seeds die?

In discussing His return, Jesus claimed that at "the coming of the Son of Man ... the stars will fall from the sky, and the heavenly bodies will be shaken" (Matt. 24:27, 29). How can stars fall to earth when only one would destroy it completely? Understood from an ancient phenomenological perspective, this passage makes perfect sense. Stars look like tiny specks, and a streaking meteorite gives the appearance they can fall to earth; and shaking the firmament would dislodge them.

In summary, the Lord Himself accommodated by using ancient science in His teaching. It is only consistent that He would also employ an ancient understanding of human origins—the *de novo* creation of the first man Adam—as an incidental vessel to deliver inerrant spiritual truths.

Let us now turn to the apostle Paul. Did he believe that Adam was a real person? *Yes, absolutely.* Paul was a first-century Jew, and like every other Jewish person at that time, he accepted the historicity of Adam.[34] Many Christians point out to me that since this apostle believed in a historical Adam, then the account of Adam in Genesis 2 and 3 must be historical. In other words, they use a "conferment argument" in that Paul's belief in Adam confers historical reality to Adam. These Christians also appeal to consistency. They assert that since Paul refers to Jesus as a historical person in Romans 5 and 1 Corinthians 15, then it is only consistent that his references to Adam must also be to a real individual in history.

Finally, my critics emphasize that the gospel appears in these New Testament passages. In fact, it is explicitly stated in 1 Corinthians 15:1–7 and is introduced by the clauses "the gospel I [Paul] preached to you ..." (v. 1) and "by this gospel you are saved ..." (v. 2). Critics then accuse me of picking-and-choosing the Bible verses I want, such as accepting the gospel and rejecting the existence of Adam. On the surface, these three criticisms are reasonable. Thirty years ago I used all of them when I was a young-earth creationist.

Let me now respond. First, concerning the conferment argument. Many Christians argue that since Paul accepted a historical Adam, then Adam must have been a real person. But what else did this apostle believe? As we noted with Philippians 2:10, Paul accepted a 3-tier universe. Does his belief confer reality to this understanding of the structure of the cosmos? And do we have to believe it also?

Second, the consistency argument claims that because Paul refers to Jesus as a historical individual in Romans 5 and 1 Corinthians 15, then Adam in these chapters must also be a real person in history as

---

34. C. John Collins offers solid evidence for this belief within the Jewish community in *Did Adam and Eve Really Exist?* (Wheaton, IL: Crossway, 2011), 72–76.

described in Genesis 2 and 3. However, this argument would be similar to using Philippians 2:6–11 and the historical fact that Jesus actually existed in order to argue for the existence of the 3-tier universe, and then to extend this ancient astronomy back to Genesis 1 and claim that God actually created a world with three tiers. This consistency argument fails to distinguish real history (the existence of Jesus) from an ancient understanding of human origins (the *de novo* creation of Adam). In other words, it is inconsistent. It conflates (blends together) actual historical events of the first century AD with an ancient biology of human origins.

Third, being accused of picking-and-choosing the Bible verses I prefer is a serious charge. But let's again consider Philippians 2:10–11. The inerrant Message of Faith asserts that Jesus is Lord over the entire creation. Am I picking-and-choosing when I embrace this inerrant spiritual truth and decide not to accept reference to the 3-tier universe? Yes, I am. But once my critics become aware of the ancient astronomy in this passage, they will do so as well, because I doubt anyone today believes the world is really made up of three tiers.

By acknowledging the ancient science in Scripture, we can view Paul's understanding of the origin of death in a new light. He definitely believed that death entered the world with Adam. This was not merely spiritual death, because in judging Adam God stated, "For dust you are and to dust you will return" (Gen. 3:19). Clearly, it is physical death. Paul also believed that the natural world had changed with the divine judgment of Adam (this is termed the "Cosmic Fall"). He asserts, "The whole creation has been groaning" because it "was subjected to frustration" and is in "bondage to decay" (Rom. 8:20–22).

Indeed, these are challenging passages to interpret. However, since Paul accepted an ancient biology of the origin of life, it is only consistent that he also accepted an ancient understanding of the origin of death, suffering, and decay. Therefore, in the same way that Scripture does not reveal how God actually created life, the Bible does not reveal the origin of biological death.

By recognizing and respecting the ancient biology of origins in Romans 5 and 8 and 1 Corinthians 15, we can understand these passages through the Message-Incident Principle as presented in Figure 6. These are inerrant spiritual truths: We are sinners, and God judges us for our sins; but the good news of the gospel is that we are offered the

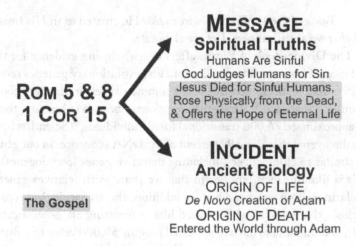

Figure 6. The Message-Incident Principle.

hope of eternal life through the sacrificial death of Jesus and His bodily
resurrection from the dead. To deliver these life-changing Messages
of Faith, the Holy Spirit accommodated and allowed Paul to use the
biology-of-the-day as an incidental vessel.

To be sure, this is a very counterintuitive way to read Scripture.
Throughout most of church history Christians have conflated the spiritual
truths in Romans 5 and 8 and 1 Corinthians 15 with the ancient biology
of origins, assuming Adam to be a real person and giving his existence
the status of an inerrant truth. However, once Christians discover the
ancient astronomy in Genesis 1, I doubt they will extend biblical inerrancy
to how God created the heavens in that chapter. I also believe that when
evangelicals become aware of Paul's 3-tier universe in Philippians 2:10,
this ancient astronomy will not be deemed an inerrant truth. And in the
future, I fully expect that we will set free the doctrine of inerrancy from
the ancient biology that has created the first man in the Bible—Adam.

Human Evolution and the Two Divine Books

At the beginning of this chapter I stated that I embrace the time-honored
complementary relationship between science and Scripture—the Two
Divine Books Model. I can now qualify my position. In contrast to most
evangelical Christians, I hold these two books in a *nonscientific concordist*
relationship. The Book of God's Works reveals *how* the Lord created

us; the Book of God's Words discloses *that* He created us in His Image and *that* we are all sinners. Let me elaborate.

The Divine Book of Works offers overwhelming evidence for the evolution of humans. The fossil record and evolutionary genetics reveal that we share with chimpanzees a last common ancestor that lived about six million years ago.[35] Along the evolutionary branch to humans, there are approximately 6,000 transitional fossil individuals.[36] Scientists have also discovered that about 99 percent of the DNA sequences in our genes are similar to chimpanzees, including defective genes (pseudogenes).[37] This is like our own families in that we share with relatives genetic similarities, both good and bad. In addition, the archaeological record discloses that humans who behaved like us (creating art, sophisticated tools, and intentional burials) appeared roughly 50,000 years ago. Burying the dead with items assumed to be needed in the afterlife signifies religious belief. Finally, science has found that the genetic variability among all people today is quite small and indicates that we descended from a group of about 10,000 individuals.[38]

The Divine Book of Words reveals that humans are the *only* creatures who bear the Image of God, and *only* humans are sinful. I suspect that the manifestation of these spiritual realities coincides with the appearance of behaviorally modern humans about 50,000 years ago. And similar to the way we do not really know when exactly each of us personally begins to bear God's Image or commits our very first sin, I believe the arrival of the first true humans is also a theological mystery.

It is worth noting that some Christians attempt to pin Adam on the tail end of evolution.[39] However, this is categorically inappropriate. It mixes the modern science of evolution with the ancient science of the *de novo* creation of Adam. This would be similar to tacking on a 3-tier universe to cosmological evolution and the Big Bang. Certainly, the

---

35. More accurately, we share a last common ancestral population.

36. Richard Potts and Christopher Sloan, *What Does It Mean to Be Human?* (Washington: National Geographic, 2010), 11.

37. Daniel Fairbanks, *Relics of Eden: The Powerful Evidence of Evolution in Human DNA* (Amherst, NY: Prometheus Books, 2010), 96.

38. Francis Collins, *The Language of God: A Scientist Presents Evidence for Belief* (New York, NY: Free Press, 2006), 126.

39. See Bruce Waltke, *An Old Testament Theology* (Grand Rapids: Zondervan, 2007); Darrel Falk, *Coming to Peace with Science* (Downers Grove, IL: InterVarsity Press, 2004); Denis Alexander, *Creation or Evolution* (Oxford, UK: Monarch Books, 2008).

temptation of scientific concordism is powerful. But I think Christians can all agree that knowing *how* the Image of God and human sin are first manifested, whether individually as a person or collectively as our species, pales in comparison to knowing *that* we have these spiritual realities.

To conclude, I do not believe that there ever was a historical Adam. Yet he plays a pivotal role in Holy Scripture. Adam functions as the archetype of every man and woman. In Genesis 2 and 3, he is an incidental ancient vessel that delivers numerous inerrant spiritual truths. His story reveals that the Creator has set limits on human freedom. We are accountable before God, and a failure to obey His commands results in divine judgment.

Adam's story is our story. Has anyone not been tempted to defy the words of the Father (Gen. 2:17; 3:6)? Have you ever wanted to hide from Jesus because you are ashamed of a sinful act (3:8)? Who has not tried to rationalize their sinfulness in the face of the Holy Spirit (3:13)? And have you blamed others for your sin ... even God (3:12)? To understand who we truly are, we must place ourselves in the garden of Eden. The *nonhistorical* first Adam is you and me. But the Good News is that the *historical* Second Adam died for our sins and frees us from the chains of sin and death. Amen.

I am grateful to Jim Ruark and Madison Trammel for their many helpful suggestions in preparing my manuscripts for this book. I am also appreciative of my assistant, Anna-Lisa V. Ptolemy, for her editorial work, as well as Nancy Rosenzweig, Grace Barlow, Randy Isaac, Dennis Venema, Peter Enns, Don Page, Keith Kowalsky, Sharon Young, Nancy Halliday, Don Robinson, Thor Ramsland, Hilary Davis, Pat McGaffingan, Shiao Chong, Chris Barrigar, and Jack Owens. And special thanks to my mom for her prayers.

JOHN H. WALTON

I applaud Denis Lamoureux's focus on a pastoral mission and his concern for the health of the church. I share the same sentiment, and I believe that it is an appropriate one to adopt when dealing with controversial issues such as this. I agree that there should be room in the evangelical faith for those who choose an evolutionary model of human origins, as long as they preserve the orthodox theology that is required by the biblical text. Therein lies the potential problem: what are the essential claims of orthodox faith?

I agree with a large percentage of what Lamoureux presents. I agree that Genesis needs to be read through ancient eyes and that concordism is hermeneutically suspect. What the Bible *claims* has authority; if the Bible does not claim something, it does not have authority. If we are reading into the text something that the text does not claim, we have departed from the authority of the text. As Lamoureux indicates, this is a matter of giving the biblical text the respect that it deserves. Concordism tries to identify that which can be identified as common truths in the convergence of the Word and the world. That pursuit has its place. But in this discussion it is more important for us to identify what the authoritative claims of the biblical text are.

That God has accommodated a human audience should hardly need defense, but of course, it does. The fact is that every act of communication requires some amount of accommodation. This is particularly true of God's communication, as he adapted his revelation of himself to human beings—and those in a particular language and a particular culture.

It is therefore appropriate to differentiate between that which is "incidental" (i.e., part of the accommodation) and that which is central to the affirmations of the text. We all make such distinctions all the time when reading Scripture. We know, for example, that the Bible is

not lining up its authority behind the spelling of "Nebuchadnezzar" —
on this it has no claims to make.

When Lamoureux demurs that Genesis 1–11 is not "real history"
but a unique type of literature, I find myself uncomfortable with the
way he has chosen to communicate his point. I agree that Genesis 1–11
is a unique type of literature. There is nothing remotely like it in the
ancient world or in the remainder of the biblical text. In that regard I
refer to it as *sui generis*. We must always remember that a genre can be
identified only when we have numerous pieces of literature that have
aspects of form and content in common. To identify a "genre" requires
that more than one exemplar exists. This is the problem with Genesis
1–11: it is without peer.

I am nevertheless uncomfortable with saying that it is therefore not
"real history." "History" can be associated with a genre ("historiography"), but "real" cannot. After all, the ancients considered their mythology to represent important realities, yet those mythologies are certainly
not in the same class of literature as their historiography. I believe that
Genesis 1–11 offers narratives deeply concerned with reality, but they
do not take the form of other historiographical works. My point is that I
would not want to leave the impression that Genesis 1–11 lacks reality.
Nevertheless, it is reality on a different plane.

All of the above pertains to hermeneutics and the general literary issues. When it comes to perhaps controversial details of biblical
interpretation, there are, again, details in Lamoureux's treatment that
I find perfectly acceptable. For example, I agree with his treatment of
the phrase "after its kind." The Israelites would recognize what we all
do: wheat grows from wheat, not from lilies; zebras are born to zebras,
not to chimpanzees. And, of course, no evolutionist would claim any
differently. One species does not give birth to another; the changes are
so minuscule as to be unnoticeable.

Other details of his exegesis I find not as agreeable, but they make
little difference. For example, in the past I had also drawn the conclusion that *raqiaʿ* referred to a solid dome, but more recently I have come to
believe differently. Methodologically the procedure that he uses to move
from the semantic domain of the verb (*rqaʿ*) to the semantic domain of
the noun (*raqiaʿ*) is unreliable. Nouns and verbs that are etymologically
related do not necessarily operate in the same semantic domain. More

importantly, however, I have come to believe that there is a different Hebrew word to refer to the solid sky, and I therefore conclude that *raqia'* refers to the air space that separates waters from waters. Nevertheless, this is still representative of ancient Near Eastern ways of thinking, so his point remains valid.

Now, however, I want to focus my attention on those things on which I disagree with Lamoureux and to explain why. Most particularly, I believe that Lamoureux makes some indefensible leaps in logic. In these cases, I may well agree with the setup that he provides, but find the leap unnecessary or only one of a number of options.

Example #1: On page 58, after suggesting that Adam is simply a "retrojection" of ancient science, he states, "And since ancient science does not align with physical reality, it follows that *Adam never existed.*" I disagree that his conclusion follows inevitably from his observation. It does *not* follow that Adam never existed; only that the forming account does not record the forming of a single, unique individual. I believe that here he has leaped farther than is necessary. On this count, I remain unpersuaded concerning his "retrojection" model.

Example #2: Again on page 58 he contends, "But consistency argues that if the creation of the heavens in the Bible reflects an ancient astronomy, then we should not be surprised that the Holy Spirit also accommodated in allowing the biblical authors to use the science-of-the-day regarding human origins." Perhaps it is accurate that we would not be surprised if the Holy Spirit accommodated the ideas of the day regarding human origins, but that does not mean that full accommodation is the only choice. The principle of consistency does not accomplish that much. Specifically, there is no tradition in the ancient Near East of one human pair being the result of God's forming. There is a tradition there about *de novo* human origins, but there are likewise sufficient differences to urge us to caution. Even if the "forming" narrative about Adam has some parallels in the ancient Near East, that does not prove that Adam is not a real person in a real past. At most it would indicate that the forming account may be an accommodation — that does not mean that the role of Adam is an accommodation. After all, there is no one with the role of Adam in the ancient Near East.

In a second category of disagreement, Lamoureux's treatment of the New Testament material is inadequate in my opinion.

Example #1: Is Jesus only accommodating the Jewish belief that Adam was a real person? The key question is "Is Jesus making a scientific point or a theological one?" If the former, it could easily be accommodation. If the latter, it cannot. Jesus' use of the mustard seed, wheat seeds dying, and stars falling from sky are good examples of accommodation, so we can acknowledge that Jesus did at times accommodate their ways of thinking. But I would say those are not examples in the same category as the way that Jesus treats Adam. Jesus is not vesting the aforementioned examples with theological significance—they are only illustrations; it seems to me that with Adam he *is* making a theological point. So we might pick apart Lamoureux's conclusion: "In summary, the Lord Himself accommodated by using ancient science in His teaching. It is only consistent that He would also employ an ancient understanding of human origins—the *de novo* creation of the first man Adam—as an incidental vessel to deliver inerrant spiritual truths." Lamoureux would have to demonstrate that these are truly in the same category. Perhaps he can, but he has not done so.

Example #2: Lamoureux insists that "since Paul accepted an ancient biology of the origin of life, it is only consistent that he also accepted an ancient understanding of the origin of death, suffering, and decay. Therefore, in the same way that Scripture does not reveal how God actually created life, the Bible does not reveal the origin of biological death." Again, the question is whether what he calls "incidentals" can be distinguished from theological affirmations. I wonder whether Lamoureux's use of "consistency" really bears up under scrutiny. The question is not whether Paul *believed* that Adam was a real person. Paul believed many things that (in our estimation) were not true about the natural world. The question is whether Paul invested theological significance in his belief.

In a third area, I disagree with how Lamoureux treats the genealogies. It is true that we must not expect that ancients used genealogies the same way we do or insist that they think of genealogies the way that we do. Nevertheless, we must be constrained by the evidence that we do have from the ancient world. To the point, there is no evidence that ancient genealogies included individuals whom they did not believe existed. Lamoureux invokes the oral nature of traditions in the ancient world, but implies that the traditions can therefore not be trusted. In contrast, we more often find that in an oral culture, memory is enhanced, not corrupted.

Finally, Lamoureux states that "it is worth noting that some Christians attempt to pin Adam on the tail end of evolution. However, this is categorically inappropriate. It mixes the modern science of evolution with the ancient science of the *de novo* creation of Adam" (p. 64). If someone accepts the evolutionary model for human origins and accepts a historical Adam, then Adam, like any of us, would be a product of evolution. Here it seems to me that he is unnecessarily mixing together the scientific (*de novo*) and the potentially historical (Adam as a real person in a real past). *De novo* could indeed be an idea that resonates with the ancient world. The Adam of the Bible, however, has no parallel there.

In conclusion, I find Lamoureux's more extreme conclusions to be unnecessary. He is trying to establish that the Bible does not offer information on the origins of humans (or other living organisms). He does so by developing a line of logic that sees the biblical texts simply accommodating ancient literature and its cognitive environment. Even though I believe that there are many ways that the Bible accommodates the ancient world, in the end one does not have to rely solely on that principle. When Lamoureux says that "Holy Scripture makes statements about how God created living organisms that in fact never happened" (p. 56), I would ask whether Scripture is even making statements about how God created living organisms. From the text of Genesis itself, I think I have reason to suggest that it is not. In this sense, he maintains that the Bible's claims can be safely set aside; I maintain that the Bible is not making those claims.

Lamoureux claims that the forming of Adam follows a *de novo* pattern found in the ancient Near East. I go beyond that to see in the *de novo* pattern an archetypal element that is found not only there, but in the biblical text itself. He and I agree that the Bible uses Adam and Eve as archetypes, but we sort things out differently. He could achieve his scientific objectives (the Bible makes no claim about the material origins of human beings) without giving up the theological specifics (he maintains only the theological generalities) and without giving up the idea that Adam and Eve were real people.

Near the beginning of his chapter Lamoureux says that the "Image of God and human sin were mysteriously manifested" (p. 43). It would be difficult to disagree with this statement no matter the details of one's interpretation. Despite that acknowledgement, some knowledge has been made available to us, however slight. Our responsibility is to sort out what we can, and it has proven profoundly complicated. I am grateful for Lamoureux's long career of trying to arrive at an understanding that does justice to the evidence and to his sincere Christian faith. Our interaction with one another can serve only to sharpen our understanding as time goes on.

C. JOHN COLLINS

I appreciate how Denis Lamoureux begins his essay with a personal word about his own background in both science and faith. I happily embrace him as my Christian brother.

At the same time, for all the Christian mutuality, intellectual respect, and personal affection I have for Lamoureux, I must here focus on evaluating his contribution. I find that I have fundamental disagreements, not only with his specific conclusions, but more importantly, with his methods and assumptions, as they apply to the interpretation of both the Bible and the sciences. I will argue that in both these arenas of interpretation Lamoureux has followed a style of reasoning that is oversimplified, specifically in that he generally poses either-or questions with only two options; he does not consider whether there are alternatives. Due to space limitations, I will attend more to these larger questions than to the specific conclusions.

As to biblical interpretation, in reading texts in a literalistic fashion and equating this with historicity, Lamoureux exemplifies the tight connection between historicity and literalism that I argue against. He tells us, for example, that while Bible writers used phenomenological language, "What the biblical writers saw with their eyes, they believed to be real, like the literal rising and literal setting of the sun" (p. 46).[40] He provides one of the standard pictures of the "3-tier universe" that (we are told) Bible writers—and ancients in general—believed to be the case. The "incidental ancient science" conveys the "Message of Faith," which tends to be a timeless principle.

To explain why I find this approach to interpretation so unsatisfying, consider C. S. Lewis's essay "The Language of Religion."[41] Lewis

---

40. I leave aside discussion of whether the Hebrew terms are "literally" *rising* and *setting*, rather than English conventions being reflected in the translations; the point is not really affected.

41. C. S. Lewis, "The Language of Religion," in C. S. Lewis, *Christian Reflections*; ed. Walter Hooper (Grand Rapids: Eerdmans, 1967), 129–41. I hope one day to develop this

notes that within any given language (say, English or French, or Greek or Hebrew) there are three different levels of language use: there is "ordinary" language, which we use in day-to-day conversation, and two specializations of it, which he calls "poetic" and "scientific."

Lewis's example clarifies the difference among these three: compare (1) "it was very cold" with (2) "there were thirteen degrees of frost," and (3) "Ah, bitter chill it was! The owl, for all his feathers, was a-cold; the hare limp'd trembling through the frozen grass, and silent was the flock in wooly fold: numbed were the Beadsman's fingers."[42]

Sentence (1) is the ordinary language way of describing a winter night. Its level of detail is adequate for the communication at hand, but rarely makes a strong claim about the actual workings of what it describes and thus does not invite a close interpretation.

Sentence (2) is scientific language, whose superiority "clearly consists in giving for the coldness of the night a precise quantitative estimate which can be tested by an instrument." Its virtue is that it allows us to predict various effects on animal and vegetable life, and to do this or that with the things we are discussing. It aims at a high level of detail with as little ambiguity as possible, seeking to explain the inner workings of things.

Sentence (3) is poetic language, and it conveys more of what it would be like to experience the cold night. Often its level of detail is higher than ordinary, and its literary and linguistic features serve the communicative purposes of the poetic text: to celebrate, to mourn, to enjoy, to enable the audience to see things differently, and so on.

There is much more to say, but for now the key thing is to recognize that the Bible consists mostly of ordinary and poetic language. In my essay I show why I do not consider this to be a barrier to successfully referring to actual persons and events (the subject matter of the Big Story). The Bible authors therefore attend very little to what I call the inner workings of the things involved.

To illustrate, consider the statements in Genesis 1 about plants and animals "each according to its kind." Lamoureux tells us that this is ancient biology according to which "living organisms were immutable" (p. 55). But this is exactly what we *don't* find in Genesis, because

---

further and bring its linguistic side up to date.

42. These are the opening lines of John Keats (1795–1821), "The Eve of St. Agnes."

Genesis 1 is not a scientific text—which becomes clear once we compare it with an actual ancient scientific work, Aristotle's treatise *On the Generation of Animals*. In Genesis we learn that plants produce seeds "each according to their kinds" (Gen. 1:11–12), and the various animals appear "according to its kind" (Gen. 1:21, 24–25). The Septuagint for this phrase is *kata genos*.[43] Aristotle notices the same phenomenon, that animals generate "according to their own kind," with a Greek phrase closely akin to that in the Septuagint, *kata tēn sungenneian*. The philosopher goes on to explain that the kinds have always existed, since, "if the products were dissimilar from their parents, and yet able to copulate, we should then get arising from them yet another different manner of creature, and out of their progeny yet another, and so it would go on *ad infinitum*. Nature, however, avoids what is infinite."[44] Genesis simply employs the farmer's observation (as I have noted) and leaves it there; Aristotle seeks a description of the process.

I argue elsewhere that the features of Genesis 1—its broad-stroke description (including its terse taxonomy of plants and animals), its rhetorically high word for the sky (the "expanse") in the context of an overall simple vocabulary, its high degree of patterning (such as the refrain for each workday)—lead me to conclude that the best name for its style is "exalted prose narrative," and its purpose is quasi-liturgical, to enable its readers to celebrate God's work of creation as a magnificent achievement.[45] To call such a text "scientific" is confusion.

We might draw a similar conclusion about the hymnlike section in Philippians 2. To see that as a "scientific" description of the world, or even as the author's portrayal of his own picture of the world, misses the point of the hymnody due to a language-level mistake.[46]

---

43. The Greek in verses 11–12 adds an amplificatory "and according to their likeness."

44. I use the Loeb Classical Library edition and adjust the English as needed.

45. Collins, *Genesis 1–4: A Linguistic, Literary, and Theological Commentary* (Phillipsburg, NJ: P&R Publishing, 2006), 43–44, 78–79, invoking Moshe Weinfeld, "Sabbath, Temple, and the Enthronement of the Lord—the Problem of the Sitz im Leben of Genesis 1:1–2:3," in A. Caquot and M. Delcor, eds., *Mélanges Bibliques et Orientaux en l'Honneur de M. Henri Cazelles* (AOAT 212; Neukirchen-Vluyn: Neukirchener, 1981), 501–12. See also Walton, *The Lost World of Genesis One: Ancient Cosmology and the Origins Debate* (Downers Grove, IL: InterVarsity Press, 2009), 91; *Genesis 1 as Ancient Cosmology* (Winona Lake, IN: Eisenbrauns, 2011), 191.

46. In the light of my argument, and contra Lamoureux's assertions, the poetic language in the hymn in no way obscures its ability to *refer* to Jesus' historical achievements.

Lamoureux assures us that a literalistic reading of these features of the text yields the authors' underlying picture of the world; his diagram includes a number of texts held to support this. What I have said above makes it unlikely that this is in any way a good reading of these texts, none of which occurs in a scientific discussion.[47]

Actually, we cannot tell, one way or the other, simply from the words used, exactly what the writers "believed" about the world. For the most part, it doesn't even matter: these authors *successfully refer to* the things they describe—and enable us to picture them—without making any kind of strong claim about the processes. As near as I can tell, the age and shape of the earth play no role in anyone's communication in the Bible; and the likely explanation for that is—besides the obvious fact that such topics are outside of the authors' purposes—what C. S. Lewis said about ordinary people in the Middle Ages: "There were ditchers and alewives who ... did not know that the earth was spherical; not because they thought it was flat but because they did not think about it at all."[48] We can say the same as well about writings from the nearby cultures.[49]

I grant that some ancients have made these mistakes: for example, Josephus (*Antiquities* 1.30 [1.1.1]) described the "expanse" with a Greek term for a "crystalline" or "icy" surface, which seems to correspond to how the pre-Socratic Greek philosopher Empedocles described the heavens.[50] But this is a common hermeneutical goof, which C. S. Lewis also found in medieval Christian writers: he says of Isidore (7th century): "A highly lyrical passage from Job (xxxix.19–25) is here being turned into a proposition in natural history."[51] That is, this is a *mistaken* reading.

Consider some examples from English. In the first *Star Wars* film, *Episode 4: A New Hope*, Luke is learning the ways of the Force. He

---

47. For comments on the supposed "primitive" world picture in the Bible, see Collins, *Science and Faith: Friends or Foes?* (Wheaton, IL: Crossway, 2003), 100–102; *Genesis 1–4*, 263–65.

48. C. S. Lewis, *The Discarded Image: An Introduction to Medieval and Renaissance Literature* (Cambridge: Cambridge University Press, 1964), 20.

49. Cf. Wayne Horowitz, *Mesopotamian Cosmic Geography* (Winona Lake, IN: Eisenbrauns, 1998), xiii–xiv. Hence the pictures and quotations from the other cultures prove nothing: We still must exegete *them*.

50. See Eusebius, *Preparation for the Gospel*, 15.42 [845b], quoting Plutarch; and see Diogenes Laertius, 8.77.

51. Lewis, *Discarded Image*, 148.

cannot block the shots from the remote droid, until Obi-Wan makes him put on a helmet with an eye cover, explaining, "Your eyes can deceive you. Don't trust them." Similarly, in *The Two Towers* (part of *The Lord of the Rings*), as Gandalf restores King Théoden of Rohan to health, he says, "Your fingers would remember their old strength better, if they grasped a sword-hilt."

Now, a modern neuroscientist could object: the *eyes* don't deceive, and the *fingers* don't remember; instead, it is the processing of the signals that takes place in the *brain*. So perhaps Obi-Wan and Gandalf simply betray some aberrant science?

But our neuroscientist is actually hindering communication. We can easily identify the experiences that Obi-Wan and Gandalf are talking about, and their words portray just what it feels like—even when we accept the neuroscientist's explanation. Actually, the more popular way of describing these activities is easier for us to picture, precisely *because* it's what it feels like!

At the same time, the referent imposes limits on "artistic license." In *Star Wars Episode 6: Return of the Jedi*, Luke has learned that Darth Vader is really his father, and he reproaches Obi-Wan's ghost for telling him that Vader had *killed* his father. Obi-Wan explains, "Your father was seduced by the dark side of the Force. He ceased to be Anakin Skywalker and became Darth Vader. When that happened, the good man who was your father was destroyed. *So what I told you was true, from a certain point of view.*" Luke's incredulous reply: "A certain point of view?" Even Alec Guinness, who portrayed Obi-Wan, could not manage a facial expression of conviction! I expect he agreed with Luke's incredulity; I certainly do.

This is the context in which Lamoureux tackles what he takes to be the problem of concordism. Again, his discussion oversimplifies with an all-or-nothing approach. I quite agree that it is misguided to expect that the Bible will align with what the sciences discover, although not for the same reason that Lamoureux states. Nevertheless, I read him as implying that there is only one kind of concordism, the literalistic kind; and since that is bad, then no concordism is possible. However, Lamoureux agrees that the Bible may refer to actual events and that it is legitimate to illuminate these texts by historical studies. In other words, there is what we call a *historical concordism* that is quite appropriate—again, so long as we observe the literary conventions of the writers themselves. In this light, the survey question about Noah's flood—"Do you think that's literally true, meaning it happened that way word-for-word; or do you think it's meant as a lesson, but not to be taken literally?" (p. 45)—is unjustifiably poor in its wording. So the right distinction is between *proper* and *improper* concordism; the abuses of the improper kind do not nullify the right use of the proper kind.[52]

Hence there is no reason to suppose that the sort of "accommodation" we find in the Bible is the sort that uses (now rejected) ancient science to teach timeless truths. This is probably a stretching of the traditional notion of accommodation anyhow. We might compare two efforts at accommodating the needs of a child's mind when we answer her question about where babies come from. One way is to say something about storks bringing the baby. A better way (which my wife used) is simply to say, "God mixes a little bit from the mom and a little bit from the dad and grows it into a baby in the mom's tummy." The second is a truthful accommodation, and is in line with the traditional notions; young children rarely ask for elaboration.

Lamoureux gives us no real reasons for his assertion that "real history in the Bible begins roughly around Genesis 12 with Abraham," other than the kind of literature we find in Genesis 1–11. I have dealt with this already; I will here simply note that the first eleven chapters are so well interwoven into the whole of Genesis that the assertion loses any critical force.

As a general rule I find that Lamoureux does not distinguish between what a biblical author *says* and what Lamoureux *reads him to be saying.* This often means that his exegesis comes without much supporting argument. For example, he tells us that "Paul also believed that the natural world had changed with the divine judgment of Adam" (p. 62), when he should inform us of why he reads Paul that way. I am quite confident that this is a *mis*reading, by the way.[53]

When it comes to the science, I think Lamoureux has likewise offered too stark an alternative. He seems to imply that since scientists believe that there is good evidence for evolution, therefore we Christians

---

52. For more on this, see Collins, *Did Adam and Eve Really Exist? Who They Were and Why You Should Care* (Wheaton, IL: Crossway, 2011), 106–11.

53. For discussion, see Collins, *Science and Faith*, ch. 10; *Genesis 1–4*, 182–84.

should accept it as "a purpose-driven natural process." As I have indicated in my essay, I think that we have excellent reasons for disputing whether a "natural" process, even *God's* natural process, is adequate to produce human beings with their distinctive capacities.[54]

It cannot be reasonable to insist *beforehand* that the process is natural all the way through, unless we already know that. But we do not know it, and Christian faith helps us to avoid the blunder in our critical thinking. As Christian philosopher Paul Helm put it,

> It is not appropriate to argue, *a priori*, what God will and will not do with and in the physical creation, but—as with any contingent matter of fact—it is necessary to investigate what God has done.[55]

Further, the assertion that "our creation in the womb is proof that the Creator uses physical mechanisms to create life" is misleading. Who disputes the use of physical mechanisms? The real question is different. From where does life originate, and are physical mechanisms adequate to do the *whole* job?

Let us suppose for the moment that the biological evidence does indeed favor *some version* of "evolutionary" theory. But since that word has several meanings (as I suggest in my essay), we still have to decide which kind of evolution is warranted. Turning to C. S. Lewis again, I find his clarity helpful in separating evolution as a scientific theory from the philosophical extrapolations some might try to make from it:

> Again, for the scientist Evolution is a purely biological theorem. It takes over organic life on this planet as a going concern and tries to explain certain changes within that field. It makes no cosmic statements, no metaphysical statements, no eschatological statements.... It does not in itself explain the origin of organic life, nor of the variations, nor does it discuss the origin and validity of reason. It may well tell you how the brain, through which reason now operates, arose, but that is a different matter. Still less does it

---

54. Lamoureux tells us that the intelligent design (ID) theorists have created a false dichotomy between design and evolution, without noting that it all depends on which kind of "evolution" we are talking about (see my essay). Further, while *some* ID advocates may fall foul of the "God-of-the-gaps" problem, not all do; see, among others, Collins, "Miracles, Intelligent Design, and God-of-the-Gaps," *Perspectives on Science and Christian Faith* 55:1 (2003): 22–29.

55. Paul Helm, *The Providence of God* (Downers Grove, IL: InterVarsity Press, 1994), 76.

even attempt to tell you how the universe as a whole arose, or what it is, or whither it is tending.[56]

As I document elsewhere, this is reasonable as well as consistent with the approach advocated by some science teachers' organizations (but not by others).[57] Lewis articulates a vision for the science that is similar to what I advocate in my essay. In the process of integrating the science into the larger story the scientist does not have a privileged position. Some scientists, not observing this, have made silly forays into public policy, arguing for such things as a reform of the justice system based on a materialist view of human nonresponsibility.[58]

Finally, and I must again be brief, Lamoureux has given us a "Message-Incident Principle" that stresses the "life-changing, spiritual truths" of the Bible. I cannot see that these "truths" do adequate justice to the overarching narrative element in the Bible. Genesis 1–11, as I contend, is integrated into the whole to provide a narrative explanation for Israel's calling in the world.[59] This story appeals to publicly accessible events as key episodes; and this public nature of the events grounds the biblical claim to speak to all people everywhere about every manner of subject in God's good creation. The Bible as a whole, not just Genesis, portrays sin as something that at some point made an entrance into God's good world, but does not belong here, and will one day be eradicated. Further, we have in the creation story a pattern for human marriage that is intended to be universally applicable; it is universally applicable because it shows how we were made.[60]

---

56. C. S. Lewis, "The Funeral of a Great Myth," in *Christian Reflections*, 82–93, at 86. I take the term "theorem" to refer either to the mathematical formulae that population geneticists were using in his day or else to "a demonstrable proposition" (see the *Oxford English Dictionary*).

57. See Collins, "A Peculiar Clarity: How C. S. Lewis Can Help Us Think about Faith and Science," in John G. West, ed., *The Magician's Twin: C. S. Lewis on Science, Scientism, and Society* (Seattle: Discovery Institute Press, 2012), 69–106, at 92–94.

58. See my discussion of one such in "A Peculiar Clarity," 94–96.

59. George Orwell's novel *1984* expresses how crucial the story and its telling are to worldview formation. The Party has a slogan, "Who controls the past controls the future: who controls the present controls the past." Hence Winston's job was to revise news accounts of previous events.

60. For some thoughts on how this provides the right background to biblical views of sexual propriety as founded in creation ("natural"), see Collins, "Echoes of Aristotle in Romans 2:14–15," *Journal of Markets and Morality* 13.1 (2010): 123–73, at 146 (with 164 n. 88), 165 n. 98.

WILLIAM D. BARRICK

Declaring that Adam was "nonhistorical . . . an *incidental*, ancient vessel" (pp. 65, 37), Denis Lamoureux tosses aside the traditional view that I and other adherents to a historical Adam hold dear. Let us be perfectly clear, however. One could argue that the historicity of Adam might not indicate anything about a person's salvation. Perhaps a born-again believer could deny Adam's historical existence without losing his or her saving relationship to Christ and everlasting forgiveness of sins. However, although it might not be a salvation issue, the matter is still a gospel issue, because it touches on matters related to our need for salvation (universal sin) and the ability of Jesus Christ to act as a representative and Savior for mankind (as the "second Adam") and as the restorer of the fallen creation. Diminishing the identification of the first Adam can have a detrimental effect on one's view of the second Adam. Questioning the accuracy of one part of Scripture always puts the whole of Scripture in doubt.

Lamoureux makes it clear that the evidence that turns him away from the traditional viewpoint involves the "*overwhelming*" (p. 40, his emphasis) nature of the evidence for evolution. It acts as the driving force behind his search for an alternative interpretation for biblical evidences. I appreciate his difficulty and also his recognition of the destructive impact that evolutionary scientists can have on the faith of Christian young people. He also possesses a clear understanding that the interpretation of the biblical evidence comprises the central issue of the debate over origins. In other words, the debate over methods of science or the opinions of scientists will not lead to a satisfactory solution. Biblical evidence should receive the bulk of our attention in this discussion of the historicity of Adam.

To introduce evolutionary creation to other evangelical believers, Lamoureux draws a parallel between ongoing procreative processes (conception and birth). As he sees it, the progressive development of the embryo presents an analogy for the physical mechanisms that the Creator employed in Genesis 1 creation — especially the creation of life itself. Such procreative processes, however, do not appear to offer an equivalent parallel. According to Scripture, God did not form Adam in a preexisting mother's womb. Genesis depicts an instantaneous special creation of one individual, Adam, from the dust of the earth. God made Eve by an equally instantaneous and special creation.

I argue that Adam bears no resemblance to the legend of Rip van Winkle, who slept for years and awoke to find a world changed by the passing of time. For Eve to have evolved out of Adam would have taken millions of years. Adam could not have slept for eons of time while God made the woman. It would require the multiplication of many miracles to keep Adam from aging while he waited for a wife to evolve.

By starting "real history" (p. 44) in the Bible around Genesis 12, Lamoureux reveals the nature of his hermeneutics. He changes his interpretive principles when dealing with Genesis 1–11, because he identifies Genesis 1–11 as a unique category of literature. Therefore he seeks interpretive standards that he considers more in keeping with the way that people of the ancient Near East spoke and wrote about the creation of the universe, the earth, and mankind.

Evolutionary creation emphasizes the use of phenomenological language in Scripture. Lamoureux believes that the ancients interpreted natural phenomena literally. In other words, they believed the sun really did rise and set. This differs from our modern phenomenological perspective, which understands that the sun merely *appears* to rise and set. A 3-tiered universe also fits within that ancient perspective, but not within our modern perspective.

Lamoureux argues that Paul's belief in a 3-tiered universe in Philippians 2 finds no inherent contradiction with the apostle's clear view of the historicity of Jesus. It works for Lamoureux to use the argument that poetry does not negate the character and historical reliability in Philippians 2. However, when it comes to Genesis 1, the "unique" character of its literary type does not allow him to look at its content as historically reliable. To me this seems inconsistent.

As an example of phenomenological language in the Genesis creation account, Lamoureux cites the meaning of "firmament" for the Hebrew *raqi'a*, which I believe to be an inaccurate and misleading translation.

"Expanse" offers a superior rendering due to the core meaning of "hammer/stretch/spread out." The lexicographical fallacy involved in this appeal to the word "firmament" (as referring to a solid physical entity) is similar to that which comes into play with attempts to attribute something physically literal for English words such as "butterfly" or "white paper" (as a reference to a governmental policy announcement). "Firmament" represents an example of the classical semantic fallacy relying on etymology as the deciding factor in determining a word's meaning.

Are the six days of the Genesis creation account an accommodation made by God to indicate an extended amount of time more commensurate with evolutionary theory? According to John Calvin, in his comment on Genesis 1:5,

> Here the error of those is manifestly refuted, who maintain that the world was made in a moment. For it is too violent a cavil to contend that Moses distributes the work which God perfected at once into six days, for the mere purpose of conveying instruction. Let us rather conclude that God himself took the space of six days, for the purpose of accommodating his works to the capacity of men.[61]

As far as accommodation is concerned, Calvin declares that God used six days as a means of accommodating himself to what man could comprehend. God created the world in six days, then rested on the seventh day from his creative work in order to provide a pattern for mankind to follow in Sabbath observance (Exod. 20:11). Calvin did not use the argument of accommodation to support an old universe or an old earth. In fact, a century prior to James Ussher's published chronology, Calvin states that "the duration of the world, now declining to its ultimate end, has not yet attained six thousand years."[62]

Another classical traditionalist, Martin Luther, likewise held firmly to his conviction "that Moses spoke in a literal sense, not allegorically or figuratively, i.e., that the world, with all its creatures, was created within six days, as the words read."[63] When Luther arrives at Genesis 1:27,

61. John Calvin, *Commentaries on the First Book of Moses Called Genesis*, 2 vols., trans. John King (Grand Rapids: Eerdmans, 1948), 1:78.

62. John Calvin, *Institutes of the Christian Religion*, trans. F. L. Battles (Philadelphia: Westminster Press, 1960), 1.14.1.

63. Martin Luther, in *Luther's Works: Vol. 1, Lectures on Genesis Chapters 1 – 5*, ed. and trans. Jaroslav Pelikan (St. Louis: Concordia Publishing House, 1958), 5.

he repeats his assertion that "the six days were truly six natural days, because here Moses says that Adam and Eve were created on the sixth day."[64] He also insisted that Genesis 2 gives information about how man was created on the sixth day.[65] Modern evangelicals who adopt a day-age theory or accept millions or billions of years for the age of the earth have clearly chosen to take a path distinctly contrary to long-trusted commentators and theologians such as Calvin and Luther.

The destruction of faith in evangelical Christians cannot be laid solely at the door of evolutionary theory. There must be some account-ability for scholars like Lamoureux who make declarations such as this: "Holy Scripture makes statements about how God created the heavens that in fact never happened" (p. 54). The statement creates tension in regard to God's truthfulness in his Word and in regard to the clarity (perspicuity) of Scripture. This type of statement goes beyond mere accommodation or phenomenological language. It strikes at the integrity and dependability of Scripture!

The parables that Jesus used in teaching the multitudes and his disciples could be his own observations of real-life people and their experiences. Lamoureux assumes that they are made up or are like old wives' tales passed on from ancient times. It is as though Jesus could not observe and think for himself, but merely parroted traditional stories and axioms. In other words, Jesus did not raise the standard of theological consideration, but rather adopted the lower standards of the pagan world around him.

When it comes to the realm of science, Lamoureux appeals to uniformitarian thought by interpreting past processes in the light of present-day processes. Let's consider the New Testament account of Jesus' creation of wine at the wedding in Cana (John 2:1–11). Note that the normal production of wine results from a natural process requiring time and fermentation. Jesus, however, instantly changed the water into the very best of aged wine—without using the natural process.[66] In order

---

64. Ibid., 69.

65. Ibid., 73.

66. According to D. A. Carson in *The Gospel of John*, Pillar NT Commentary (Grand Rapids: Eerdmans, 1991), 168, John might again (cf. 1:1–18) refer to the Genesis creation account by recording a week of days (John 1:19–2:1) that come to a climax with the miracle at Cana on the seventh day. We cannot be dogmatic on this point, since it assumes that John's readers are familiar with the Hebrew Bible and might read it over several times with care. However,

to be consistent, Lamoureux would have to deny the miracle at Cana on the same grounds that he denies instant creation in Genesis 1 — after all, modern evolutionary science is antagonistic to both. Is that really the way we ought to read the Bible and apply modern thinking to its interpretation? The traditional young-earth creation view of the historicity of Adam seeks to distinguish itself by avoiding any appearance of either questioning or denying the supernatural, miraculous character of either the original Genesis creation or Jesus' creation of wine at Cana. For us it is inconsistent to accept the latter, but not the former.

Toward the end of his essay, Lamoureux hints at his possible rejection of the doctrine of original sin. It would seem to be consistent, as he himself points out, with the view that a historical Adam never existed. After all, if Adam and Eve are not the real heads of the human race, no foundation remains to establish the sinfulness of all mankind without exception. Therefore some people might not be objects of wrath "by nature" (Eph. 2:3). If that is true, then they do not need the sacrificial death of Christ for their salvation. Again, such a view denies the credibility of Scripture in more than just the creation account in Genesis.

A side issue, but still related to the integrity and authenticity of the biblical record of creation, involves Lamoureux's statement about the absence of any mention of writing in the book of Genesis. This is as good a time as any to point out that absence of evidence is not evidence of absence. It is a dangerous precedent to set when the interpreter of Scripture assumes that something does not exist if the text does not mention it.

In the end, Lamoureux admits that his understanding of Romans 5 and 8, as well as 1 Corinthians 15, is "a very counterintuitive way to read Scripture" (p. 63). That is the major weakness of the evolutionary creation viewpoint: it insists on a counterintuitive way of reading the biblical record so as to not read it for what it appears to actually say. In summary, the evolutionary creation viewpoint bases its conclusions on a full, unquestioning faith in secular evolutionary theory and on the concept of accommodation with regard to the written record in Scripture. Victims to this approach include the historicity of Genesis 1–11,

---

both the simpler reading discussed above and Carson's suggestion of a more nuanced reading indicate the significance of the literal, historical creation account to Jesus, his ministry, and the apostolic writings.

instantaneous special creation as a divine act, divine revelation, and a consistent hermeneutic.

Such casualties in the realm of biblical interpretation set the stage for even higher casualties among believers — especially among young people. The cost of this viewpoint is too high to be acceptable. The evolutionary creationist might still be a born-again believer with sins forgiven, but at what loss to a fuller view of God, God's Word, and even of the Savior himself?

A REJOINDER

DENIS O. LAMOUREUX

I have enjoyed this exchange with Drs. Walton, Collins, and Barrick. I thank Zondervan for affording us the opportunity to share our views. This book offers readers a fine resource for developing their position on the historicity of Adam.

My approach to Adam is based on the notion that the Bible is not a book of science. In contrast, my three colleagues embrace scientific concordism in varying forms. I contend that Adam reflects an ancient understanding of human origins, similar to the ancient scientific idea of the firmament. No one today believes in the existence of a hard dome overhead, and consistency argues that neither should we believe in the *de novo* creation and existence of Adam.

Regarding my understanding of the Hebrew word *rāqia'* (firmament), Walton and Barrick are correct in saying that caution is required when considering the etymology of words (pp. 67, 81–82). However, my position does not rest *only* on the etymology of *rāqia'*. The context of the numerous biblical passages that I cited supports my view. *Taken together*, the 42 verses presented in Figure 2 (p. 48) only make sense in a 3-tier universe with a firmament. My position is also consistent with the astronomy accepted in the ancient Near East (Figures 4 and 5, p. 52). Finally, Christian tradition up to the seventeenth century believed that *rāqia'* referred to a solid firmament (e.g., Luther and the King James Bible).

Readers will note that none of my colleagues dealt with *katachthoniōn* (the underworld) in Philippians 2:10. I believe that the evangelical method of biblical interpretation entails dealing with *every* word in the Word of God, not merely with those words that conveniently fit into our traditional assumptions.

Walton states that I often appeal to consistency in my chapter and offers three examples in his rebuttal. Astonishingly, he asserts, "The principle of consistency does not accomplish that much" (p. 68). I will let readers decide if the notion of consistency is worth accepting.

In identifying a critical difference between us, Walton proclaims that the historicity of Adam bears "theological significance" (p. 69). Yet he agrees with me that "Jesus' use of the mustard seed, wheat seeds dying, and stars falling from the sky are good examples of accommodation" (p. 69). But why is the Lord's use of the *de novo* creation of Adam in Matthew 19:4–6 not an accommodation as well? Walton's position strikes me as inconsistent.

My treatment of biblical genealogies was not as clear as it could have been, and Walton judiciously challenges me. I believe that real people are behind the genealogies in Genesis 1–11 and that these lists of individuals were connected to the *de novo* creation of Adam. For more on my view of biblical genealogies, see www.ualberta.ca/~dlamoure/genealogies.html.

Collins complains that my proposed Message-Incident Principle does not "do adequate justice to the overarching narrative element in the Bible" (p. 79). He stumbles over my use of the term "ancient science," since he prefers the category "ordinary language" (p. 73). I have no objection to his terminology.

However, Collins actually embraces my interpretative principle by distinguishing between a "world picture" and a "worldview." In his book *Genesis 1–4*, he defines "worldview" as "one's basic religious stance toward the world" and adds that he "can share a worldview with some ancient [person] whose world picture involved a stationary earth with an orbiting sun."[67] Therefore, Collins could agree with me by saying that the *de novo* creation of Adam is "ordinary language" and an ancient "world picture" of human origins held by the biblical writers.

According to Barrick, "Diminishing the identification of the first Adam can have a detrimental effect on one's view of the second Adam [Jesus]" (p. 80). Not true. In my book *Evolutionary Creation* I revealed, "The Jesus I knew and loved as a young earth creationist is the very same Jesus I know and love today as an evolutionary creationist."[68]

Barrick claims that evolution is "the driving force behind" (p. 80) my interpretive approach to Genesis. Not true. If he had read my chapter with care he would have recognized that my PhD in theology came

---

67. C. John Collins, *Genesis 1–4: A Linguistic, Literary, and Theological Commentary* (Phillipsburg, NJ: P&R Publishing, 2006), 261–2.
68. *EC*, 367.

before my PhD in biology (pp. 39–42). I rejected young earth creation in seminary, but I remained a staunch anti-evolutionist. It was at that time "I concluded that young earth creation is un-biblical."[69]

Evidence that Barrick completely misunderstands my view of Adam appears in his assertion, "For Eve to have evolved out of Adam would have taken millions of years. Adam could not have slept for eons of time while God made the woman" (p. 81). Was that in my chapter? No. This quotation reveals the entrenchment of scientific concordism in the mind of Barrick.

To defend his position, Barrick calls on "long-trusted commentators and theologians such as Calvin and Luther" (p. 83). But as I will present, Luther was a geocentrist who believed in the firmament and the heavenly sea (pp. 233–35). According to Calvin,

> We indeed are not ignorant, that the circuit of the heavens is finite, and that the earth, like a little globe, is placed in the centre [geocentricity].... The primum mobile [the last sphere with stars attached to it] rolls all the celestial spheres along with it.[70]

Prior to understanding gravity, astronomers believed that planets were embedded in moving heavenly spheres. Are we to trust Calvin and Luther regarding the structure of the heavens and earth? No. Why then should we trust their sixteenth-century understanding of human origins?

I am disappointed by Barrick's thinly veiled questioning of my salvation. For example, "*Perhaps* a born-again believer could deny Adam's historical existence without losing his or her saving relationship to Christ and everlasting forgiveness of sins" (p. 80, my italics). I will not dignify such remarks with a response.

Preferring to end my contribution to this book on a positive note, I will simply say that I am humbled by Drs. Walton and Collins for their generous affirmations of my evangelical Christian faith. Amen.

---

69. *EC*, 351.

70. John Calvin, *Commentary on Genesis*, Vol. 1 (1554; Grand Rapids: Christian Classics Ethereal Library, 2007), 24–25, 114.

A HISTORICAL ADAM:
ARCHETYPAL CREATION VIEW

JOHN H. WALTON

I*n my view, Adam and Eve are historical figures — real people in a real past. Nevertheless, I am persuaded that the biblical text is more interested in them as archetypal figures who represent all of humanity. This is particularly true in the account in Genesis 2 about their formation. I contend that the formation accounts are not addressing their material formation as biological specimens, but are addressing the forming of all of humanity: we are all formed from dust, and we are all gendered halves. If this is true, Genesis 2 is not making claims about biological origins of humanity, and therefore the Bible should not be viewed as offering competing claims against science about human origins. If this is true, Adam and Eve also may or may not be the first humans or the parents of the entire human race. Such an archetypal focus is theologically viable and is well-represented in the ancient Near East.*

Introduction

My view is that Adam and Eve were real people in a real past; they were individual persons who existed in history. The basis for this conclusion comes from the fact that in the Old Testament Adam becomes part of a genealogy, and in the New Testament a real event featuring real people is the clearest reading to explain the entrance of sin and death. Nevertheless, I also believe that the biblical text is most interested in Adam and Eve as archetypes — those who represent humanity. In particular, I believe that the "making" accounts in Genesis 2 reflect their roles as archetypes and therefore give us no scientific information about human origins.

To begin, it is important that I clarify that an archetype is different from a prototype, as I use these terms. A prototype is the first in a series that serves as a model for subsequent production. It establishes a pattern but is otherwise unrelated to the later products. In contrast, an archetype serves as a representative of all other members of the group, thus establishing an inherent relationship. In this specific instance, Adam as a prototype would be designated the "Primeval Man," whereas Adam as an archetype would be designated "Everyman," representing all.

Another important point of clarification to make is that the role of someone as an archetype does not preclude their historical existence. An archetype can be a real person in a real past, though not all archetypes are. In the view that I present here, I believe that Adam and Eve were real people who existed in a real past in time and space; but I believe that both in Genesis and in the New Testament, there is more interest in them as archetypes (notwithstanding their reality). Abraham was a real person in a real past, but the New Testament shows its interest in him as an archetype when it identifies him as a father of all who believe (Rom. 4:11–12). Jesus was a real person in a real past, but is portrayed as an archetype as the second Adam (Rom. 5:12–21). In this same passage, Adam (designated the first man) is used as a contrasting archetype.

I would not want to diminish in any way the importance of Adam and Eve being real people. At the same time, I will be developing the perspective that we miss the mark if we do not see that all biblical authors are more interested in them as archetypes. When dealing with authoritative text, it is the author's intentions that take on the most significance. If we find that the author's interests are in the archetypal rather than the genetic role of Adam and Eve, that might influence our understanding of the claims the text is making.

Archetypal Role of Humanity in Genesis 1

The humanity referred to in Genesis 1, whether referring to one couple or to corporate humanity, is described in archetypal terms: they are made in God's image, and they are represented as male and female. As such, they describe and represent all of humanity throughout time, as do the roles given them (subdue, rule, etc.). In ancient Near Eastern literature the image of God is not generally ascribed to all humanity (exception, a passing reference in the Instruction of Merikare—see more later). Even though the designation usually refers to the king, even there it is archetypal as it connects to the royal personage.[1]

Archetypal Role of Adam in Genesis 2

Adam. The first evidence of the archetypal importance of Adam is the fact that he is called "Adam," the Hebrew word for humankind.[2] We have to recall from the start that whoever Adam is, however he came to be, and whenever he lived, he did not speak Hebrew. Hebrew as we know it developed as a language only sometime after the Israelites came to the land of Canaan after the Exodus. Thus, the Hebrew designation "Adam" is a literary designation given relatively late. We cannot think of it as the actual personal name of this historical person. In that sense then, even the name is archetypal rather than historical.

Richard S. Hess has done a thorough study of the thirty-four occurrences of 'adam in Genesis 1–5.[3] Of these occurrences, twenty-two have the definite article (which in Hebrew is never attested on a personal name). Only five occurrences clearly refer to a personal name (all without the definite article: 4:25; 5:1a, 3, 4, 5; note also the anomalous 4:1, which by context may suggest a personal name but uses the definite article). The others without the definite article refer to generic humanity; corporate, en masse (i.e., people including both male and female; 1:26; 2:5; 5:1b, 2; and oddly, 1:27 with the definite article). I believe that the definite article in all but Genesis 1:27 and 4:1 is used to designate the archetypal individual (the bulk of them [14 times] in 2:7–25; see also the confrontation in the garden, 3:8, 9, 12, and the result, 3:22, 24).[4] In these examples, everything that this archetypal individual does he performs as a representative for all humanity or on behalf of all males.

---

1. See the detailed discussion in John H. Walton, *Genesis 1 as Ancient Cosmology* (Winona Lake, IN: Eisenbrauns, 2011), 78–84.

2. The root meaning "humankind" has cognates in other Western Semitic languages such as Phoenician, Ugaritic, and Aramaic.

3. Richard S. Hess, "Splitting the Adam: the usage of 'adam in Genesis i-v," in *Studies in the Pentateuch*, ed. J. A. Emerton, in VTSup XLI (Leiden: Brill, 1990), 1–15.

4. Three occurrences feature the ל preposition pointed by the Masoretes with a shewa and are therefore presumed to be indefinite, though one wonders whether that is correct with all other occurrences through chapters 2 and 3 being definite. (Only one vowel change differentiates definite from indefinite when the preposition is present.)

Formed from dust. The most obvious statement about Adam—and the one most important to this discussion—is the statement that God formed (*yaṣar*) him from the dust (*'apar*) of the earth. Is this intended to be a statement about the material origins of the first human being? Traditionally, it has been common to think about this statement as describing a material process of special creation characterized by discontinuity with any previously existing creature. Yet there are limits to how far this concept should be taken. Most would not contend that reference to the ingredient "dust" dictates the chemical composition of the human body. That being the case, it would appear that a Pinocchio concept is envisioned in which the sculpture or image is made (it would not matter what it was made of) and then that image is brought to life (now bearing no resemblance to dust at all).

One of the difficulties with this way of thinking is that dust is characteristically resistant to being molded. If a sculpting process is being used, clay would be a much more likely ingredient to use (cf. Job 4:19; 10:9; 33:6, *homer*). Another is that if the dust was only to be transformed, it has nothing to say about the material process and, in fact, plays no role at all.

The verb *yaṣar*, however, need not be thought of as suggesting a sculpting process. We only need to look at the verb's range of usage to see that it does not require a material context. Especially noteworthy is Zechariah 12:1: "The LORD, who stretches out the heavens, who lays the foundation of the earth, and who forms [*yaṣar*] the human spirit within a person. . . ." Here Zechariah is speaking specifically about the creation narrative and sees the "forming" as pertaining to the spirit rather than the body and thus not referring to material origins.

The same concept is represented in Egyptian reliefs where Khnum, the craftsman creator deity, is shown shaping a human on the potter's wheel (here it is clay, not dust). The context of the relief and the text that accompany it, however, make it clear that it is not the material formation of the human that is conveyed, but the shaping of the pharaoh to be pharaoh. He is being designed for a role. This imagery pertains to the function he is destined to have and not to the process by which he was created as a material individual. One could say that his "royal spirit" is being formed to highlight similarity to Zechariah 12. In Egyptian thinking this is not referring merely to his training or preparation;

rather, it is an indication of his election and sponsorship by the gods who have ordained him for this task. It reflects his high calling and his exalted status.

Returning to the role of "dust" in Genesis 2, we can reasonably deduce from the passage itself that dust carries an archetypal rather than a material significance. Genesis 3:19 explains this significance (in case we might have failed to grasp it in 2:7) when it states, "Dust you are and to dust you will return." Dust refers to mortality, and everyone is formed from dust.[5] Psalm 103:14 substantiates this as the psalmist says that the LORD "knows how we are formed, he remembers that we are dust." This verse uses the same vocabulary as Genesis 2:7 and indicates that humankind (archetypally) is formed from dust. In fact then, it would not be a distortion to say that each of us is formed from dust (that is, we are all frail and mortal).

The conclusion of this line of reasoning is that being formed from dust does not refer to the material origins of any of us, nor does the fact that we are formed from dust preclude that we were born of a woman by a natural process. Following that line of reasoning back, we could also suggest that Adam being formed from dust does not preclude him being born of a woman. In other words, the statement in Genesis 2:7 is not essentially a statement about material discontinuity. It is a statement about our nature. The New Testament confirms this when it contrasts the archetype human as being from "dust of the earth" while Jesus as an archetype is "of heaven" (1 Cor. 15:47). Thus I conclude that being formed from dust plays an archetypal role in the context, with a debatable inference regarding material origins or discontinuity. If the text is not addressing material origins or asserting material discontinuity, there is no biblical claim being made about the mechanics or process of material human origins.

Taken and placed in a garden. Genesis 2:8 provides a summary statement introducing the next section of text (2:9–17), which fills in the details. Genesis 2:15 provides a fuller explanation of 2:8 and makes a statement

---

5. Additional evidence that dust equals mortality is that in the garden an antidote—the tree of life—was provided. No tree of life would be needed if people were created immortal. Mortality was the natural human condition, but God had provided a mechanism by which people could find life. That life is represented in the tree, but finds its source in God (cf. Deut. 30:15–19). Cf. also Paul's statement in 1 Corinthians 15:48.

whose significance is often missed. This verse says that God "took" (*lqḥ*) the archetypal human (definite article) and "caused him to rest" (*hiphil* of *nwḥ*) in the garden. "Rest" is a loaded term that certainly implies more than simply settling or dwelling somewhere. But the use of *lqḥ* is even more arresting. Took him from where? In similar contexts the use of this verb has an opposite problem. When Enoch walks with God and God "takes" him, we are left wondering where he takes him (Gen. 5:24).

Further insight can be gained from an interesting parallel wording in the Gilgamesh Epic. In tablet XI the flood hero, Uta-napishti, disembarks from the ark to be met by a group of the gods discussing how he was spared, whether he should have been spared, and what they were to do with him now. In lines 203–6 the decision is made and a blessing conferred:

> "In the past Uta-napishti was one of mankind,
> But now Uta-napishti and his woman shall be like us gods!
> Uta-napishti shall dwell far away, at the mouth of the rivers!"
> They took[6] me and settled me far away, at the mouth of the
> rivers.[7]

The setting to which the flood hero is "taken" is an Edenic setting ("at the mouth of the rivers") where he will have an existence "like the gods." It is not a dwelling with the gods, but it is removed from the strictly mortal realm. (Note that Gilgamesh had to cross the river of death to get there.) His being "taken" is seen as a blessing. This sort of understanding would also make sense for Enoch in Genesis 5.

On the basis of Genesis 5 and Gilgamesh 11, I would propose that Adam, the archetypal human, is being removed from the everyday realm of human existence and placed in a specially prepared place (the mouth of the rivers) as a blessing.[8] If other people are around, he is being elected from them to play a special role. From Genesis 4:14, 17 we could reasonably deduce that there are other people around—in fact, that may be the easiest reading. Regardless of whether or not other people were

---

6. This uses the Akkadian cognate to Hebrew *lqḥ*, *leqû*.

7. Andrew George, trans., *The Babylonian Gilgamesh Epic* (Oxford: Oxford University Press, 2003), 1:716–17.

8. The identity of two of the rivers of Eden as the Tigris and Euphrates would not detract from this view. Significant bodies of water are part of cosmic space.

present, the text has shown us that the forming of the archetypal human is directed toward a particular role that he will play. The second half of verse 15 tells us about the nature of this blessing and elect role.

Priestly role. The last two words in the Hebrew text of Genesis 2:15 delineate the role being given to the archetypal human by means of two infinitives constructed from the roots 'abad and šamar. The former has been used in the near context to refer to "working the ground" (2:5; 3:23), and the pair in Genesis 2:15 are traditionally interpreted as pertaining to manual labor in the garden (agricultural work such as landscaping, pruning, and harvesting).

Certainly, as Genesis 2:5 shows, 'abad could point in that direction, given the appropriate direct object. The second verb, šamar, however, would not fit so easily into the category of agricultural work. It is used regularly in the Pentateuch to refer to Levitical responsibility for guarding sacred space. With that prompting, we then also notice that 'abad is used throughout the Pentateuch to refer to priestly service in sacred space (note particularly Num. 8:15). Both verbs are used together in reference to caring for sacred space in Numbers 3:8–9.[9]

The significance of this conclusion must not be underestimated. The role of the archetypal human, if a priestly role, is a representative role—thus affirming the archetypal interests of the text.[10] This representation would extend to all humans alive at the time (if there are any) in that he was chosen from among them to serve this role on their behalf, and for all humans yet to come. The themes of election (e.g., Abram, David) and representative priesthood (the Aaronic priests) are well-known in Old Testament theology.

Thus, we also find that as pharaoh is being formed for the royal role in the Egyptian reliefs (an exaltation theology), so here the archetypal human is being formed for a priestly role (arguably an election theology). The "forming" in Genesis 2:7 then finds credibility for being understood as role/function oriented rather than as a statement of material origins of humanity.

---

9. For a more extensive discussion see John H. Walton, *Genesis*, NIVAC, vol. 1 (Grand Rapids: Zondervan, 2001), 172–74.

10. A distinction should be realized between archetypal representation and priestly representation. All share in the archetype's profile, but not all are priests—the priest *does*, however, represent all.

Archetypal Role of Eve in Genesis

Deep sleep. It has also been commonplace to interpret Genesis 2:21–22 as describing the material origin of Eve. A number of elements in the text, however, may readily admit to other interpretations that would lead to different conclusions.

As the section opens, God causes Adam to fall into a deep sleep. It is easy for us to think of this as a necessary anesthesia for some significant surgery. Nonetheless, a little thought reminds us that removal of a rib is not any sort of standard surgery in either the ancient or the modern world. Furthermore, they knew nothing of anesthesia. Beyond those observations, interpreters have always been curious about what significance a rib would have.

Such questions should first lead us to investigate what is going on in biblical text when someone is in a deep sleep. The text here uses the noun *tardemâ* (seven occurrences in the Old Testament), related both morphologically and semantically to the verbal root *rdm* (seven occurrences in OT). This deep sleep sometimes refers to an individual being oblivious to what is taking place in the waking world (usually a potential threat, Judg. 4:21; 1 Sam. 26:12; Jonah 1:5–6). Other times it refers to someone whose deep sleep gives them awareness of something going on in the spiritual realm (Gen. 15:12; Job 4:13; Dan. 8:18; 10:9). In my estimation, the latter is more likely here. There is no potential threat, and there is an important spiritual reality that is conveyed. As Genesis 15:12, which features the ratification of the covenant, indicates, such visions can be used to make highly significant spiritual or theological points. If this is a vision, it need not refer to a material event. Before we draw such a conclusion, however, another key interpretative element calls for careful attention.

Rib. The Hebrew term here, *ṣelaʿ*, never refers to anatomy anywhere else in the Hebrew Bible.[11] In its roughly forty occurrences it refers to a "side" and is typically directional (north side versus south side) or structural (sides of the ark or sides of the temple).[12] What is most important to note is that the term generally refers to one side of something of

---

11. The Akkadian cognate *ṣelu* does refer to anatomy, particularly in the medical texts and divination texts. Although it is occasionally translated "rib(s)," it typically refers to the side or to the rib cage, *CAD* Ṣ:124–26. Even so, it is common for it to refer to one of a pair. It is also used directionally and structurally as in Hebrew.

12. See Exodus 25:14; 36:31–32; 1 Kings 6:5; Ezekiel 41:5–9. For full discussion see *TDOT* 12:401.

which there are only two sides, that is, these "sides" tend to come in pairs.[13] The result of this analysis suggests that God takes one of the two sides of the archetypal man to build the archetypal woman.

If this is so, it is clear that this process is unlike any surgery, despite the fact that God then "closed up the place with flesh." In this interpretation, God puts the archetypal man into a deep sleep so that he can show him in a vision something important about the nature and identity of the woman to whom he is about to introduce him. When the man awakes, he immediately understands that she is "bone of my bones and flesh of my flesh." Bone and flesh are both involved, thus indicating that the text is not to be understood as referring simply to a rib. Then, as a final piece of evidence, the text itself identifies the archetypal significance through the words of the narrator: "That is why a man leaves his father and mother and is united to his wife, and they become one flesh" (Gen. 2:24). This is true of all mankind and all womankind. The vision has shown the archetypal man that woman is essentially related to him. If this is the case, these verses need not be understood as recounting the material origins of the first woman. Communication through a vision underlines this, and the idea that half of Adam is removed fairly requires it. God is showing the man how he should think about the helper that he is about to provide and then brings this woman to him (just as the man had been taken and brought to the garden).

Mother of all living. While it can be readily observed that Eve is given archetypal significance in the only two references to her in the New Testament (2 Cor. 11:3; 1 Tim. 2:13), we should note that the designation "mother of all the living," given to her in Genesis 3:20, is also archetypal. At the same time, it does not demand a biological or genetic role, as we can see from the similar statements in Genesis 4:20–21, where Jabal is "the father of those who live in tents and raise livestock" and Jubal is "the father of all who play stringed instruments." Since these refer to archetypal roles, not biological relationships, we can see that the terminology of biological relationship can be used in archetypal ways. This does not prove that Eve's name does not indicate that all human beings came from her; it merely offers other reasonable alternatives from within the near context.

---

13. It should be noted that there are likely other technical uses; cf. the ongoing controversy concerning the architectural detail of 1 Kings 6:15–16.

Having provided strong evidence in favor of interpreting the form-ing account and naming account of Eve as archetypal, I must also state that giving birth to sons in Genesis 4:1 and the information in the New Testament references indicate that we should think of her as a real indi-vidual who existed in a real past even though her primary significance in Genesis 2–3 is as an archetype. It is true that the text *could* be refer-ring to the biological as well as the archetypal, but neither one can be assumed; both must be demonstrated. I am proposing that the primary interests of the text are in the archetypal. I have offered arguments that the evidences in this passage that have traditionally been taken as refer-ring to material origins are credibly and perhaps preferably interpreted as archetypal. If that is so, biological claims would not be understood as affirmed within the authority of the text.

Archetypal Humanity in the Ancient Near East

So far, although a few illustrations from the ancient world have been mentioned, I have been drawing conclusions from the biblical text based on the biblical text. With these conclusions in mind, we can now turn to the ancient Near Eastern texts pertaining to human origins to discover the ideas that existed in the world in which Israelites lived.

Accounts of or allusions to human origins are found in Sumerian, Akkadian, and Egyptian texts. Most of the accounts are brief (a couple of lines), with the longest ones (Enlil and Ninmaḫ and Atraḫasis) extending for several dozen lines.

Sumerian	Akkadian
• Song of the Hoe[14] • Hymn to E'engura[16] • Enki and Ninmaḫ[18] • KAR 4[19]	• Atraḫasis[15] • Enuma Elish[17]

14. *COS* 1.157. Also called "Praise of the Pickax"; see R. J. Clifford, *Creation Accounts in the Ancient Near East and the Bible*, CBQMS 26 (Washington: Catholic Biblical Association, 1994), 31.
15. *COS* 1.130.
16. Clifford, *Creation Accounts*, 29–30.
17. *COS* 1.111.
18. *COS* 1.159.
19. Clifford, *Creation Accounts*, 50–51.

Egyptian[20]
• Pyramid Texts 445, 522 (Khnum on potter's wheel) • Coffin Texts (CT II: 43, spell 80).[21] • CT spell 1130[22] • Instruction of Merikare[23]

Nowhere in the ancient texts are human origins depicted in terms of a single couple being created as progenitors of the entire human race. Consequently, if the biblical text includes that idea, it is not doing so in conformity with its ancient Near Eastern environment. I hasten to note, however, that such nonconformity would make perfect sense. In the ancient Near East people are created as slave laborers for the gods, so it would be illogical to make only two. In contrast, the Old Testament has a very different view of the role of humanity, in which there would be no compulsion for mass production.

These observations do not mandate that the biblical account must initiate humanity with a single couple. It merely suggests that if this is so, this is unique in its cognitive environment. Despite that important possible distinction, archetypal representation could be intended whether accounts feature mass production or focus on one couple. We have seen the archetypal indicators in the biblical text, so we now turn our attention to the archetypal nature of the ancient Near Eastern accounts.

1. *Ingredients.* No consensus exists in the ancient world concerning the ingredients of creation stories, yet at the same time the designated ingredients are consistently archetypal. In two Sumerian accounts, Song of the Hoe and Hymn to E'engura, people break out from the ground. Another account refers to clay (Enlil and Ninmaḫ). Some Egyptian Pyramid texts refer to clay on a potter's wheel while others use a product from the living creator deity (tears in the coffin texts, from the god's body in Merikare).[24]

---

20. James P. Allen, *Genesis in Egypt* (New Haven: Yale University Press, 1988); Ewa Wasilewska, *Creation Stories of the Middle East* (London: Jessica Kingsley, 2000); James K. Hoffmeier, "Some Thoughts on Genesis 1 & 2 and Egyptian Cosmology," *JANES* 15 (1983): 39–49.

21. *COS* 1.8.

22. *COS* 1.17; see also 1.9.

23. *COS* 1.35.

24. In Egyptian the word for tears (*rmwt*) is very similar to the word for people (*rmtn*), Jacobus van Dijk, "Myth and Mythmaking in Ancient Egypt," *CANE*, 1707. In text, see

Akkadian accounts uniquely refer to products from a slain rebel deity. In Atraḫasis both flesh and blood are used, whereas only the blood is mentioned in Enuma Elish and KAR 4. Only in Atraḫasis is there a combination of common and divine materials.[25] In addition to material ingredients, allusion to divine infusion may be represented by means of the mother goddess giving birth to humans (Enlil and Ninmaḫ) or by the divine breath (Coffin Texts, Merikare). The variety of materials reflects the differences that each account wants to emphasize and explain in the archetypal profile. The commonality we find in the cognitive environment is that people are portrayed conventionally as being created out of elements that will explain their archetypal roles.

Archetypes

All these provide a profile defining the archetypal nature of humanity, particularly pertaining to connectivity, relationships, and roles — arguably the most significant aspects of reality. To be clear, they have no concern for materiality or material origins. One of the clearest examples of archetypal thinking is found in Enki and Ninmaḫ, in which the mother goddess, Ninmaḫ, undertakes the challenge of creating archetypes of certain handicapped or defective classes of humans for which Enki, the god of wisdom, has to find a role. Although these are individuals, they function as archetypes and are textually significant only as archetypes. The focus on roles and functions is obvious, since functionality is the basis of the contest between the deities.

Not only can we see that corporate human origins are represented archetypally, but we also find evidence of creation of humans for notable roles that shows us a proclivity to think in archetypal terms. In this excerpt of a Neo-Babylonian text we can see that a transition is made from corporate common humanity ("lullu-man") to the archetypal king:

> Belet-ili, you are the mistress of the great gods.
> You have created lullu-man:

Coffin Text spell 1130 in *COS* 1.17 p. 27.

25. The bilingual version of Enki and Ninmaḫ suggests that mixture may also occur there. See W. G. Lambert, "The Relationship of Sumerian and Babylonian Myth as Seen in Accounts of Creation," in *La circulation des biens, des personnes et des idées dans le Proche-Orient ancien*, ed. D. Charpin and F. Joannès, (RAI 38; Paris: Editions Recherche sur les Civilizations, 1992), 129–35.

Form now the king, the thinking-deciding man!
With excellence cover his whole form,
Form his features in harmony, make his whole body beautiful!
Then Belet-ili fulfilled her commission with the major gods
    contributing specific attributes.
The great gods gave the king the battle.
Anu gave him the crown, Ellil ga[ve him the throne],
Nergal gave him the weapons, Ninurta ga[ve him shining
    splendor],
Belet-ili gave [him a handsome appea]rance.
Nusku gave instruction, imparted counsel and sto[od by him in
    service].[26]

This piece illustrates the same concept as the Egyptian iconography and texts concerning pharaoh being formed on the potter's wheel to be king! Creation pertains to role and function, and even though an overarching materiality is evident in the wording, it is thoroughly archetypal in focus and interest.

One other noteworthy example from the ancient Near East that demonstrates archetypal thinking is the Tale of Adapa, the most significant of the primeval sages (*apkallu*) who were credited with bringing the arts of civilization to humanity. We should note that Adapa is identified as a "priest of Enki" and thus has a representative role. He has wisdom but lacks immortality. Through a series of circumstances he is ushered into the presence of the god Anu, where he unwittingly refuses food that would give him immortality. Some interpretations suggest that through his choice humanity loses a chance at immortality.[27] If this is accurate, this priestly individual represents all humankind, both in his time and as a species. The text is unclear whether Adapa's eating of the food offered by Anu would gain immortality only for him or for all humanity. Only in the latter situation would he fulfill an archetypal role that would be comparable to that played by the archetypal man in Genesis. The text of Adapa is not clear on this issue, but one factor that would suggest that

---

26. Translation from Clifford, *Creation Accounts*, 70. Text published in W. Mayer, "Ein Mythos von der Erschaffung des Menschen und des Königs," *Orientalia* 56 (1987): 55–68.

27. Shlomo Izre'el, *Adapa and the South Wind* (Winona Lake, IN: Eisenbrauns, 2001), 120–23. On p. 120 Izre'el indicates that although Adapa is presented in the text as a "single human being," he "definitely symbolizes humanity or, rather, the essence of being human."

all of humanity is affected by Adapa's choice is Anu's exclamation "Alas for inferior humanity!"[28] after Adapa refuses the food.

The cumulative effect of this discussion is the understanding that it was commonplace in ancient Near Eastern literature to think about human origins in archetypal ways and to focus on the functions of humanity. This would not demand that we read Genesis archetypally, but since we have seen that our investigation moves in that direction, we now see that such a way of thinking would be natural in the ancient world.

The Message of the Archetypes in Genesis contrasted to Ancient Near East

Interpretation of human origins in Genesis as archetypal does not strip the account of its meaning; rather, it brings to our attention the essential theological teaching of the passage.

Humankind was created with mortal bodies. As discussed above, dust is equated with mortality in the text (Gen. 3:19), in the canon (Ps. 103:14), and by logic (a tree of life would otherwise be unnecessary). In Adam we were all created mortal.

Humankind was provisioned by God. Genesis 2:9, 16 indicate that the garden provided food for the humans that were in the garden. This is not an indication that God provided food for all humanity in every place and every time, but that the food growing in sacred space was God's provision for humans. This stands in contrast to the idea that humans were providing for the needs of God. In the ancient Near East, gardens adjoined sacred space and were used to feed the gods—a task, in their view, for which humanity was created. In Genesis 2 the important archetypal statement is that humankind has not been created to meet God's needs; rather, God is meeting their needs. This is a key departure in the archetypal picture of humanity.

Humankind was given the role of serving in sacred space (which implies relationship with God). When the archetypal man was taken and placed in the garden as a priestly representative, a couple of archetypal affirmations were made. First and foremost, service in sacred space per-

---

28. Adapa B 68; Izre'el, *Adapa*, 20–21. For discussion see Tryggve N. D. Mettinger, *The Eden Narrative* (Winona Lake, IN: Eisenbrauns, 2007), 104–7.

tains most significantly to maintaining a relationship between God and people. The archetypal nature of humanity is found in the idea that we have not been created as slaves to meet the needs of the gods (ancient Near Eastern model), but that ultimately God wants to be in relationship with us as we dwell in his presence (sacred space).

Second, however, is that this is represented in "already/not yet" terms. That is, the archetypes are placed there as representatives of others (whether in their time or in future times), implying perforce that not all are there. The objective, as evident in the theological developments across the canon, is to expand that circle of those in relationship to God so that it becomes broadly inclusive. Thus we find Israel identified as a "kingdom of priests" (Exod. 19:6) and eventually Christians identified as a "holy priesthood" (1 Peter 2:5). God's desire is for us all to be in relationship with him in sacred space—the eventual outcome in New Creation (Rev. 21).

Humankind was given a role ordering the animals. God brings all the animals to the archetypal man as a first step after it is noted that "It is not good for the man to be alone" (Gen. 2:18). This observation comes on the heels of the commissioning to priestly service in the garden (Gen. 2:15). The companion that is envisioned is not focused on a search for a reproduction partner (otherwise, the initial focus on the animals would be nonsense), but for a coworker in the task of maintaining and expanding sacred space. In this task humanity is fulfilling the role of vice-regent, having been delegated by God to continue the ordering process. The naming of the animals is undertaken as part of that commission. In naming, a creative/order-bringing act, the roles of animals, and their place in the ordered system are being identified. This is an ongoing task of humanity. In the process, the archetypal man found none that could suitably fill the ordained role of humanity in sacred space (Gen. 2:20).

Humankind genders work together to fulfill their God-given role. Genesis 2 makes important countercultural statements about gender roles that help us to see that they were not just serving as an etiology for the situations of Israelite society that already existed.[29] Israel did not have women priests, and even if Israelite society gave higher status to women than neighboring

---

29. It is important to note that an etiology differs from an archetypal story in that etiology focuses on how some situation came to be (and continues to exist today), whereas an archetype is explaining the essential nature of something that can be either ideal or actual.

societies, it was undoubtedly a patriarchal society. But Genesis 1–3 shows no sign of patriarchy, and the archetypal woman is given a role as coworker in sacred space, placed in equal relationship with God.[30]

Humanity was divided into male and female and so would seek reconnection in new family relationship. Many Protestant wedding liturgies assert that Genesis 2:24 is establishing the institution of marriage. If it is doing that, it would certainly be identifiable as archetypal, but I am not convinced that it is focused on establishing an institution. Contextually, it is explaining why a man would leave the closest biological relationship (with parents) to form a new relationship (with his wife).

The answer has been given in the preceding verses: the relationship between husband and wife has a stronger claim than biological derivation. A man may be biologically derived from his parents, but he is archetypally (ontologically) related to his wife. The husband/wife bond is more elemental, and it trumps the parental bond. They again become one flesh in reestablishment of the archetypal model. The narrator's statement does not refer to the emotional bond of love,[31] but to the essential bond built into our nature.[32]

I am not suggesting that these elements have not been seen by past interpreters. Certainly the long held Reformed tradition of "federal headship" converges with this view in important ways. But perhaps at times this recognition of archetypal significance has been occluded by the pervasive attention to human origins. When questions about material origins dominate our thinking, we tend to see the above elements as connected to an individual, Adam, rather than to all humanity through its archetype. While it is true that both material and archetypal elements could be the intention of the text, the two need not be bundled together, though interpreters have often assumed that they must be bundled. My point is that we have to be willing to separate them as we examine whether they are both inherent in the claims of the text.[33]

---

30. For fuller discussion see the extended treatment in Walton, *Genesis*, NIVAC.

31. Recall that Genesis 2:24 is an accurate statement whether marriages are arranged or are pursued for love.

32. Marriage is then seen as premised on the ontological nature of gendered humanity and represents a return to an original state. "One flesh" is not primarily a reference to carnal experience, though carnal experience is one of the reflections of the ontological relationship (1 Cor. 6:16).

33. It must be left to theologians to figure out the details of the transmission of original sin. My view is certainly not Pelagian, but neither is it reflective of the Reformed tradition.

Archetypal Role of Adam and Eve in the New Testament

Only a handful of New Testament passages address Adam and Eve, and we will deal with each one briefly. We will see that each one shows an interest in Adam and Eve as archetypes. The New Testament authors believe Adam and Eve to be real individuals in a real past (as do I), but the theological use that is made of them is archetypal.

Acts 17:26. On Mars Hill Paul confronts the Athenians about the "Unknown God" that they worship. He turns their attention to the Creator God and the fact that this God is noncontingent: Everything and everyone owes their existence to him, and he owes his existence to no one (Acts 17:24–25). In verse 26 Paul moves the argument from creation to history, a point that he introduces by stating that "From one man he made[34] all the nations."

If Paul were referring to Adam, we would expect him to use other vocabulary rather than "nations" to refer to all people. In that regard, his choice of the word "nations" (*ethnos*) is rather odd. In fact, however, here the word choice is key because the Old Testament does talk about one man from whom the nations came—and that is Noah through his three sons. Comparing Paul's words to Genesis 10:32—"From these [the sons of Noah] the nations [Septuagint: *ethnos*] spread out over the earth after the flood"—we see that Paul's statement could easily be seen as a paraphrase of what is stated in Genesis 10. If this is so, it is quite plausible that this verse could be a reference to Noah. If this is true, this verse could be removed from the discussion about Adam as the genetic/biological forebear of all humanity.[35]

Romans 5:12–14. Here the text affirms that sin entered the world through one man and that death came through sin.[36] It does not claim that humans were created immortal, only that humans are now subject to death because of sin. I have demonstrated above that being made

---

34. Notice Paul's use of *poieō* here even though "making" the nations is an organizational act, not a material one.

35. Even with regard to Noah this verse makes limited claims. The point Paul is making is that in our common humanity we all have a thirst for God, and indeed, we are *all his* offspring (obviously not a biological/genetic statement). Our commonality does not require a genetic relationship to Noah any more than it requires a genetic relationship to God. Furthermore, this verse makes no statement about material origins.

36. Note that Paul's interest is not death in the larger world of life (cells, plants, bugs, or sentient creatures), but why it is that people are subject to death.

from dust indicates that we were made mortal, subject to death. The opportunity for release from our natural mortality was provided by an antidote, the tree of life. Sin brought expulsion from the garden and loss of access to the tree of life. Therefore, sin doomed us to death — that is, with no antidote we would have no alternative but to succumb to our mortality, which was already ours naturally.

This text does not comment on how or when sin came to all and all sinned. While it articulates an idea of original sin, it does not work out the details.[37] The archetypal nature of Adam is evident in two ways here: first, he is seen as a pattern of Christ; second, Adam represents all people in Paul's treatment (through him all sinned). Adam and Christ are related as archetypal representatives.

The text does appear to claim a historical event, but nothing here necessitates that Adam was the first human being or that we all must be related biologically or genetically to Adam. Likewise, there is no suggestion of sin being passed through biological relationship (in contrast to the common view of seminal transmission). No claims are made about material origins. This important section of Scripture, then, affirms the reality of sin and death entering human experience in an event and thereby implies a historical Adam. At the same time we should note that no scientific claim is made about biological/genetic relationship or material discontinuity.

First Corinthians 15:22. Death came through a man, and the solution to death comes through a man — that is, both Adam and Jesus were human. Since we all die "in Adam" the way that we are all made alive "in Christ," we can presume that our circumstances in either case are not determined by biological descent but through the representation of the archetypes, Adam and Christ.[38] Again we should note that in these verses there is neither a claim to genetic relationship to Adam nor any statement about material human origins.

---

37. I have neither the space nor the expertise to address the doctrine of original sin in this article. I am, nevertheless, aware of ongoing contemporary theological research that is more favorable to the view of Irenaeus over that of Augustine. In general this direction would favor what I call the "radiation" model rather than the biological model. The radiation model is based on the analogy that if someone were to open a door to what had been a sealed source of radiation, the entire area and population would be irradiated. This must be left to others to decide.

38. My use of "representation" language parallels the standard federal headship view of the Reformed tradition. However, I differ from those federal headship advocates in that I question the complicity of biological or seminal connection as being asserted in the text.

First Corinthians 15:45. Here Adam is called the "first" man, but in the context of the contrast with Christ as the "last" Adam, it cannot be seen as a claim that Adam was the first biological specimen. Since Christ was not the last biological specimen, we must instead conclude that this text is talking about the first archetype and the last archetype. We might say that Adam was an initial archetype replaced by the ultimate archetype in Christ. It is insufficient to bring in biology simply because Christ was biologically descended from Adam. This is confirmed in the remainder of the passage, as it contrasts the natural and the spiritual. The archetypal element of dust is specifically explained as making the archetypal man earthly in comparison to the heavenly nature of Christ. It describes human nature.

The biblical point is to contrast and compare Adam to Jesus and our relationship to both. Paul makes no claims about genetic relationships of all people to Adam or about material origins — only that we share the "dust" nature of the archetype.

Second Corinthians 11:3. This verse implies that there was a historical Eve, but it refers to her archetypally as an analogy about how easily people may be deceived. No claims are made about genetic relationships or human origins.

First Timothy 2:13–14. Paul mines Genesis for an illustration to address the situation in Ephesus. He accurately reflects the textual data that Adam was formed first and Eve was the target of the deception. No claims are made about how humanity was formed, about genetic relationships, or the mechanisms or timing of material origins. Like all of the previous New Testament passages, Adam and Eve are used as archetypes to make a point about all of humanity, here providing an illustration of how a deceived woman can lead a man into error.

In summary, the New Testament can be seen to indicate that there was a historical point in time when sin and death became human realities. It is further clear that Adam and Eve were the principal parties in this real event in a real past. Even though the use made of Adam and Eve is archetypal, they are treated as real, individual persons. Having noted that, however, I have tried to demonstrate that no claims are made in the New Testament that all humans are biologically descended from Adam and Eve and therefore genetically derived from them.

I acknowledge that most Jews in the first century would have believed that all people were descended from Adam; but they also believed the earth was flat. I do not see any authoritative assertion of Scripture that all people are descended from Adam, and his material origin has no meaningful weight in Paul's arguments.

Finally, pertinent observations about the comparison of the archetypes of Adam and Christ are instructive. Despite the fact of the virgin birth, Jesus was biologically and genetically human,[39] yet he did not inherit sin. This suggests that sin is not passed biologically and genetically. Furthermore, the archetypal role of Jesus for humanity does not require his biological descent or ancestry with each individual human. If Adam's archetypal role is comparable, we would see no need for it to be founded in biological descent.[40] In fact, Jesus is characterized by material continuity with the rest of humanity (genetics)—at least in the sense that he is fully human as we are—but with spiritual discontinuity. This could suggest that humanity might be distinguished by a spiritual discontinuity even if there were material continuity.

Literary Issues in Genesis 1 – 3 and Human Origins

When we consider the biblical view of human origins in the early chapters of Genesis, one of the key questions is whether or not Adam and Eve are presented in the text as the only humans on earth. This question has traditionally been raised in connection with Genesis 4, where Cain is afraid that "whoever finds me will kill me" (Gen. 4:14) and where Cain not only marries a wife but later builds a city (v. 17)—all more easily explained if there are other people who already exist.

---

39. Note that Jesus must have had a full set of DNA, though the fact of the virgin birth makes it a mystery how he got the part that usually comes from a father. He was fully human, but in an extraordinary way, thus indicating some level of biological discontinuity.

40. One could argue that, like Christ, there could be a level of biological continuity (genetic patterns?) as well as a level of biological discontinuity. This is not impossible, but we would need a statement from the text such as we have with the virgin birth of Christ. This would be the logical path were one to continue thinking of Adam and Eve as being characterized by biological, material discontinuity—but it is certainly a hard sell in the area of genetics. Note also that the whole cosmos is affected by sin even though there is no biological or genetic relationship. This would be another point supporting the "radiation" model of original sin (see previous note). I reject the Pelagian view and am intrigued by the view of Irenaeus, though more research and perhaps qualification would be needed.

The toledoth *transition between the first and second account.* An important factor in this question that has not been adequately explored concerns the relationship of the first account (Gen. 1:1—2:3) and the second account (Gen. 2:4—3:24). Critical scholarship has long considered these two accounts as competing traditions from different sources that at a late stage in the redactional process came to be incongruently next to each other with unresolved tensions. Traditional interpretation considered the second account synoptic to the first account as an explanation giving more detail of the sixth day.

I propose a third option as viable, given its considerable explanatory power, that being that the second account might be considered a sequel to the first. If this is so, the second account is not detailing the sixth day, but identifying a sequel scenario, that is, recounting events that potentially and arguably could have occurred long after the first account.

In such a case, Adam and Eve would not necessarily be envisioned as the first human beings, but would be elect individuals drawn out of the human population and given a particular representative role in sacred space. The first account would simply refer to the creation of humanity as a corporate species with no details of mechanism or time span. This would, incidentally, correlate to the standard ancient Near Eastern view, where the question of human origins is discussed in corporate terms.

Nevertheless, we would not adopt a corporate interpretation of Genesis 1 just because the ancient Near Eastern accounts did it that way.[41] Instead, we should seek out internal literary evidence for or against the interpretation. This evidence can be developed from an investigation of the common narrative transitionary formula in Genesis: "This is the account of ..." (ʾelleh toledoth). This toledoth formula serves at times to introduce sections that are historically synoptic, but the formula also functions as an introduction to the next sequential time period (see chart).

The transitions sometimes join two genealogies, sometimes two narratives, and sometimes move from genealogy to narrative or narrative to genealogy. The transition in Genesis 2:4 is from narrative to narrative, and the only other transition of that type is Genesis 6:9. In 6:9

---

41. Reasons for mass production of humanity exist in the ancient Near East that are not true of the Bible—primarily, that in the ancient Near East the gods are creating slave laborers and would therefore want to produce many.

Genesis Reference	Type	Relation
5:1	Genealogy →Genealogy	synoptic
6:9	Narrative →Narrative	sequel
10:1	Narrative →Genealogy	sequel
11:10	Narrative →Genealogy	synoptic
11:27	Genealogy →Narrative	sequel
25:12	Narrative →Genealogy	sequel
25:19	Genealogy →Narrative	synoptic
36:1	Narrative →Genealogy	sequel
36:9	Genealogy →Genealogy	synoptic
37:2	Genealogy →Narrative	synoptic

the two narratives are sequential, not synoptic. In fact, we should note that all five examples of synoptic relationship occur when brothers are the linked subjects (e.g., Cain/Seth, Ishmael/Isaac, Esau/Jacob).

These observations would suggest that the most natural interpretation of the text would see the second account as reflecting a scenario later than the first account and that the second account is not therefore a discussion of what transpired on the sixth day. That actually resolves a long-standing problem, as interpreters have struggled to figure out how all the events of the second account could possibly have taken place in a twenty-four-hour period. This problem was among those cited as evidence for both the Day-Age Theory (in which it was contended that twenty-four hours was insufficient for all of chapter 2 to transpire) and the Source Theory (in which the two accounts were viewed as competing and contradictory).

The conclusion drawn from this literary analysis is that the text is not making an overt claim that Adam and Eve should be identified as the people in the first account if it presents the second account as sequential to the first. I would hasten to add that neither does it rule out that the first account could be talking about Adam and Eve alone or include Adam and Eve as part of a larger group. It simply does not address the issue. As a result, one could easily maintain that the opening chapters of Genesis do not make a claim as to whether or not Adam and Eve were the first people.

Genesis 2:5–6. As in Genesis 1:2, Genesis 2:5–6 sets up a preliminary scenario. This establishes the "before" picture that gives us direction into the passage and that we expect to be resolved by the time we reach the end of the account.

Genesis 1:2 describes an inchoate cosmos that is not yet ordered or functioning as sacred space or as the home in which people can dwell in relationship with their Creator. It concludes with God taking up his rest and rule in the cosmos in which he has brought order and installed people made in his image with sacred space functioning on their behalf.

Genesis 2:5–6 describes an inchoate terrestrial realm where there is no productivity under the control of humanity. Domesticated crops are not yet present, and neither rain nor irrigation is available. This description does not pertain to a prior material ecology any more than Genesis 1:2 does. Instead, it reflects an old world science contrasting non-order to order. Since a third inchoate situation is introduced in Genesis 2:18 and resolved by the end of the chapter by means of the activities of verses 18–24, the inchoate situation described in Genesis 2:5–6 should be seen as resolved in 2:7–17.

Interpreters who have been inclined to see the second account as synoptic have struggled with the problem that Genesis 2:5–6 does not offer a description of the situation at the beginning of day 6. As a sequel, it can stand on its own as offering an introduction to the issues that are going to be addressed in the account and will stand in sharp relief against the situation at the end of the account. This being the expectation, we note that the account does not end with rain or with human irrigation. As in the first account, however, all of the identified non-order is not going to be resolved here; rather, the first steps are going to be taken to resolve it. Among the negations identified in the inchoate situation is the lack of "sprouting" (at least of certain classes of food-producing plants), the absence of humans to work the ground, and the apparent inadequacy of watering ("springs" rather than rain?). The conclusion I drew in my Genesis commentary will suffice here to make the point:[42]

---

42. Walton, *Genesis*, NIVAC, 163–65, quoting from 165. Conclusions rely on the analysis of David Toshio Tsumura, *The Earth and the Waters in Genesis 1 and 2*, JSOTSup 83 (Sheffield, UK: JSOT Press, 1989), 87–89, 110–16.

The thrust of verses 5–6 in an interpretive paraphrase is as follows: "No shrubs or plants were yet growing wild (for food) because God had not yet sent rain; and people were not yet around to work the ground (for irrigation), so the regular inundations [of river systems] saturated the ground indiscriminately (thus no food was being grown)." A creation text from the city of Nippur sets the scene for creation in a similar way by saying that waters did not yet flow through the opening in the earth and that nothing was growing and no furrow had been made.[43]

As resolution, God forms humanity with the task of working, causes plants to sprout in the garden, and waters the ground. Even as these actions address the initial situation, each takes a different tack and offers unexpected resolutions. Humans are given the task of working in sacred space rather than working the ground. The classes of plants mentioned in Genesis 2:5 are not sprouting in the garden; instead, it is trees of every sort in sacred space. Finally, the watering is not accomplished by rain, but by a water system flowing from God's presence.

Consequently, we can see that God's initial resolution of the inchoate situation is not by introducing a whole new terrestrial ecosystem. Instead, he provides sprouting food and a watering system to chosen human beings serving in sacred space. On the premise of relationship with God in sacred space, the eventual resolutions will be expected to come about.

The main point to be made in this discussion is that through these observations we can see that the second account introduces further inchoate situations, each to be addressed in context. It is not addressing the inchoate situation of the first account, therefore commending the view that the second is a sequel account, not a synoptic account. With this evidence that the two accounts are better understood as sequential, the claim that Genesis 2 deals with the first two people or the only people is weakened.

In turn, if Genesis does not make the claim that Adam and Eve are the first and only people and does not give an account of material human origins, then there is no biblical claim concerning the genetic role of Adam and Eve or of material human origins. If the Bible makes no such claims, then the Bible will not stand opposed to any views that

---

43. Clifford, *Creation Accounts*, 28.

science might offer (e.g., evolutionary models or population genetics), as long as God is not eliminated from the picture.

Continuity, Discontinuity, and Genetics

Three discrete questions can now be identified:

Are Adam and Eve real people in a real past?[44]
Are Adam and Eve the first human beings and the ancestors of all?
Is there material discontinuity between Adam and other species?

If #2 is answered affirmatively, then #1 is true, and #3 should be answered affirmatively as well. If #3 is answered affirmatively, then likely both #1 and #2 would be considered true. Those have traditionally been clustered affirmations. What is important to note, however, is that if #1 is answered affirmatively, #2 and #3 could be true but are not necessarily true. This is to say that if the Bible makes an overt claim to #1 (as I believe it does), it is not necessarily making a claim concerning #2 and #3.

A legitimate, close reading of the texts at least allows for, and in some cases would favor, dissociating the scientific claims of #2 and #3 from the biblical claims of #1. Furthermore, with #1 alone, adequate support can be given for the origination of sin and death in Adam. Consequently, someone who answered only #2 and #3 negatively could not be accused of rejecting the Bible or the faith. This does not mean that such a person should accept the scientific consensus uncritically, but interpreters would not be in a position to say that specific biblical texts or theology in general demand the rejection of the scientific consensus. Any science must be weighed on its merits, but the Bible would not predetermine the outcome.

Hypothetical Scenario

I will now present a hypothetical scenario that someone could adopt if they were persuaded by the modern scientific consensus that humans are the product of a process of change over time from a common ancestor

---

44. With this comes the more extensive affirmation that they existed in this story—they were specially designated by God to a priestly role as representatives of the human race; they failed as they disobeyed the command of God in an act by which they intended to arrogate to themselves the role of being the center of order. I consider this a historical event that had real consequences at a point in time for humanity.

(i.e., any of several evolutionary models) by a variety of mechanisms known and unknown, and that our genetic heritage is diverse (rather than from one human pair), and who further were convinced that such a process has been divinely guided.

I do not present this as a hypothesis that I have adopted (as I continue to await further scientific clarity and support), but as an example of how one could accept all of the biblical and theological affirmations, including a personal Adam and Eve as real people in a real past, and still opt for the scientific consensus in matters pertaining to human origins. Such conclusions are informed by a close reading of the Bible that takes Genesis seriously as a piece of ancient literature rather than being dismissive of the biblical text.[45]

If someone who takes the Bible and theology seriously were to believe that evidence supports the idea that hominids evolved, it would be essential for them to understand evolution as a guided process by a Creator God (e.g., something like Evolutionary Creation). Sometime in that process—perhaps at that moment that geneticists refer to as the bottleneck when humanity nearly became extinct—God undertook a special act of creation that gives the entire human population the image of God. This would constitute a creative act (giving a role and a function) and represents a gain that could not be achieved through evolution.

Even after being endowed with the image of God, people are dying (due to their inherent mortality, subjection to death—formed from dust). Although engaging in activities that we would label sinful, they are not being held accountable (based on Romans 5:13, "sin is not charged against anyone's account where there is no law"). They would therefore be in a state of original innocence (wrong not held against them or punished) rather than a state of original righteousness (no wrong being committed). Accountability would not come until the fruit of the tree of the knowledge of good and evil was eaten.

Sometime later, perhaps tens of thousands of years, individuals whom the Bible designates as Adam and Eve are chosen by God as

---

45. Inerrancy states that we accept as without error all that the text affirms, and that is my position. It has long been recognized that this needs to be nuanced in relation to the accommodation that God made to the ancient culture in his communication. See lengthier treatment of these issues in Walton, *Lost World of Genesis One* (Downers Grove, IL: InterVarsity Press, 2009) and in Walton and D. Brent Sandy, *Lost World of Scripture* (IVP, 2013).

representative priests in sacred space. As representatives for all humans living then and to come after, their role offered hope to all for the possibility of life in God's presence. In this view, though people outside the garden were still dying and were not yet accountable, God provided the potential for wisdom and life through Adam and Eve: archetypes and representatives of all humanity.

A comment about the "good"-ness of creation is necessary here pertaining to this hypothesis. As I have proposed elsewhere, if Genesis 1 is viewed as an account of functional origins rather than as an account of material origins, when God sees repeatedly that "it was good," he is indicating that it is ready to function as sacred space (established by observing what is not good). In this case "good" is not indicative of perfection (either moral or design), but of order. The presence of humans who were subject to an inherent mortality and were not yet accountable does not nullify this order. Placing Adam and Eve in sacred space provided an opportunity for greater order to be established, but that opportunity was forfeited when they sinned and disorder entered the cosmos. Their sin and the punishment for it do not mean that creation was no longer good.

When Adam and Eve ate from the tree of the knowledge of good and evil, they chose to see themselves as the source and center of order, life, and wisdom ("you will be like God" [Gen. 3:5] and "they have become like God" [3:22 paraphrased]). In that choice, they brought disorder into the world, gained accountability for themselves and all humans through them (beginning of sin), and lost the hope of life for themselves and all humanity (so we are all doomed to death through that sin). They were cast out of sacred space and out of relationship with God. They and all humanity with them are now in sin and subject to death because, having lost access to the antidote, they are doomed to their inherent mortality. Accountability and disorder have become the lot of humanity.

In this scenario Adam and Eve are real individual persons living in a real past, but they are neither the first people nor the biological/genetic ancestors of all. Furthermore, in this scenario neither Adam and Eve specifically, nor humankind in general, is brought about in an act of material discontinuity. Nevertheless, (accountability for) sin and death come to all humans through them.

Summary and Conclusion

I have been building the case that even though Adam and Eve are portrayed in the text as real, individual persons in a real past, the main interest of the text in both testaments is to portray them as archetypes for all of humanity. I have further proposed that the "making" accounts in Genesis 2 are part of the archetype profile and that, as such, they contribute neither to our understanding of the material origins of the individuals, Adam and Eve, nor to the material origins of humanity.

The profile of Adam and Eve as individuals is important for the theological points about the human experience of sin and death. Those theological points do not require the scientific conclusions that Adam and Eve were the first people, the only people, or the progenitors of the entire human race. They are our first parents archetypally even if they may not be so materially.

It has been common for many Christians to believe that human evolution is a godless alternative to origins. On this we must be clear: Godless people are going to choose evolution as their origins model, but evolution is not inherently godless; godless people are going to configure evolution as purposeless, but even the immensely complex process of evolution could be guided purposefully by an infinitely powerful and sovereign God.

When people find the current scientific consensus persuasive (e.g., that humanity, along with all other species, evolved from a common ancestor or that humanity today derives from a diverse genetic stream rather than from one initial couple), they are not of necessity thereby denying biblical claims. In the interpretation that I have presented, the Bible makes no claims about the mechanisms of human origins or ultimate genetic ancestry. Indeed, I contend that we would not expect it to do so because the Bible is not revealing science, it is revealing God.[46] In the pages of Scripture I cannot find one example of God giving revelation about the mechanisms and processes of the ancient world that everyone in the ancient world did not believe. God appears to be

---

46. Information in the Bible may certainly converge with science, but there is no revelation in the text that changes how Israelites think about the mechanisms or processes of the natural world; nothing gives them a view that anyone else in the ancient world would not have shared. Certainly God could have chosen to reveal both himself and science, but there is no evidence that he did so.

content to communicate in terms of what the Israelites believed about the material cosmos.[47] We dare not read our science between the lines lest we intrude on the authority granted to the communicators in the Israelite context.

Although the Bible is not making scientific claims, it sometimes makes historical claims that carry implications concerning what happened at some point involving operations in the natural world (such as the plagues or the parting of the Red Sea). As such it makes claims that would have had an empirical foundation. In these, we must first notice that the text affirms only that God did those things; it does not identify the mechanisms by which God did them. If someday we were to be able to identify natural cause and effect explanations for those, God's role would not be diminished. Nonetheless, some acts attributed to God or Jesus will always defy natural explanations.

But in the case of the "making" accounts of Adam and Eve, I am claiming something different. I am proposing that the text not only makes no scientific claim about material human origins, but is also making no historical claim about material human origins (recall that inerrancy is related to claims, i.e., affirmations of the text). The historical Adam was made from dust in the same way that any of us are made from dust; he and we are mortal. These biblical statements relate to the archetypal profile.

The historical profile of Adam and Eve becomes important, not in the "making" accounts, but in the fall account: sin and death come to all of us through the historical actions of Adam and Eve. Even here this real event in a real past becomes significant archetypally. The theology is important, but the theology is built on the archetypal profile—we are all represented in Adam and Eve.

This view adheres to inerrancy in that it is distinguishing between claims that the Bible makes and, more importantly, to claims it does not make. It accepts the existence of a historical Adam and Eve and honors the doctrine of original sin associated with a historical event, though it works with an alternate model of the transmission of original sin. It

---

47. Inerrancy allows for accommodation. God did not dispel ancient views of cosmic geography (e.g., pillars of the earth, waters above), but communicated using those ideas. He was not revealing a new cosmic geography. See lengthier treatment of these issues in Walton, *Lost World of Genesis One*, and in the forthcoming *Lost World of the Word*.

does not promote evolution nor accept evolution, though the view offers a biblical and theological interpretation that would allow us to accept evolution if we are so inclined.

Finally, this view offers a path to integrating faith and science as it suggests through a close reading of Scripture as an ancient text that the Bible may not be making the scientific claims that many have thought it did.

DENIS O. LAMOUREUX

I want readers to know that John Walton is not only a valued colleague in science-religion scholarship, but also my friend. He has been instrumental in expanding my knowledge of the conceptual world of the Holy Spirit-inspired authors of the Old Testament. Of course, there are differences in our approaches to the opening chapters of Genesis. But I believe that we have many more agreements than disagreements, and I contend that the former are essential to Christianity, whereas the latter are secondary and incidental.

The Material Origins versus Functional Origins Thesis

Walton's chapter is rooted in his unique thesis about biblical creation accounts. In *The Lost World of Genesis One* (2009), he concludes,

> Genesis 1 has been presented as an account of *functional origins* (specifically functioning for people) rather than an account of *material origins* (as we have been generally inclined to read it). As an account of *functional origins*, it offers no clear information about *material origins*.[48]

Nearly thirty times in his chapter, Walton repeats his thesis that Scripture does not deal with material origins, giving readers the impression that it is a well-established concept in Old Testament scholarship. The advantage of his approach is that it sidesteps the chronic conflict between modern science and Christian faith. As Walton elaborates, "If Genesis 1 is not an account about material origins, then it offers no mechanism for material origins, and we may safely look to science to consider what it suggests for such mechanisms."[49]

---

48. John H. Walton, *The Lost World of Genesis One* (Downers Grove, IL: IVP Academic, 2009), 163, my italics.
49. Ibid.

The question must be asked, "Is Walton's thesis true?" My answer is "no." I had the privilege of learning about this theory firsthand from Walton when I gave a lecture at Wheaton College in 2002. My initial reaction was one of surprise, because I had never heard of any other scholar holding such a position. Yet I was open to the possibility since I knew that ancient texts often have ancient ideas that are strange to modern readers (e.g., the firmament). So for the last eleven years, every time I have read an ancient account of origins, I have read it with Walton's thesis in mind. Regrettably, I cannot agree with him. Creation accounts are not limited to functionalities. Instead, they feature *both* functional origins and material origins.

Walton addresses this possibility. He notes, "In a last effort to cling to a material perspective, they [skeptics of his thesis] ask, why can't it be both? It is easy to see the functional orientation of the account, but does the material aspect have to be eliminated?"[50] Walton answers, "A material interest cannot be assumed by default, it must be demonstrated.... The comfort of our traditional view is an insufficient basis for such a conclusion. *We must be led by the text.*"[51]

Fair enough. Let's look at the biblical text and consider the second day of creation in Genesis 1. According to Walton,

> Day Two has a potentially material component (the firmament, *rāqîʻa*), but no one believes there is actually something material there—no solid construction holds back the upper waters. If the account is material as well as functional, we find ourselves with the problem of trying to explain the material creation of something that does not exist. The word *rāqîʻa* had a meaning to Israelites as referring to a very specific object in their cosmic geography. If this were a legitimate material account, then we would be obliged to find something solid up there (not just change the word to mean something else as concordists do). In the functional approach, this component of Old World science addresses *the function of the weather*, described in terms they would understand.[52]

---

50. Ibid., 93.
51. Ibid., 94, my italics.
52. Ibid., 94–95, my italics.

Walton further explains that the function of the firmament "was to serve as a mechanism by which precipitation was controlled—the means by which weather operated."[53]

It must be pointed out that the Old Testament has two well-known Hebrew words for rain, *geshem* (30 times) and *māṭā* (38 times), and two words for clouds, *'ānān* (82 times) and *'āb* (22 times). One would expect that if the second day of creation were dealing with precipitation and weather, at least one of these terms should appear. But they do not. In addition, the word *rāqî'a* (firmament) is found 17 times in the Old Testament, and never once is it associated with the Hebrew words for rain or clouds, nor does the context have anything to do with precipitation or weather.

Note that Walton chastises concordists in the passage above, since they "change the word [*rāqî'a*] to mean something else." He adds that such an approach "manipulate[s] the text to say something that it had never said. We cannot think that we can interpret the word 'expanse/firmament' as simply the sky or the *atmosphere*."[54]

However, only two years after the publication of *The Lost World of Genesis One*, Walton changed his position in *Genesis 1 as Ancient Cosmology* (2011). Appealing to another Hebrew word, he states,

> I propose that *šēḥāqîm* pertains to the solid sky, a common component of ancient Near Eastern cosmology.... I propose that *rāqî'a* refers to the space created when the *šēḥāqîm* were put in place. This would explain why the birds and sun and moon are seen to be *in* the *rāqî'a*.[55]

Walton now believes that the *rāqî'a* includes the atmosphere because birds are *in* it. But this is not in the Hebrew Scriptures. Literally translated, Genesis 1:20 states that birds fly "across [the] face of" the *rāqî'a*. In other words, birds fly *in front of* the *rāqî'a*, not *in* it. And with "*šēḥāqîm* pertain[ing] to the solid sky," Walton now has "the problem of trying to explain the material creation of something that does not exist."

---

53. Ibid., 57.

54. Ibid., my italics.

55. John H. Walton, *Genesis 1 as Ancient Cosmology* (Winona Lake, IN: Eisenbrauns, 2011), 157, italics original. For example, *šēḥāqîm* appears in Job 37:18: "Can you join him [God] in spreading out of the skies [*šēḥāqîm*], hard as a mirror of cast bronze?"

In light of Walton's pointed criticism of concordists, readers can decide whether or not he has "changed/manipulated" the meaning of *rāqîʻa* in Genesis 1. You can also determine if Walton has forced his functional versus material thesis *into* Scripture (eisegesis), and whether or not it is a false dichotomy.

Ancient Science

Walton recognizes that Scripture includes an ancient understanding of the physical world. In his chapter he states,

> Genesis 2:5–6 describes an inchoate terrestrial realm.... it reflects an *old world science* [p. 111].... God did not dispel *ancient views of cosmic geography* (e.g., pillars of the earth, waters above), but communicated using those ideas [p. 117, fn. 47].... I acknowledge that most Jews in the first century would have believed that all people were descended from Adam, but they also believed *the earth was flat* [p. 108].... [T]here is no revelation in the text that changes how Israelites think about the *mechanisms* or *processes of the natural world*; nothing gives them a view that anyone else in the ancient world would not have shared [p. 116, fn. 46, *my italics*].

Walton definitely accepts the presence of ancient science in Scripture. In particular, he affirms ancient geography ("pillars of the earth") and ancient astronomy ("waters above"). He also believes that the Israelites "shared" with other ancient cultures ideas "about the mechanisms or processes of the natural world." And since this is "old world science," then obviously Scripture deals with the material universe. Walton's statements in this passage undermine his thesis that the creation accounts in Genesis focus only on functional origins rather than *both* material and functional origins.

Moreover, since Walton admits the presence of ancient geography and ancient astronomy in the Bible, it is only consistent that the biblical authors also embraced ancient biology, including ancient biological "mechanisms or processes." As we saw in my chapter, one of the mechanisms ancient Near Eastern people believed to be involved in the creation of humans was an artificial craftsman-like fashioning of the first people using earth (p. 58). This process is found in Genesis 2:7 when "the LORD God formed a man from the dust of the ground."

Consequently, the existence of Adam is based on "old world science," and like the firmament it doesn't align with physical reality.

Archetypes

Walton insightfully states, "Interpretation of human origins in Genesis as archetypal does not strip the account of its meaning; rather, it brings to our attention the essential theological teaching of the passage" (p. 102). Using my categories, biblical archetypes are *incidental* vessels that deliver *inerrant* spiritual truths. Walton is also correct in asserting, "An archetype can be a real person in a real past, *though not all archetypes are*" (p. 90, my italics). The italicized clause certainly fits well with my view that Adam never existed. As an archetype, Adam functions to deliver Messages of Faith regarding the human spiritual condition.

Archetypical interpretation is the key to Walton's position on Adam. He claims, "The most obvious statement about Adam—*and the one most important to this discussion*—is the statement that God formed (*yasar*) him from the dust (*'apar*) of the earth" (p. 92, my italics). Walton then qualifies, "Dust refers to mortality ... being formed from the dust does not refer to material origins" (p. 93). This is the Achilles heel of his position. If it can be shown that Walton's archetypal interpretation of the term "dust" falls short, then his belief that Genesis 2:7 does not refer to the material origins of Adam can be dismissed.

Here are three reasons why I disagree with Walton's archetypal interpretation of dust. First, to use his terminology, "the clearest reading to explain" (p. 89) Genesis 2:7 is that this verse is referring to how God actually made Adam. In fact, most Christians throughout history have understood this verse to mean the material origins of Adam.

Second, *de novo* (quick and complete) creation was the origins science-of-the-day in the ancient Near East. As we noted above, Walton recognizes the presence of "old world science" in the Bible. In order to be consistent, Walton should accept the *de novo* creation of Adam from dust as an ancient understanding of material human origins.

Third, to appreciate the use of the term "dust" in Genesis 2:7, we need to think like ancient people. What would they have seen sometime well after the death of a person? That the body had turned to dust. Therefore, to think we are made of dust was a perfectly reasonable idea from an *ancient phenomenological perspective*. This ancient scientific concept lies behind God's condemnation of Adam: "By the sweat of your brow you will eat your food until you return to the ground, *since from it you were taken;* for dust you are and to dust you will return" (Gen. 3:19). This verse only makes sense in the context of the material origins of Adam.

To conclude and recast Walton's words, dust does not refer to mortality; being formed from the dust refers to the material origins of Adam.

In reading Walton's archetypes, the question naturally arises: how do we determine when an archetype is being used in Scripture? Many of his proposals seem *ad hoc*, even eccentric. Are we to believe that Adam was assigned a "priestly role" (p. 95) in Genesis 2? Nothing could be further from the truth. The role of priests in the Old Testament was to declare the Word of God, sacrifice for sin, and uphold the covenant. None of these activities appear in Genesis 2. Instead, Adam broke God's Word, he inaugurated sin, and there is no mention of a covenant.

Or consider Walton's archetypal interpretation of the creation of Eve. He proposes that Adam's "deep sleep" could be a vision, and "it is clear that this process is unlike any surgery, despite the fact that God then 'closed up the place with flesh'" (p. 97). Walton's qualification "despite the fact" rings hollow, since elsewhere in his chapter he endorses "the clearest reading" (p. 89), "the easiest reading" (p. 94), and "the most natural interpretation of the text" (p. 110). In light of these examples, Walton's interpretive approach opens the door to each and every whimsical archetype imaginable.

Genesis 1 and 2: In Sequence or Two Sources?

I am grateful that Walton raised the issue of the relationship between the first two chapters of the Bible. I wanted to deal with this in my chapter, but the word limit prohibited it. This is a critical issue that every Christian needs to consider because the implications are significant to our interpretation of Genesis 1 and 2.

Walton correctly notes that the traditional (synoptic) approach is to view Genesis 2 as a detailed account of the events on the sixth day of creation in Genesis 1. He then dismisses the position of "*critical* scholarship," which sees "these two accounts as *competing* traditions" that are "*contradictory*" and "*incongruently*" next to each other," resulting in *"unresolved tensions"* (p. 109, my italics). Note the negative language. Walton argues for a "third option" (p. 109) and suggests that Genesis 2 is sequential in time to Genesis 1.

Walton's glossing over of Genesis 1 and 2 as coming from two different sources is typical of evangelical theological education. As a seminarian, I was told the theory about sources was "liberal" and "irrational." Being a student, who was I to challenge my professors? But that was my mistake. I should have taken the time to carefully examine this theory.

This is what I suggest: Don't trust me, and don't trust Walton. Examine source theory yourself. It claims there were originally two separate accounts of origins, each with a creation story and a flood story. An editor then combined them. In particular, he interwove the two flood accounts together into what has become Genesis 6–9. In doing so, he took a few verses from the first account, then a few verses from the second, then a few verses from the first, then a few verses from the second, etc. To be sure, this seems bizarre. But if this is true:

(1) Each reassembled flood account should make sense.

(2) The terminology in the creation and flood accounts of each original source should be similar, because it would have been composed by the same author.[56] To assist your research, I have placed the two reassembled flood accounts online: http://www.ualberta.ca/~dlamoure/sources.html.

If you come to the conclusion that there are two separate sources behind the Genesis creation and flood accounts, as I have, this will have no impact on your belief that the Bible is truly the Word of God. It only indicates that similar to the ancient science in Scripture, the Holy Spirit used ancient literary techniques in biblical revelation. Instead of purported "contradictory" accounts with "unresolved tensions," the opening chapters of Genesis offer two inspired divine revelations that are *complementary*. In this way, God is both the transcendent Creator of the universe (Gen. 1) and the immanent Lord of our lives (Gen. 2).

---

56. For an excellent introduction to source theory, see Richard E. Friedman *The Bible with Sources Revealed* (New York: HarperSanFancisco, 2003).

C. JOHN COLLINS

It is always a treat to interact with John Walton; his creativity certainly keeps us on our toes. When it comes to Genesis, I agree with almost everyone else that Genesis records some sort of "material origins," and I do not grasp exactly why Walton keeps making a disjunction between material and functional. The things in the world do indeed have their divinely assigned functions, and these functions depend at least partly on the physical properties of the things (e.g., iron and cotton are candidates for the functions of knife and swab).

It is probably more helpful to say that Genesis, like many other ancient origins stories, gives little attention to the processes and mechanisms by which the various kinds of things came to have their properties and functions. I will not belabor this overall point here, as there are other places where it has been addressed.[57] Instead I will focus on his take on Adam in relation to the rest of humankind.

In proposing that we treat Adam as an archetype, there are two exegetical and theological factors that Walton's case rests on: first, that the formation of Adam and Eve in Genesis 2 need not be the same as the "creation" of humankind in Genesis 1; second, that Adam—whom Walton takes to have been a real person—therefore need not be at the beginning of humankind. This second point may lead to revising our notions of how the sin of Adam and Eve came to affect us all. I will argue that neither of his factors will withstand scrutiny.

---

57. See the essays in J. Daryl Charles, ed., *Reading Genesis 1–2: An Evangelical Conversation* (Peabody, MA: Hendrickson, 2013), particularly those by Collins and Averbeck, and their responses to Walton's contribution therein. Averbeck argues that "material origins" are in fact relevant to the other cultures' origin stories. But even if these other cultures actually did lack an interest in material origins (for some reason that must remain mysterious), that does not establish that *Moses* would tell a story that also lacked it.

Traditional rabbinic readings have taken the activities of Genesis 2 to be an elaboration of the sixth "day" of Genesis 1.[58] More importantly for us, it is also clear that Jesus read the two passages together: in Matthew 19:3–9 (see Mark 10:2–9), he combines Genesis 1:27 with 2:24 (see discussion in my essay). I have supplied a grammatical justification for this traditional approach by showing how Genesis 2:4–7 links the two stories, and how the well-known chiastic structure of Genesis 2:4 invites us to read the two passages in harmony.[59]

Several of the links between Genesis 1 and Genesis 2–3 mentioned in my essay are relevant here as well. For example, the reversal of "blessing" (1:28) to "cursing" (3:17), and the ironic "multiply" (1:28; 3:16). I think that the "not good" of 2:18 has the literary effect of alerting us that we are not yet at the "very good" of 1:31.[60] Further, the account of Adam's offspring (5:1–5) both continues the characters of Genesis 2–4 and clearly echoes Genesis 1:26–27: for example, the verb "create," and the "likeness" and "image." Indeed, while 5:1 is rightly rendered as "when God created *man*" (because of its echo of 1:27), it could easily be "when God created *Adam*" (because the Hebrew for "man," *adam*, lacks the definite article).

A number of texts, in both the Hebrew and the Greek, exhibit a reading of Genesis 1–2 that sees them as complements. For example, Psalm 104 is widely acknowledged to be a poetic reflection on the creation story of Genesis 1 in order to celebrate how this created order still continues in human experience.[61] Nevertheless, verse 14 "plants for man to *cultivate*" (or, "plants for the *work* of man"; cf. also v. 23) uses a characteristic term from Genesis 2–3, "work" (Heb. *'abad*, Gen. 2:5, 15; 3:23). In 1 Corinthians 15:45, we have a citation of Genesis 2:7;[62] then in verse 49 Paul says, "Just as we have borne the *image* [Gk. *eikōn*]

---

58. See Yehudah Kiel, *Sefer Bere'shit 1–17* (Da'at Miqra'; Jerusalem: Mossad Harav Kook, 1997), מד, n. 7, for details. We may add Tobias 8:6 and Wisdom 10:1, as well as Josephus, *Antiquities*, 1.34. A rationale for this comes from Richard Hess, "Genesis 1–2 in Its Literary Context," *Tyndale Bulletin* 41:1 (1990): 143–53, who argues that the pattern of "doublets" in Genesis 1–11 is for the second element to focus on some details of the first.

59. Collins, "Discourse Analysis and the Interpretation of Genesis 2:4–7," *Westminster Theological Journal* 61 (1999): 269–76.

60. See Collins, *Genesis 1–4: A Linguistic, Literary, and Theological Commentary* (Phillipsburg, NJ: P&R Publishing, 2006), 75.

61. See ibid., 85–86.

62. For discussion of what is going on here, see ibid., 146–47.

of the man of dust, we shall also bear the *image* of the man of heaven," which evokes Genesis 1:27; 5:3: that is, to Paul the person of Genesis 2:7 is the same as the first man of Genesis 1:27.[63] Similarly, Paul is able to characterize Christ as both the new Adam (1 Cor. 15:45) and as the ideal "image of God" (2 Cor. 4:4; Col. 1:15–16),[64] which is probably why Luke traces his ancestry back to Adam and then to God.[65]

We add to this the idea that God makes fresh starts on humankind after the disobedience of Adam and Eve: particularly in Noah, and then in Abraham and Israel.[66] They are God's way of retrieving what was lost, not only for themselves but also for the world. Israel, both in its land and especially in its temple, is to be a kind of reconstituted garden of Eden, whose role is to anticipate God's presence restored for all humankind.[67] This theme appears in Isaiah 43:1, 7:

> But now thus says the LORD,
>   he who *created* you, O Jacob,
>   he who *formed* you, O Israel:
> "Fear not, for I have redeemed you;
>   I have called you by name, you are mine....
> everyone who is called by my name,
>   whom I *created* for my glory,
>   whom I *formed* and *made*."

The terms for how God established Israel—*created* (cf. Gen. 1:27), *formed* (Gen. 2:7), and *made* (Gen. 1:26)—bring together the terms of Genesis 1–2, to make it clear that Israel is God's new start on humankind, the proper heirs of the first humans in Genesis 1–2.

Consider further that God's goal for his redeemed creation is "a new heaven and a new earth" (Rev. 21:1), using terms from Genesis 1:1; 2:1, 4;

---

63. This is why Walton's suggestion that the designation "first man" in 1 Corinthians 15:45 "cannot be seen as a claim that Adam was the first biological specimen," though on the surface reasonable, fails to account for the whole context of the passage.

64. For discussion see Collins, *Genesis 1–4*, 64.

65. I expect that Adam as "son" of God ties in to the idea of the Davidic king as "son" of God; the role of the Davidide is to embody true humanity. I touch on this theme in Collins, *Genesis 1–4*, 24 n. 42, 29 n. 47.

66. Besides the brief mention in my essay, see also Collins, "Reading Genesis 1–2 with the Grain: Analogical Days," in Charles, ed., *Reading Genesis 1–2*, 73–92, at 74–75.

67. See Christopher J. H. Wright, *The Mission of God: Unlocking the Bible's Grand Narrative* (Downers Grove, IL: InterVarsity Press, 2006), 334, 340.

in this scene there will be "Eden come to its full fruition" (argued in my essay).

Therefore it is best to take Genesis 1 and 2 as complementary accounts that really do aim to record the making of the first humans. The argument in my essay shows why I think of this material as ordinary and poetic language (in the terms of C. S. Lewis's "Language of Religion"; see my comments on Lamoureux). That is why Walton's emphasis on "functions" gets traction — not because there is no "interest" in materials, but because the texts focus on persons and events, without specifying mechanisms. Yet this hardly excludes a material component.

I note that Walton's treatment of the verb in Genesis 2:7 ("form") lacks appropriate lexical rigor. No doubt other things can be formed (as in Zech. 12:1); but the specific syntactical structure in Genesis 2:7 employs what some call a double accusative, which is common for verbs that denote making or preparing: the first accusative ("the man") is the object of the verb, the thing made; the second accusative ("dust from the ground") is the stuff out of which the thing is made.[68] I suggest in my essay that the forming from dust (v. 7) reflects the "simple, obvious fact that the human body is made of the common elements of the soil"; and then when we die, our bodies lose their distinctive "form" and return to these common elements (Gen. 3:19). This explains more readily than Walton's suggestion the relation between dust and mortality. I see no point in taking this as a chemical formula for our bodies; nor am I certain that it absolutely excludes some intermediate steps (although a purely "natural" process is inadequate), on which I say more below. It is true that other accounts from the ancient world use the image of shaped mud, to which something special is added, to make humans, which is another good reason not to follow a strictly literalistic hermeneutic here.[69]

---

68. See, for example, Gesenius-Kautsch-Cowley, §117*hh*; Waltke-O'Connor, §10.2.3*c*; Joüon-Muraoka, §125*v*.

69. I note that Walton acknowledges that "an overarching materiality is evident in the wording" of other ancient accounts (p. 101). For my take on the way the other cultures include this theme, see Collins, *Did Adam and Eve Really Exist? Who They Were and Why You Should Care* (Wheaton, IL: Crossway, 2011), 153–54, where I conclude: "The existence of this motif can help us focus on what Genesis 2:7 is asserting about the first man, namely his special origin that sets him apart from the other animals (in the light of 1:26–27, that includes the image of God). It also leaves us careful about applying too firm a literalism in relating the words of Genesis 2:7 to a physical and biological account of human origins, although it does insist that the process was not a purely natural one."

130 FOUR VIEWS ON THE HISTORICAL ADAM

Under Walton's scenario, with Adam as possibly not the first human, he envisions Adam as a real person given a real test, as a representative and archetype of all humankind. He suggests that the humans before Adam, "even after being endowed with the image of God," would have been dying and "engaging in activities that we would call sinful." This resembles the scenario offered by Denis Alexander in his *Creation or Evolution: Do We Have to Choose?*, which I have discussed more fully elsewhere.[70] Walton's scenario is hard to reconcile with several considerations.

First, there is the simple affirmation that "God made man *upright*, but they have sought out many schemes" (Eccl. 7:29), which should help us in thinking about the meaning of "good" in Genesis 1. Walton tells us that the term "is not indicative of perfection … but of order." To speak of "perfection" is indeed unnecessary; I would say that instead it refers to what pleases God, what answers to his purpose. That this should include moral innocence comes, not only from the sense of the word, but also from "upright" (v. 29), as well as from Paul's insistence that "everything created by God is *good*" (1 Tim. 4:4).

There is the further difficulty that Walton's scheme raises serious questions about the justice of God in accounting the sin of this couple to their contemporaries, without having some kind of natural relationship between them. We can at least understand how children can "inherit" their citizenship from their parents; if my children, say, move to Australia and become citizens there, the children born to them will be Australians. On the other hand, it makes no sense, say, for a drill sergeant to punish all the men in a unit when one of them is unruly. For instance, in the film *Full Metal Jacket*, Sergeant Hartman does just that when Private Lawrence ("Gomer Pyle") goofs up, and the recruits take it out on Lawrence—but the sergeant is the one in the wrong (and this leads to Lawrence's breakdown, and to his murder of Sergeant Hartman and his own suicide).

Walton rejects a "genetic" model of sin's transmission. However, I doubt that many traditional theologians have advocated such a model. Indeed, there is no reason to believe that our genes define us; nor do we

---

70. Denis Alexander, *Creation or Evolution: Do We Have to Choose?* (Oxford: Monarch/ Grand Rapids: Kregel, 2008). I summarize and evaluate his scenario in Collins, *Did Adam and Eve Really Exist?*, 125–28.

need a medically detectable mechanism for passing along sin. Humans in a "people" share mutual connections that we cannot see or even properly describe; hence Paul's use of the "body" idea (borrowed from Hellenistic political philosophy) expresses quite well the notion of corporate solidarity found in the Hebrew Bible. Paul uses the terms "in Adam" and "in Christ" (1 Cor. 15:21): to be "in" someone is to be a member of that people whom that someone represents. In both cases, the "in" relationship also involves some kind of solidarity and participatory union (natural in the case of Adam, and supernatural in the case of Christ). There is no evidence that this representation can be as arbitrary as Walton seems willing to allow.[71]

In sum, then, I do not see how Walton's approach accounts for the unified origin of humankind, or for the foreignness of sin in God's plan.

I also consider Walton's idea of a "special creation" of humans that "gives a role and a function" to be inadequate. I cannot here go into everything that I take the Bible to mean by "the image of God," but whatever we think it is, if we read Genesis well, attending to the literary technique of showing (as against telling), we must see the image as something that clearly distinguishes humans from every other "living creature."[72] Whatever distinctive functions we humans exercise, and especially "dominion" (Gen. 1:26; cf. Ps. 8), requires that we have the capacities that everyone recognizes as setting us apart from the other animals. The "special creation," whatever material it operates on, must impose new features on both body and soul of the new creation; the body-soul unity is needed as the vehicle of this image.[73]

Walton mentions in a couple of footnotes an interest in Irenaeus's approach to the transmission of Adam's sin, and he encourages more research. I would welcome such research, having found similarities

---

71. Some of what Walton refers to as "Reformed" views of federal representation suffer from arbitrariness; this is due, not to the notion itself, but to the excessive focus on the legal idea of "imputation" without attention to the also important notion of participatory union.

72. Richard Briggs has helpfully brought considerations from speech-act theory into biblical interpretation; but in his "Humans in the Image of God and Other Things Genesis Does Not Make Clear," *Journal of Theological Interpretation* 4:1 (2010): 111–26, he fails to recognize that an author's "showing" can be a part of his illocutionary force. In the case of reading Genesis, one simply must notice the similarities and differences between humans and other animals in the presentation and draw the proper conclusions.

73. For the argument that humans are not body only, nor simply bodies containing souls, but a body-soul tangle, see Collins, *Science and Faith: Friends or Foes?* (Wheaton, IL: Crossway, 2003), ch. 8 (with notes and comments in the back).

between my own views and those of Irenaeus;[74] but we can only imagine Irenaeus's surprise that anyone would appeal to his work in support of a theological construct that disputes Adam's place as the first human. Irenaeus is quite clear that Genesis 1:27 is paralleled in Genesis 2 and that the agent of temptation was an apostate angel (Satan). He describes wickedness as spreading, without explaining the mechanism; he is also clear that "the Fall of Man was the occasion by which the growth of Man toward the future completion of the image of God in Man was brought to a stop," which then spread through Adam and Eve to their descendants.[75]

To conclude, then, Walton wants to make Adam out to be an archetype. I am not sure exactly what he means by that term, but he certainly has not intended to imply "nonhistorical," which I appreciate.[76] However, when he says "the role of someone as an archetype does not preclude their historical existence" (p. 90), I think he has the relation backward: a historical person can easily be an archetype, which is why Adam's temptation and sin has *both* its own historical particularity and consequences *and* a paradigmatic role with which we can identify. (This is one reason I suggest that "anachronism" is an important literary device in Genesis, so that Israel—and thus we—may see ourselves as the heirs of these events.)[77]

But the paradigmatic gets its power from the historical: this event has set a pattern by which we can understand temptation and sin. There are other paradigms as well, most notably marriage, where "a man" (any man) "shall leave his father and his mother and hold fast to his wife, and they shall become one flesh": the first marriage sets the pattern for every one that follows, an ideal toward which we strive (painfully, now that the "fall" has happened).[78]

---

74. See Collins, *Did Adam and Eve Really Exist?*, 65.

75. See Anders-Christian Jacobsen, "The Importance of Genesis 1–3 in the Theology of Irenaeus," *Zeitschrift für antikes Christentum* 8.2 (2005): 299–316 (quoted from 310). Important passages from Irenaeus include *Against Heresies* 3.22.3–3.23.8; 5.15.4; 5:23.1–2; *Demonstration of the Apostolic Preaching*, 11–18.

76. It is not at all clear what Walton means by identifying Abraham as an "archetype" in Romans 4:11–12. Paul's argument depends on a narrative—namely, that believing Gentiles are incorporated into Abraham's family and thus become his "heirs" (vv. 13–14). That is, Abraham's relationship to Christian believers is a historical one, as our "father" and head of the people through whom God will bless the world.

77. See, for example, Collins, *Did Adam and Eve Really Exist?*, 59–60, 113–14.

78. Walton doubts that this marriage is indeed paradigmatic, but see my discussion in Collins, *Genesis 1–4*, 142–45.

Walton (p. 113) wants to accommodate those who might be persuaded by the modern scientific consensus that humans are the product of a process of change over time from a common ancestor (i.e., any of several evolutionary models) by a variety of mechanisms known and unknown, and that our genetic heritage is diverse (rather than from one human pair), and who further were convinced that such a process has been divinely guided.

As I say in my essay, the biologists and paleontologists may explore their own fields of study, and may God bless them in it; at the same time, when they wish to integrate their conclusions into the larger story of human life, they do not automatically speak with expert authority. In particular, Walton is wise to clarify that the mechanisms are "known and unknown"; there is no *a priori* right to exclude the possibility that some (or even much) of God's guidance of this process involves factors that go beyond the natural (see also my comments on Lamoureux's essay, invoking C. S. Lewis). When it comes to human origins, there is excellent reason to be persuaded that God's guidance has indeed done so! Hence I believe that the criteria for scenarios that I have set out do a better job of allowing science and Scripture to illuminate each other. If someone thinks that his biological studies support a kind of evolutionary story, let these freedoms and limitations safeguard his good reasoning.

WILLIAM D. BARRICK

Every serious Bible student will find much in John Walton's essay that will augment his or her understanding of Scripture's metanarrative. This includes his cosmic temple analogy in addition to the archetypal roles of Adam, Eve, Cain, Abel, Enoch, Noah, Abraham, Jacob, Moses, and Jesus, just to name a few. Both approaches deserve examination and reward the reader with theological insights that help to unite the overall message of Scripture. In Adam's case, the statement about his origin in the dust of the earth certainly heightens the reality of his (and our) mortality. The dust does, indeed, serve as an indication of one element in mankind's nature.

As Walton himself notes, these archetypal observations per se do not deny the historicity of Adam and Eve as real people in real history. In fact, I would argue that the Genesis account regarding Adam's original material (dust) reflects the actual process and its material, as well as acting as a referent to his mortality. In other words, the Creator himself purposefully chose the medium in order to convey a theological message beyond the historical account. Sculptors often intend a subliminal message by means of the material they form into an object of art—it is not merely a matter of the resulting statue's durability. A sculpture of Churchill in wood just does not send the same message about his character and significance that a bronze or stone statue of the British prime minister would convey. If a mere human sculptor can possess such thoughtful expression through his work, why not the Creator of all things and all life?

Genesis provides clues concerning Adam's role by means of the verbs 'abad and šamar, as Walton observes. Common sense would seem to dictate that God's creation of the first man established the divine intent for mankind as a whole. Just as God created each of the first animals to reproduce and multiply after their own kind, so God created mankind to reproduce after its kind. Why create an individual head of the race who exhibits neither the intended character nor the intended function of his descendants? Possessing such functions, however, does not negate the accuracy of the biblical account regarding Adam's historical individuality as first man and biological head of the human race.

Just as Walton admits that Jesus exists both as an archetype and as a literal historical individual about whom the biblical record reveals an accurate, reliable history, so we ought to understand the same of Adam. Why accept the virgin conception of Jesus, but not Adam's special creation from dust? Consistency would seem to demand that a denial of the latter should be accompanied by a denial of the former.

Admitting that we can gain much theological insight from Walton's cogitations on the one hand does not mean, on the other hand, that his treatment of the historical Adam is a guaranteed outcome. Whether we are discussing the material origin of Adam or the nature of his sleep when God took a portion of Adam's flesh and bones, the archetypal interpretation need not affect the accuracy of the traditional interpretation of the biblical record. The author's careful attention to detail in the Genesis record ensures the literality and reality of the events. Genesis 2:7 ("Then the LORD God formed a man from the dust of the ground and breathed into his nostrils the breath of life, and the man became a living being") specifies the agent (God), the object (a man — not men), the actions (formed and breathed), the medium (dust and breath — not other humans), and the result (a single living being). Likewise, the fact that the created man was alone (v. 18) provides the reason for the creation of a woman whom God forms from the man's side. The text's comment that God "closed up the place with flesh" (v. 21) serves to emphasize that it simply happened in the way the account declares. That little detail speaks volumes regarding the historicity of Adam and Eve as specific individuals who originated exactly as the text specifies. It seems pointless and desperate to conclude that what the text describes did not take place.

In the words of James Boice,

> ... the human race is not one minor or accidental part of an eternal
> order of things but rather a specific and valuable part of creation,
> for which the other parts were brought into existence. The entire

human race descended from one original pair, Adam and Eve, and therefore one, despite subsequent division into national or ethnic groups.[79]

Apparently Walton dismisses the concept of the seminal headship of Adam, focusing only on his federal or representative headship. However, all mankind receive the Adamic nature by natural generation. Genesis 5:3 ("Adam ... had a son in his own likeness, in his own image") speaks of more than just the continuation of the image of God in mankind. As Kenneth Mathews points out, "Adam has endowed his image to Seth, including human sinfulness and its consequences."[80] We do not each fall by means of our first sin. We are all born fallen, as fallen children of Adam, with a sin nature transmitted through our parents. We are endowed with the sin nature at conception (Ps. 51:5), going astray from the womb (Ps. 58:3). Our inherited nature makes us sinners and, as sinners, we sin. Only the unique conception and birth of Jesus kept him free from receiving the same sin nature.

The biblical text breaks with its ancient Near Eastern environment by speaking of an original head of the human race. The student of the Scriptures and its attendant theological implications would expect exactly this of divine revelation for the people of God living in a fallen world. Myth and legend play no role in the biblical representations of God's creation of Adam and Eve. This nonconformity to ancient myths and legends extends even to biblical attention to the material origins of both the man and the woman. Again, since Walton accepts both the archetypal and historical realities of Jesus, one would expect him to favor the reality of both the virgin conception of Jesus as well as his sacrificial death by crucifixion. If so, it would appear that Walton has no viable reason for not taking Adam's historical details as equally unique and historically real.

If, indeed, the ancient Near Eastern cultural context directed readers to the archetypal sense of creation accounts, the same readers would see in the biblical account the archetypal implications. Despite

---

79. James Montgomery Boice, *Foundations of the Christian Faith: A Comprehensive & Readable Theology*, rev. ed. (Downers Grove, IL: InterVarsity Press, 1986), 544.

80. Kenneth A. Mathews, *Genesis 1 – 11:26*, NAC (Nashville: Broadman & Holman, 1996), 310.

that direction, however, they would find that the Hebrew Scriptures departed from their expectations by providing details that would be unique to ancient Near Eastern literature—namely, the existence of actual individuals and events in real time.

Did the Hebrews accept the identical cosmic geography of other ancient Near Eastern peoples? Did every ancient culture really believe that the world is a flat disk?[81] The God of Israel, Yahweh, is not like the ancient Near Eastern gods. He has revealed what his world is in such a way that his people, his true followers, have always possessed a different worldview and a different cosmology. As Walton himself observes concerning peoples in the ancient Near East, "it is important to realize that their cosmic geography was predominantly metaphysical and only secondarily physical/material. The role and manifestation of the gods in the cosmic geography was primary."[82] Godly Hebrews worshiped the true God and accepted his revelation of creation and cosmic geography, not the pagan concepts characteristic of the anti-Yahweh cultures surrounding them.

Interestingly, modern evangelicals who adopt the worldview of evolutionary science tend to abandon the divinely revealed worldview, which has always stood at odds with the way the pagan world has thought and believed. The modern evolutionary worldview, too, is still primarily a metaphysical and theological choice and only secondarily physical and material.

Walton agrees that "the text *could* be referring to the biological as well as the archetypal" (see p. 98, his emphasis). He is correct in stating that both require demonstration. His arguments for denying the biological claims of the text are, however, unconvincing. His argument from silence in the New Testament, by which he concludes that there is no need to consider all humans as biological descendants of Adam and Eve, is dubious.

So, too, Walton's treatment of the *toledot* formula in Genesis falls short of providing conclusive evidence for a much later set of events

---

81. According to John H. Walton, *Ancient Near Eastern Thought and the Old Testament: Introducing the Conceptual World of the Hebrew Bible* (Grand Rapids: Baker Academic, 2006), 171–72, an Egyptian sarcophagus and a Babylonian world map "confirm the unanimity with which all parties considered the earth to be a flat disk."

82. Ibid., 167.

for Genesis 2:5–25, because the transition in Genesis 2:4 is unique to the remaining *toledoths* in Genesis. Genesis 1:1–2:3 is an introduction to the entire book, not a prior *toledoth*.[83] Like the isolated *toledoth* in Numbers 3:1–4, Genesis 2:4–25 is contemporaneous with at least one part of the preceding text unit.

Yes, we ought to insist that modern readers pay attention to more than just the material origins of the man and the woman in the Genesis account. But we must disagree with any disregard to their material origins, because those origins have an impact on biblical concepts regarding the character of God (wholly truthful, all-powerful, and all-wise), the character and nature of mankind (universally sinful due to Adam's disobedience and Adamic biologically and theologically), the reality and nature of sin (originating in Adam and universal),[84] and the necessity and extent of Christ's sacrificial death as the solution to the state of fallen mankind and a sin-corrupted and Creator-cursed universe (to make both spiritual and physical restoration).

Where Walton tends to see only the archetypal in the Genesis text, young-earth creationists accept the necessity of preserving both the archetypal and the material elements of the biblical text.

By reducing the "good"-ness of creation solely to the aspect of function rather than morality and/or design, Walton tosses aside the fact that the biblical reference to the tree of the knowledge of good and evil anticipates "a moral, ethical capacity, the ability to know the essence of these values and the differences between them."[85] Functionality appears as part of the meaning of "good" in some parts of the biblical creation account, but it does not eliminate either morality or divine design. The physical creation reflects the moral character of God, and his goodness cannot be limited to mere function.

---

83. See Jason S. DeRouchie, "The *Toledot* Structure of Genesis: A Textlinguistic, Literary, and Theological Analysis" (paper presented at the National Meetings of the Evangelical Theological Society, San Francisco, 2011), 9: *"Genesis 1:1 – 2:3 provides the prefatory lens into the* toledot *units …"* (emphasis his).

84. Walton's "radiation" model for addressing the doctrine of original and universal sin might find either support or illustration in Romans 8:19–22 with its strong hint that Adam's disobedience had an impact on all of creation, not just on mankind.

85. Eugene H. Merrill, *Everlasting Dominion: A Theology of the Old Testament* (Nashville: B&H Publishing Group, 2006), 183.

A REJOINDER

My colleagues disagree with me — otherwise we could not have a "four views" book. Much of what is said in their responses offers little more than a reaffirmation of their disagreements rather than a refutation of my arguments. In this brief rejoinder I will focus on comments in which my colleagues have suggested that my methods are flawed rather than on those where they simply indicate that they are unpersuaded.

I doubt that any of our positions are very different with regard to the theological affirmations of the text. We all believe that people are created by God in his image, that sin is real and we are all subject to it, and that Christ's death was necessary to resolve the sin issue. I will address their concerns in ten categories.

History of Interpretation: It is no argument to say that people did not interpret Genesis 1 and 2 in the way that I do before. The church fathers did not have the tools available today, nor did they have the exegetical objectives. The rabbis were in the cognitive environment of the Hellenistic world, not in the one shared by the Israelites and the ancient Near East. Jesus is another matter, but the fact that Jesus addresses Genesis 1 and 2 together does not mean that they operate synoptically.

Relationship to ANE: It is true that the accounts of human origins in the ANE feature *de novo* creation of people. But even then their interests are not anything like what we would call scientific; they have no such category, and as I demonstrated, their interests are archetypal.

Dust as Material: The dust people turn into in the grave is material, but that does not mean that this account of human origins has material interests. Psalm 103 shows that we are all made from dust, but that does not describe our material origins even though we all return to material dust when our bodies disintegrate.

Priestly Roles: The objection that priests teach the Word of God and offer sacrifices and that Adam does not do either is a reductionistic assessment of the role of priests. The major role of the priests is to preserve sacred space, which Adam was tasked to do. Priests' teaching and their rituals are part of their role, but not all of it.

Vision of Eve: The closing up of the flesh in the vision still does not make this a material surgical procedure that actually happened.

Relationship of Genesis 1–2: Lamoureux dismisses my treatment as "typically evangelical" in favor of the apparent inevitability of source theory. Source theory has significant problems, and these have been addressed in the book I did with Brent Sandy, *The Lost World of Scripture* (Downers Grove, IL: InterVarsity Press, 2013).

Collins and I have no disagreement about the complementarity of Genesis 1–2, but that does not mean that Genesis 2 pertains to day 6. Psalm 104 talks about both chapters, and well it should. Recall that I do not consider Genesis 1–2 as deriving from different sources or competing traditions. Genesis 1 tells how sacred space functions for humanity; Genesis 2 tells how humans began to function in sacred space. Genesis 1 tells us how the cosmos became sacred space; Genesis 2 tells us where the center of sacred space was located (Eden).

Lexical Issues: Collins's comparison to God making, forming, and creating Israel seems to me to support my position rather than to argue against it. Clearly, the texts he cites do not pertain to material origins of Israelites.

It is another matter when he claims that my analysis "lacks lexical rigor." That would indeed be a serious drawback, but his following discussion really does not address my lexical rigor. I fully recognize that there is a double accusative in Genesis 2:7 (the only occurrence of this verb with a double accusative), but that changes nothing. Collins would claim that the double accusative serves to indicate what was formed (Adam) and what he was formed from (dust). I fully agree, but that does not mean that forming pertains to the question of material origins. Adam *was* formed from dust; we are all *formed* from dust. The question concerns the semantic range of the verb translated "formed," and any lexical study demonstrates that the word frequently pertains to something other than materiality. My claim is that Adam being formed from dust does not pertain to the material origins of this single human being, but pertains to the mortality of all of us.

Other Statements of Scripture: The linkage that exists between various sections in Genesis 1–5 is no surprise and likewise no refutation of my position. The most important one concerns the implications of Genesis 5:1, referring to Adam in the image of God. But of course I agree that Adam is in the image of God, and Collins admits that Genesis 5:1 refers to "mankind." Another suggestion was that Ecclesiastes 7:29—"God made man upright" (ESV)—would contradict my position about the original state of humanity. I disagree, because the Hebrew word translated "upright" is frequently used to refer to those who are largely innocent, and that would be the case here. Such a statement would therefore not require original sinlessness, only original innocence.

Theological Issues: Collins treats new heaven and new earth as a restoration of Eden, whereas I would consider it to be a climax in which the cosmos finally achieves the level of order that only began in Genesis 1. It is the story of sacred space reaching its intended culmination. For my colleagues who are concerned about the spread of sin and God's justice, I would note that a priest's actions can have consequences for all. We must acknowledge, however, that this issue is full of mystery in any model; one can have just as many questions about God's justice in the inheritance model in which Adam is the father of all in a genetic sense.

Overall Sense: Collins questions whether my approach "accounts for the unified origin of humankind, or for the foreignness of sin in God's plan." I contend that the most important aspect of human origins is in their identification as God's images and in that origin we are unified. In my view, sin is originally foreign to humankind, not because they were perfect or totally righteous, but because they were not yet accountable. I would suggest that Paul thinks the same way (Rom. 5:13).

A HISTORICAL ADAM:
OLD-EARTH CREATION VIEW

C. JOHN COLLINS

In this chapter I argue that the best way to account for the biblical presentation of human life is to understand that Adam and Eve were both real persons at the headwaters of humankind. By "biblical presentation" I refer not only to the story in Genesis and the biblical passages that refer to it, but also to the larger biblical story line, which deals with God's good creation invaded by sin, for which God has a redemptive plan; of Israel's calling to be a light to the nations; and of the church's prospect of successfully bringing God's light to the whole world. That story concerns the unique role and dignity of the human race, which is a matter of daily experience for everyone: All people yearn for God and need him, must depend on him to deal with their sinfulness, and crave a wholesome community for their lives to flourish.

I argue that the nature of the biblical material should keep us from being too literalistic in our reading of Adam and Eve, leaving room for an Earth that is not young, but that the biblical material along with good critical thinking provides certain freedoms and limitations for connecting the Bible's creation account to a scientific and historical account of human origins.

Introduction

Traditionally Christians, like the Jews from whom they arose, have read the story of Adam and Eve in the opening chapters of the Bible as describing the first pair of human beings, from whom all other humans descend. They have also taken the account of the "disobedience" in

Genesis 3 as narrating the origin of all human sin: that is, these readers have supposed that God first made humans morally innocent, and that the events of Genesis 3 transformed the moral condition of Adam and Eve and thus of all humankind after them.[1]

This is a standard belief in the ancient Christian writers, whether from the East or West, even when they do not have the same way for describing exactly *how* the disobedience of Adam and Eve transformed the human moral condition.[2] Of course, their own surrounding cultures often disputed their beliefs! Today there are also voices, both outside the church and within it, that raise questions for us as to whether we should hold this ancient belief any longer. First, there is the age-old objection: "How could anything someone else did, long ago, have any bearing on my life here and now? Even if Adam and Eve really lived and disobeyed God and were booted out of the garden: What of it? Why should that affect anything important about *me*?"[3]

Second, there is the widely acknowledged conclusion that the material in Genesis 1–11 closely parallels what we find in other ancient

1. This essay draws on and develops material found in my writings *Did Adam and Eve Really Exist? Who They Were and Why You Should Care* (Wheaton, IL: Crossway, 2011); "Adam and Eve in the Old Testament," *SBJT* 15:1 (2011): 4–25; and "Adam and Eve in the Old Testament," in Michael Reeves and Hans Madueme, eds., *Adam, the Fall, and Original Sin* (Grand Rapids: Baker/Nottingham: Inter-Varsity Press, forthcoming), with those publishers' permission. In 2009 I participated in a forum on historical Adam and Eve at the annual meeting of the American Scientific Affiliation, with Daniel Harlow and John Schneider, who argued that we should *not* take them as historical persons. Our revised papers were published in the journal *Perspectives on Science and Christian Faith* 62.3 (2010).

2. That is, we make a big mistake if we think of a position *in general* on the role of Adam and his sin as a distinctively western or Augustinian issue. The Greek-speaking fathers typically hold some version of the idea above: e.g., Irenaeus (later second century AD; see Anders-Christian Jacobsen, "The Importance of Genesis 1–3 in the Theology of Irenaeus," *Zeitschrift für antikes Christentum* 8.2 [2005], 299–316); Origen (AD 185–254), *Homily on Luke*, at Luke 2:22 ("stains of our birth"); Athanasius (AD 293–373), *On the Incarnation*, 1:3–5 ("the loveliness of their original innocence"); Eusebius (c. AD 315), *Preparation for the Gospel*, 7.8 [307d] ("Adam ... *fell from* [Greek, *apopiptō*] his better lot"); John Chrysostom (AD 347–407), *Homilies on Romans*, x ("He [Adam] *having fallen* [Greek, *piptō*], even those who did not eat from the tree, all of them, became mortal because of him"); and Theodore of Mopsuestia (AD 350–428), *Catechetical Homilies*, 14 ("we fell and sin corrupted us"). Also outside the influence of Augustine are the Syriac speaker Ephraem the Syrian (AD 306–73), *Commentary on 1 Corinthians*, 1:30 (speaking of the forgiveness we need as mediated through baptism); Latin-speaking Tertullian (c. AD 160–220), *On the Soul*, 16, 40–41 ("corruption" that came from the sin of Adam); and Cyprian (d. AD 258), *Letters*, 58.5 (to Fidus: the sin of Adam affects even newly born infants).

3. J. Matthew Ashley, "Original Sin, Biblical Hermeneutics, and the Science of Evolution," in Jitse van der Meer and Scott Mandelbrote, eds., *Nature and Scripture in the Abrahamic Religions* (4 vols.; Leiden: Brill, 2008), 2:407–36, discusses this impulse in the "modern" period, which leads to a rejection of traditional notions of "original sin."

stories, particularly those from Mesopotamia. Someone might say, "If we do not treat these other stories as history, why should we treat Genesis any differently? In fact, what makes us think that the Bible writers themselves meant to produce anything different from those other stories?"[4]

Third, we have the dominant theories of the modern sciences. The astrophysicists tell us that the universe began with a "big bang" about 13–14 billion years ago. This is or is *not* a problem, depending on whether we think Genesis gives a time line. Now, my own view of the "days" in Genesis 1 is that they are God's workdays, analogous to human workdays and not necessarily the first six days of the whole universe. Genesis 1 presents God *as if* he were a workman, going through his week, so that we can celebrate the creation as a magnificent achievement. This means that how long those days were, or how they relate to time as we know it—let alone how they might match what we find in the fossils—is not important for Genesis. For this reason I do not think the Bible specifies a time line, and thus I do not object to the standard theories of cosmology and geology.[5]

A more serious challenge comes from the science of evolutionary biology, with its narrative (as some construe it) of how human beings arose through a purely natural process of evolution. Further, studies of DNA have seemed to imply that we cannot get the genetic diversity we find in the human population if humanity began with only two people.[6] Many wonder whether the different varieties of humankind actually arose in separate places, independently of each other—thus implying that we are not a unified kind.

In this brief space I offer some reasons for retaining a version of the traditional Christian belief about Adam and Eve. I argue that this position does the best job of accounting for not only the Bible's overarching story line, but also our own everyday experience as human beings—an

---

4. See, for example, the questions raised by Peter Enns, *The Evolution of Adam: What the Bible Does and Doesn't Say about Human Origins* (Grand Rapids: Brazos Press, 2012), 37.

5. I have given my reasons in C. John Collins, *Science and Faith: Friends or Foes?* (Wheaton, IL: Crossway, 2003), especially chs. 5–7, 15.

6. Many resources along these lines can be found at the website of the BioLogos Foundation—biologos.org—associated with Francis Collins, director of the Human Genome Project. The research behind this goes back to Francisco Ayala et al., e.g., "Molecular Genetics of Speciation and Human Origins," *Proceedings of the National Academy of the Sciences* 91 (July 1994): 6787–94.

experience that includes sin as something that must be forgiven by God and by our fellow human beings; and sin as something that we must struggle against, because it defiles and disrupts a good human life.

Here is my plan. First, I consider the word "history," to be sure that we know what we mean by it. Second, I mention briefly a few "preliminaries" for Genesis 1–11. Third, I take us on a quick tour of the biblical story line, to see how Adam and Eve are woven into its very shape. Fourth, I examine some aspects of general human experience that show why the biblical story is the only thing that makes sense of the world. Finally, I offer some guidelines and some freedoms and limitations for our thinking about our first parents.

1. What Exactly Is "History"?

The first thing we must do is nail down what meaning we intend to use for that troublesome word "history." If you and I do not mean the same thing by the words we use, we will be talking past each other; and then we will have Inigo Montoya (in *The Princess Bride*) chiding us, "You keep using that word. I do not think it means what you think it means."

That happens with this word: a text might be "historical" by one person's meaning, and "not historical" by someone else's.[7] For example, some scholars say that an account is historical *only* if we tell it in its proper sequence and leave out imaginative elements. Some say that "history" applies only to the kind of thing that trained historians write. Others limit the word "history" to accounts that leave out all reference to actions of God or the gods. Now, this last group does not necessarily deny that God or the gods took part in the story—and this means they could end up saying, "This narrative is not *historical*, but that doesn't mean that it didn't happen"! This is confusing, and we should do better than that.

I have mentioned that some think that "history" leaves out the imaginative elements; that is, if a story is historical, it invites a literalistic approach to interpretation. In fact, this is a point of agreement between many strict young-earth creationists and many who reject historicity as a proper category at all for Genesis. For example, Douglas Kelly, a young-earth creationist, tells us, "the text of Genesis is clearly meant to

---

7. For more discussion, see V. Philips Long, *The Art of Biblical History* (Grand Rapids: Zondervan, 1994), especially 58–87 (chap. 2).

be taken in a literal, historical sense."[8] On the other hand, Peter Enns, whom we can call an "evolutionary creationist," makes the same equation: he writes of "a strictly literal/historical reading of Genesis."[9]

But there is nothing in the meaning of the word "history," nor in the principles of human behavior, that requires this tight connection between historicity and literalism of interpretation. Language is a means of social interaction, and we typically gear our level of expected literalism to the communication event we are engaged in. When a word or sentence is *about something in the actual world*, linguists call this *referring*. A careful speaker or writer chooses how to describe the person, thing, or event, with an eye toward conveying a dispositional stance toward it: e.g., to enable the audience to admire, or despise, or mourn over the referent.

In ordinary English a story is "historical" if the author wants his audience to believe the events really happened. That is, "history" is not really a *kind of literature* (or *genre*); it is a *way of referring*, of talking about events in the real world. This means that a variety of literary types can recount "history," and each type uses its own conventions for doing so.[10] Indeed, a *poem* can be historical. For example, Psalm 105 recounts some of the events in Exodus, mentioning only eight of the ten plagues and with a slightly different order. But that hardly nullifies the historicity of Psalm 105.

Further, some literalistic critical scholars have found tension between the ways in which Judges 4:17–24 and 5:24–30 describe the death of the Canaanite general Sisera.[11] Surely, when we recognize that Judges

---

8. Douglas Kelly, *Creation and Change: Genesis 1.1–2.4 in the Light of Changing Scientific Paradigms* (Fearn, Ross-shire, UK: Christian Focus, 1997), 51; see also pp. 41–42. This is apparently also a premise for Kelly's fellow young-earth creationist Kurt Wise, in his *Faith, Form, and Time* (Nashville: Broadman & Holman, 2002): e.g., on p. 44 he equates "taken at face value" with "intended to convey history."

9. Enns, *Evolution of Adam*, xv. See also Denis Lamoureux, *Evolutionary Creation: A Christian Approach to Evolution* (Eugene, OR: Wipf & Stock, 2008), e.g., 150: "Therefore, since the heavens are not structured in this way [i.e., according to a literalistic reading of Genesis 1], Gen 1 cannot be a historical account of the actual events that created the heavens."

10. Already in the fourth century BC, Aristotle recognized that one can tell "history" in metric verse: see his *Poetics*, 9.1–3.

11. E.g., George F. Moore, *Judges*, ICC (Edinburgh: T & T Clark, 1895), 163–64; see also G. A. Cooke, *The Book of Judges*, Cambridge Bible for Schools and Colleges (Cambridge, UK: Cambridge University Press, 1913), 66. Moore supposes that there were originally two different accounts.

5 is a *song*, whose purpose is to celebrate Israel's victory as an expression of God's favor to his people, we can see that Judges 5:25–27 portrays the killing of Sisera *as if* it were a great triumph, a humiliation of a great warrior as he dies at the hands of a tent-dwelling woman. The imaginative description does not compete with the prose telling in Judges 4, and to fail to see this is clumsy. In the same vein, Matthew 21:33–46 (cf. Mark 12:1–9; Luke 20:9–19) is a "parable" that presents a highly idealized telling of Israel's story, highlighting their repeated rejection of the divinely appointed representatives (which sets the pattern for their rejection of Jesus, the "son"). The idealization does not obscure the audience's ability to recognize the story and get the point (vv. 45–46).

Thus we can say that an author is making "historical" *claims* when he purports to refer to persons and events. An account has "historical" *value* if the persons and events are real and the intended dispositional stance is appropriate.

So then, I will use the ordinary language sense of "history," with the understanding that the following principles hold:

1. "historical" is not the same as "prose," and certainly does not imply that our account has no figurative or imaginative elements;
2. "historical" is not the same as "complete in detail" or "free from ideological bias," neither of which is possible or desirable anyhow;
3. "historical" is not necessarily the same as "told in exact chronological sequence" unless the text claims that for itself.

2. Preliminaries: Genesis 1 - 11 Is a Unity

a. Genesis 1 - 11 Has Parallels in the Ancient Near East

An attentive reader intuitively sees a transition between Genesis 1–11 and the rest of Genesis. Even though there is no grammatical shift,[12] nevertheless the narrator slows down in the Abraham story: he has been covering large stretches of time in brief narratives, whereas now he is taking more narration time to cover less elapsed time in more detail.

---

12. As noted in R. W. L. Moberly, *The Theology of the Book of Genesis*, Old Testament Theology (Cambridge, UK: Cambridge University Press, 2009), 121.

Stories from other cultures in the ancient Near East further confirm our intuition.[13] Although there are important materials from *all* the cultures of the ancient Near East, those most directly pertinent to Genesis 1–11 come from Mesopotamia. Specialists on the ancient Near East find the most promising parallels with Genesis 1–11 to include the Sumerian King List (c. eighteenth century BC), the Atrahasis Epic (c. eighteenth century BC), and the Eridu Genesis / Sumerian Flood Tale (c. 1600 BC).[14] (Another story, Enuma Elish, or the Babylonian Epic of Creation, once seemed a promising source for comparisons as well, and some biblical scholars still turn to it; Assyriologists, however, seem less willing to endorse much of a comparison than formerly.)[15]

---

13. Archaeological activity since the middle of the nineteenth century has certainly multiplied the availability of these ancient sources. However, Peter Enns is deeply mistaken when he asserts, "These discoveries *for the first time*—and irrevocably—placed Israelite religion in a larger context" (*Evolution of Adam*, 35, italics added). Jewish writers from the Second Temple period, and early Christian writers as well, already knew of these issues. For discussion of a particular question—the flood story—see my "Noah, Deucalion, and the New Testament," *Biblica* 93:3 (2012): 403–26. What these discoveries *have* changed is access to earlier versions of these stories, in their ancient tongues, rather than in Greek translation.

14. See, for example, David T. Tsumura, "Genesis and Ancient Near Eastern Stories of Creation and Flood: An Introduction," in Richard S. Hess and David T. Tsumura, eds., *I Studied Inscriptions from Before the Flood: Ancient Near Eastern, Literary, and Linguistic Approaches to Genesis 1–11* (Winona Lake, IN: Eisenbrauns, 1994), 27–57 (especially pages 44–57); Richard Averbeck, "The Sumerian Historiographic Tradition and Its Implications for Genesis 1–11," in A. R. Millard, James K. Hoffmeier, and David W. Baker, eds., *Faith, Tradition, and History: Old Testament Historiography in Its Near Eastern Context* (Winona Lake, IN: Eisenbrauns, 1994), 79–102; Kenneth A. Kitchen, *On the Reliability of the Old Testament* (Grand Rapids: Eerdmans, 2003), 423–25; and Anne Drafkorn Kilmer, "The Mesopotamian Counterparts of the Biblical *Nephilim*," in Edgar W. Conrad, ed., *Perspectives on Language and Text* (Winona Lake, IN: Eisenbrauns, 1987), 39–43. Richard S. Hess, "The Genealogies of Genesis 1–11 and Comparative Literature," *Biblica* 70 (1989): 241–54 (reprinted in Hess and Tsumura, *I Studied Inscriptions*, 58–72), adds some helpful cautions about the differences between the biblical genealogies and the king lists. Tikva Frymer-Kensky, in "The Atrahasis Epic and Its Significance for Our Understanding of Genesis 1–9," *Biblical Archaeologist* 40.4 (1977): 147–55, supports the parallel between the biblical flood story and Atrahasis over, say, Gilgamesh; at the same time, with her helpful observations about the contrast between the biblical and Mesopotamian accounts, I do not find all of her specific exegetical points on Genesis to be compelling.

15. W. G. Lambert has argued for a reduced interest in Enuma Elish; see his article, "A New Look at the Babylonian Background of Genesis," *JTS* n.s. 16:2 (1965), 287–300. He contends (291), "The first major conclusion is that the *Epic of Creation* is not a norm of Babylonian or Sumerian cosmology. It is a sectarian and aberrant combination of mythological threads woven into an unparalleled compositum. In my opinion it is not earlier than 1100 B.C." See also Alan R. Millard, "A New Babylonian 'Genesis' Story," *Tyndale Bulletin* 18 (1967), 3–18, and Kitchen, *On the Reliability of the Old Testament*, 425.

A further argument that the notion of *Chaoskampf* (such as that found in Enuma Elish) is absent from Genesis 1 comes from Gordon H. Johnston, "Genesis 1 and Ancient Egyptian Creation Myths," *Bibliotheca Sacra* 165.658 (2008): 178–94; he contends that the Egyptian

Kenneth Kitchen lays out the connections among these sources in the table "Genesis 1–11 and Writings from Mesopotamia."[16]

Sumerian King List	Atrahasis Epic	Eridu Genesis	Genesis 1–11
1. Creation assumed; kingship came down from heaven	1. Creation assumed; gods create humans to do their work	1. Creation; cities are instituted	1. Creation (Gen. 1–2)
2. Series of eight kings in five cities	2. Noisy humans alienate deities	2. [Alienation]	2. Alienation (Gen. 3), genealogies (Gen. 4–5)
3. The flood	3. The flood; ark	3. The flood; ark	3. The flood; ark (Gen. 6–9)
4. Kingship again; dynasties follow, leading to –	4. New start	4. New start	4. New start; then genealogies, down to –
5. "Modern times"	(5. "Modern times," implied)	(5. "Modern times," implied)	5. "Modern times"

There is much to say about the connections and about the ways in which Genesis 1–11 is both similar and dissimilar to these other sources, but space forbids. The point of interest for now is that this overarching pattern from Mesopotamia provides a literary and ideological context into which Genesis 1–11 speaks; and it does so *as a whole*.

So what does this parallel tell us about the function of Genesis 1–11? The Mesopotamian sources provide what Assyriologist Wil-

---

stories are a promising backcloth for Genesis. While I do not doubt the relevance of the Egyptian material, I find the pattern of the Mesopotamian material to provide the best overall parallel. Similarly, John H. Walton, in "Creation in Genesis 1:1–2:3 and the Ancient Near East: Order out of Disorder after *Chaoskampf*," *Calvin Theological Journal* 43.1 (2008): 48–63, rejects both *Chaoskampf* and "theomachy," but goes on to argue that Genesis 1 is a "temple cosmology," as in his popular work *The Lost World of Genesis One: Ancient Cosmology and the Origins Debate* (Downers Grove, IL: InterVarsity Press, 2009) and in his academic *Genesis 1 as Ancient Cosmology* (Winona Lake, IN: Eisenbrauns, 2011).

Nevertheless, Bruce Waltke (see Bruce Waltke and Cathi J. Fredricks, *Genesis: A Commentary* [Grand Rapids: Zondervan, 2001], 23) still finds what he considers important parallels in Enuma Elish, as does Enns, *Evolution of Adam*, e.g., 38–43. The factors mentioned here spoil both Waltke's and Enns' cases.

16. This table is based on my work *Did Adam and Eve Really Exist?*, 141.

liam Hallo calls "prehistory"—the period of human existence before there are any secure written records—and "protohistory"—the earliest stages for which there are records.[17] Further, it appears that the Mesopotamians aimed to accomplish their purpose by founding their stories on what they thought were *actual events*, albeit told with a great deal of imagery and symbolism. As Kenneth Kitchen, an Egyptologist, put it:

> As to definition [for the flood story], myth or "protohistory," it should be noted that the Sumerians and Babylonians had no doubts on that score. They included it squarely in the middle of their earliest historical tradition, with kings before it and kings after it.
>
> The ancient Near East did not historicize myth (i.e., read it as imaginary "history"). In fact, exactly the reverse is true—there was, rather, a trend to "mythologize" history, to celebrate actual historical events and people in mythological terms. The ancients (Near Eastern and Hebrew alike) knew that propaganda based on real events was far more effective than that based on sheer invention.[18]

While Kitchen uses the term "propaganda" for the authors' purpose, we might use the more neutral observation that these stories serve as the front end of the worldview story for Mesopotamian culture.[19]

Our *worldview* describes the way we lean into life: how we relate to God, to others, and to the world around us. It is how our deepest self answers the big questions, "Where did I come from? Why am I here? and Where am I going?" Our worldview comes to us through the Big Story we—and the communities we belong to—embrace. The story enlists the members of a community to play a meaningful part in the story as it unfolds. If the worldview story is well told, it captures the imaginations of those who own it, thereby driving them on and holding their loyalty.

17. William W. Hallo, "Part 1: Mesopotamia and the Asiatic Near East," in William W. Hallo and William K. Simpson, eds., *The Ancient Near East: A History* (Fort Worth: Harcourt Brace College Publishers, 1998), 3–181, at 25.

18. Kitchen, *On the Reliability of the Old Testament*, 425–26, 262, 300.

19. On this function in Mesopotamia, see Gordon Wenham, *Psalms as Torah* (Grand Rapids: Baker, 2012), 42–52; he draws on the work of David Carr, *Writing on the Tablet of the Heart: Origins of Scripture and Literature* (Oxford: Oxford University Press, 2005), 31–34.

Some think that this phenomenon is a feature primarily of premodern and prescientific peoples,[20] but they are mistaken; modern western culture does just the same. For example, the prominent evolutionary biologist George Gaylord Simpson (1902–84) drew this conclusion from his study of evolution: "Man is the result of a purposeless and natural process that did not have him in mind."[21] This is in fact a story, albeit a bleak one, that claims to put our lives in perspective. Actually, if it is the true story of the world, it sounds like a heightened version of what Macbeth described in Shakespeare's play, once he discovered that Lady Macbeth had committed suicide: "Life's ... a tale told by an idiot, full of sound and fury, signifying nothing."[22]

How did this work in Mesopotamia? Consider the way the Epic of Atrahasis tells us how humankind came to be created: there were the senior gods and the junior gods, and the junior gods were doing all the hard physical labor. These junior gods got tired of the work and went on strike, and thus the gods made humankind to take over this hard labor. It is likely that this kind of story explains to the average Sumerian what he is here for—to take his place in a stratified society, and to do the work his superiors tell him to do. That is, this way of telling the story preserves the social order.

The Mesopotamian stories include divine action, symbolism, and imaginative elements. The purpose of these stories is to lay the foundation for a worldview without being taken in a "literalistic" fashion. Consider, for example, the Sumerian King List. It begins, "When kingship was lowered from heaven, kingship was (first) in Eridu."[23] There are five dynasties, in the five leading cities of Sumer; then the flood "swept over," and afterward kingship is lowered again from heaven. There is little reason to doubt that the author thought he was writing about real people and real events. Nevertheless, he tells us that the kings before

20. E.g., Peter Enns, *Inspiration and Incarnation: Evangelicals and the Problem of the Old Testament* (Grand Rapids: Baker, 2005), 40, and, to a lesser extent, Don Pederson, "Biblical Narrative as an Agent for Worldview Change," *International Journal of Frontier Missions* 14:4 (1997): 163–66.

21. George Gaylord Simpson, *The Meaning of Evolution* (New Haven: Yale University Press, 1967), 365.

22. William Shakespeare, *Macbeth*, V.v.26–28.

23. For a helpful discussion, see A. R. Millard, "King Lists," in Piotr Bienkowski and A. R. Millard, eds., *Dictionary of the Ancient Near East* (Philadelphia: University of Pennsylvania Press, 2000).

the flood ruled for an enormous amount of time, ranging from 18,600 years (the last king before the flood) to 43,200 years. After the flood, the reigns shorten, but are still quite long—e.g., 1,200 years, 690 years, and so on; they show a shortening trend until Gilgamesh, who reigned for 126 years, and his son, who reigned for 30 years (the first reasonable number).

No one really knows what to make of the extraordinarily high numbers. Perhaps there is a rhetorical device being employed, to which we are not (yet) initiated: for example, involving base 60 or 360. There are further questions as to whether the dynasties mentioned in the list were strictly sequential; some seem to have been in parallel. No one knows whether the compiler of the list was aware of this.

But our (and presumably the Babylonians') inability to take these numbers and the sequences "literally" does not entitle us to call the list "unhistorical."[24] It is better to say that it has a historical core and that this core is presented with various rhetorical purposes in mind that go beyond the simple conveyance of information—even if we do not know all the devices to achieve that rhetorical purpose. The genre conventions require that we be careful in discerning what the historical referents are.

So it is fitting to find in Genesis an alternative front end to the worldview story, which aims to tell the story the right way. The biblical alternative story certainly does correct many elements of the other stories available (and probably attractive) to Israel: Genesis tells of one true God, who alone made and rules the heavens and the earth and all that is in them. In this story there is nothing left for any other god—if it even exists—to do. Further, the other cultures had "Wisdom Literature," and this presupposes that there is coherence to the world; Genesis provides the true explanation for this, namely, that the one good God made it all as the right kind of place for human beings to live and love and serve.

Moreover, far from humankind being made to relieve God of work he did not like doing, it is dignified with his image (Gen. 1:27) and with the task of ruling the creation in a wise and benevolent way (vv. 26, 28).

24. Contrast Daniel Harlow, "After Adam: Reading Genesis in an Age of Evolutionary Science," *Perspectives on Science and Christian Faith* 62.3 (2010): 179–95, who, at 185–87, notices symbolic and pictorial elements in both Genesis and the Mesopotamian stories and oddly pronounces them both unhistorical.

Human "work" at the beginning was to enjoy caring for Eden and to spread its blessings throughout the world.[25] The painful toil people now experience is not a proper part of the creation; it results from human disobedience, which requires divine redemption: Genesis 5:29 explicitly links later generations' "painful toil" (Heb. *'itstsâbôn*) to God's "curse" that followed the disobedience of Adam and Eve (Gen. 3:16, 19).

Further, Genesis appears to trace all humankind back to a common source. That is, the genealogies of Genesis 5 and 10 present Adam and Eve as the ancestors of a wide range of "families of the earth" — in fact, *all* the families so far as the audience is concerned.[26] By affirming human unity in Adam and Eve, Genesis lays the foundation for Israel's calling to bring light to the world. When God called Abram in Genesis 12:2 – 3, he promised,

> I will make of you a great nation, and I will bless you and make your name great, so that you will be a blessing. I will bless those who bless you, and him who dishonors you I will curse, and in you all the families of the earth shall be blessed.

That is, God called Abram, not simply in order to bless him and his family, but in him to bring blessing to the whole world. Abram's family, Israel, was to be the vehicle of God's light to the Gentiles, as they lived faithfully in God's covenant.[27]

This story *should* also foster a respect for common human dignity in those who believe it — though we must admit, not everyone who has *professed* such belief has shown this respect. For example, God does not endorse a stratified society for his people, treating people differently depending on their social or economic status (cf. Lev. 19:9 – 18); even slaves are human beings.[28]

---

25. This idea is the main theme in Gregory Beale, *The Temple and the Church's Mission* (Downers Grove, IL: InterVarsity Press, 2004).

26. Enns, *Evolution of Adam*, 65 – 70, makes the astounding claim that in Genesis Adam is the source specifically of Israel and not of all humankind — a view that overlooks this point. Indeed, it is entirely reasonable to suppose that Genesis portrays Adam anachronistically, in a form that an Israelite can identify with, so that the people of Israel can see themselves as God's new humanity (or new family of Adam) for the sake of bringing God's blessing to the world.

27. See, for example, Christopher J. H. Wright, *The Mission of God: Unlocking the Bible's Grand Narrative* (Downers Grove, IL: InterVarsity Press, 2006), 199 – 221.

28. For a sensible discussion, see Christopher J. H. Wright, *Old Testament Ethics for the People of God* (Downers Grove, IL: InterVarsity Press, 2004), 333 – 37.

The point to take away is this: We have gained a great deal when we notice that Genesis really does have parallels with the stories that come from other ancient Near Eastern cultures. One of these gains is to realize that "history" is an appropriate category for such a tale; another is to recognize that no one expected the stories to be read in a thoroughly literalistic fashion.

b. Genesis 1 - 11 Is a Unity on the Literary Level

Certainly the parallels between Genesis 1–11 and these Mesopotamian stories argue that we should read these eleven chapters together. Another argument for the propriety of reading them together comes from the literary and linguistic links between pericopes within them.

Well-known links for the whole of Genesis 1–11 include those between Adam and Noah, presenting Noah as a "new Adam" (compare Gen. 9:1 with 1:28).[29] Further, there are clear links between Genesis 1 and 5, such as 1:26–27 and 5:1–5 (the life of Adam), and between Genesis 4 and 5, such as 4:25–26 and 5:3–11 (Seth and Enosh). There may be a link between the genealogy descended from Cain (4:17–22) and that from Seth (5:6–32), especially in the names Enoch, Methushael/Methuselah, and Lamech (cf. 4:18 with 5:18, 21, 25), although this is uncertain.[30]

Genesis 9–11 are coherent with the previous pericopes, since these chapters record the sequel to the Great Flood, with the descent of various peoples from the family of Noah (cf. 10:1), as linked by the genealogies (cf. 11:10, picking up the line of Shem), with 11:10–19 paralleling 10:21–25 (through Peleg), and 11:20–26 bringing the line down to Abram, Nahor, and Haran (who, with their descendants, will feature in the rest of Genesis).

---

29. See, e.g., William Dumbrell, *Covenant and Creation: A Theology of the Old Testament Covenants* (Carlisle, UK: Paternoster, 1997 [1984]), 27; Tremper Longman III, *How to Read Genesis* (Downers Grove, IL: InterVarsity Press, 2005), 117–18; Waltke, *Genesis: A Commentary*, 127–28.

30. See my *Genesis 1–4: A Linguistic, Literary, and Theological Commentary* (Phillipsburg, NJ: P&R Publishing, 2006), 201, where I suggest that maybe the contrast between the two families is prominent. Perhaps this indicates as well that the decline we see in Cain's family was not an inevitable outcome of being human; rather, it flowed from the moral orientation of the members, which in turn is influenced by the orientation of the head member of the list. We might also suspect that the author saw the orientation of Cain's line as becoming dominant and perhaps drawing Seth's descendants away from God, so that "the wickedness of man was great in the earth" (6:5 ESV).

Within Genesis 1–4 there are also clear linkages. First, Genesis 2–4 are commonly assigned to the J-source, with a few redactions; their overall unity is not controversial.[31] Second (see below), Genesis 2:4–25 serves to elaborate the sixth "day" of Genesis 1. Third, the common assertion that the P creation story (Gen. 1) is free of anthropomorphisms is mistaken;[32] this story actually depends on an anthropomorphism, namely, the portrayal of God as one who goes through his work week and enjoys his Sabbath rest.[33] Genesis 2 contributes its own anthropomorphism to this pattern, depicting God as if he were a potter "forming" the first man (2:7) and a worker who "builds" the first woman (2:22, ESV margin).

Finally, several verbal links show that whatever separate origins the individual pericopes might have had, they have been edited in such a way as to exhibit coherence. For example, in 1:28 we read, "And God *blessed* them. And God said to them, 'Be fruitful and multiply.'" In Genesis 3 the "blessing" (*brk*) has turned to "curse" ('*rr*), the proper antonym. And whereas the blessing was for them to *multiply* by having children, after their disobedience God said to the woman that he will "surely *multiply* your pain in childbearing"—that is, the arena of blessing was turned into one of pain and danger. The genealogical chapter 5 (in v. 29) also refers to God's "curse" on the ground (3:17): " . . . and [Lamech] called his name Noah, saying, 'Out of the ground that the LORD has *cursed* ['*rr*], this one shall bring us relief from our work and from the *painful toil* ['*itstsâbôn*, cf. 3:16, 17] of our hands.'"

Further, three "enigmatic" first person plurals, by which God addresses "us," appear through Genesis 1–11, namely, 1:26; 3:22; and 11:7. Many suppose that these (or at least the first) are God addressing his angelic council, although I judge the best explanation to be a "plural of self-address."[34] The specific conclusion here does not matter for my

---

31. See Richard Elliott Friedman, *The Bible with Sources Revealed: A New View into the Five Books of Moses* (New York: HarperCollins, 2003), and my discussion in *Genesis 1–4*, 227–28.

32. Asserted in, e.g., Friedman, *Bible with Sources Revealed*, 12; S. R. Driver, *The Book of Genesis*, Westminster Commentary (London: Methuen, 1904), xxv.

33. I have argued this in a number of places, e.g., in *Science and Faith: Friends or Foes?* and *Genesis 1–4*, 77.

34. For relevant discussion, see Collins, *Genesis 1–4*, 59–61. More recently, Lyle Eslinger argues that these plurals reflect a heightened focus on the divine-human difference; see his "The Enigmatic Plurals Like 'One of Us' (Genesis i 26, iii 22, and xi 7) in Hyperchronic Perspective," *VT* 56.2 (2006): 171–84. I am not convinced and thus retain what I find to be a simpler and more exegetically based explanation.

purpose; the point is that this is a distinctive feature of this stretch of material, from supposedly separate sources.

Once we recognize how Genesis 1–11 is integrated into the whole flow of the book of Genesis, and how these chapters parallel basic worldview-shaping materials from Mesopotamia, it is no surprise to find that whoever put these chapters together did so in such a way that they display their unity at the literary and linguistic level.

c. Genesis 1 - 11 Sets the Stage for Genesis 12 - 50

The purpose of Genesis is to identify the people of Israel, who followed Moses, as the heirs of God's promises to Abraham. We find in Genesis 12 that God called Abraham so that his family would be the vehicle of blessing to "all the families of the earth"—and, since Genesis 10 recounts the various "families" (or "clans," Heb. *mishpâkhôt*) of the earth, this means to all Gentile peoples everywhere. So Genesis 1–11 clarifies that the God who has called Abraham is in fact the one true God, the Maker of heaven and earth, for whom all humankind yearns.

3. The Biblical Story Line

Now we can consider whether the Bible presents Adam and Eve as "historical" persons. How would we answer that, especially since we are wary of being overly literalistic? I have proposed three basic criteria:[35]

1. *How does the person or event impact the basic story line?* I contend that the biblical authors were self-consciously interpreting their world in terms of an overarching worldview story. Does treating the persons or events as "merely symbolic" distort the shape of the story?
2. *How have other writers, especially biblical ones, taken this person or event?* Any notion of biblical authority requires me to respect what biblical writers see; common sense requires me to check what I see against what others see, especially those who are closer to the original time and culture than I am.[36]

---

35. Collins, *Did Adam and Eve Really Exist?*, 19.
36. I will take up my own "notion of biblical authority" in the final section.

3. *How does this person or event relate to ordinary human experience?* The biblical writers, like other authors from the ancient world, were trying to enable their audience to live in the world as they found it. There are many intuitions we all share, such as our craving for God, our need for forgiveness, and our yearning for human community governed by love and justice. Most cultures tell stories to give a historical reason for these needs, and some explanation for how they can be met, mollified, explained away, or denied. The biblical approach to these rings true.

In the past few decades, many theologians have come to realize that the Bible has an overarching story line, which unifies all the different parts.[37] And that story line serves as the Big Story of the world — a Big Story that tells us who we are, where we came from, what is wrong, and what God is doing about it. This is why "history" matters: Biblical faith is a narrative of God's great works of creation and redemption, and not simply a list of "timeless" principles.

And what is that story line? Here is one way to summarize it:

> The Old Testament is thus the story of the one true Creator God, who called the family of Abraham to be his remedy for the defilement that came into the world through the sin of Adam and Eve. God rescued Israel from slavery in Egypt in fulfillment of this plan, and established them as a theocracy for the sake of displaying his existence and character to the rest of the world. God sent his blessings and curses upon Israel in order to pursue that purpose. God never desisted from that purpose, even in the face of the most grievous unfaithfulness in Israel.

---

37. These include: N. T. Wright, *The New Testament and the People of God* (Minneapolis: Fortress, 1992); Craig G. Bartholomew and Michael Goheen, *The Drama of Scripture: Finding Our Place in the Biblical Story* (Grand Rapids: Baker, 2004); Michael D. Williams, *Far as the Curse Is Found: The Covenant Story of Redemption* (Phillipsburg, NJ: P&R Publishing, 2005); Albert M. Wolters and Michael W. Goheen, *Creation Regained: Biblical Basics for a Reformational Worldview*, 2nd ed. (Grand Rapids: Eerdmans, 2005); Christopher J. H. Wright, *The Mission of God: Unlocking the Bible's Grand Narrative* (Downers Grove, IL: InterVarsity Press, 2006). For a brief summary of this approach, see C. John Collins, "The Theology of the Old Testament," in Lane T. Dennis et al., eds., *The ESV Study Bible* (Wheaton, IL: Crossway, 2008), 29–31 (which includes applications to reading the New Testament as well).

This overarching story serves as a grand narrative or worldview story for Israel: each member of the people was to see himself or herself as an *heir* of this story, with all its glory and shame; as a *steward* of the story, responsible to pass it on to the next generation; and as a *participant*, whose faithfulness could play a role, in God's mysterious wisdom, in the story's progress.

The New Testament authors, most of whom were *Jewish* Christians, saw themselves as heirs of the older story and as authorized to describe its proper completion in the death and resurrection of Jesus and the Messianic era that this ushered in. These authors appropriated the Old Testament as Christian Scripture, and they urged their audiences (many of whom were *Gentile* Christians) to do the same. There is debate over just how the New Testament authors used the Old Testament as Scripture, but the simplest summary of their stance would be to say that they saw the Old as constituting the earlier chapters of the story in which Christians are now participating.[38]

As before, there is much to say on this point; but for now I will note one advantage. We can discuss individual Bible passages; this is certainly good, and I have done that elsewhere. I am confident that texts from the Old Testament, the New Testament, and Second Temple Judaism consistently testify to a unified origin of humankind in Adam and Eve.[39] But when we are thinking about the story line, we can keep our eyes on the big picture. Some have gone as far as to suggest that the story of Adam and Eve is relatively inconsequential for the whole Old Testament (which implies that its role in the New Testament represents a departure from the Hebrew writers' intentions).[40] Now, I consider this argument mistaken, but I will not take time here to examine passage after passage. For our purposes, a good way to show that this suggestion

38. Collins, "Theology of the OT," *ESV Study Bible*, 30b.

39. My *Did Adam and Eve Really Exist?* contains much discussion of particular texts. See also my essays on "Adam and Eve in the Old Testament."

40. E.g., Claus Westermann, *Creation* (London: SPCK, 1974), 89, as cited with approval in W. Sibley Towner, "Interpretations and Reinterpretations of the Fall," in Francis A. Eigo, ed., *Modern Biblical Scholarship: Its Impact on Theology and Proclamation* (Villanova, PA: Villanova University Press, 1984), 53–85, at 72. See further Enns, *Evolution of Adam*, 80; and James Barr, *The Garden of Eden and the Hope of Immortality* (Minneapolis: Fortress, 1992), throughout. (Harlow, "After Adam," 187, follows Barr in this point.)

is mistaken is to demonstrate how the story of Adam and Eve serves as an underlying assumption behind the biblical story line—and that it also underlies several key Bible passages.

Good thinking about the biblical story line needs to start with Genesis 12:1–3, God's call of Abram, as we have seen: Abram's family, Israel, was to be the vehicle of God's light to the Gentiles, as they lived faithfully in God's covenant.

But what does this require as a foundation, if it is to be true? It requires that *all* the Gentiles *need* God's light, because they are estranged from him; and it requires that there be something in those Gentiles that can be enlivened to respond to that light, just as in Israel. In other words, these Gentiles have a common origin with Israel and a common set of human capacities as well as a common need.

Furthermore, this estrangement from God is *unnatural*; it is out of step with how things *ought* to be. Something has come into human experience that produced that estrangement, and that something is *sin* (cf. Eccl. 7:29).[41]

In the biblical story sin is an alien intruder; it disturbs God's good creation order. This comes through clearly in the way that the Levitical sacrifices deal with sin: they treat it as a defiling element, which ruins human existence and renders people unworthy to be in God's presence—and that is dangerous. The sacrifices work "atonement," "redemption," and "ransom," addressing sin as a defiling intruder that incurs God's displeasure (e.g., Lev. 16).[42]

The unnaturalness of sin also comes through in how wisdom books such as Proverbs connect moral goodness with mental savvy—and wickedness is a kind of stupidity or folly (e.g., Prov. 12:1). That is, living in line with God's will is sensible, while living out of step with God is foolish. Humans were meant to live sanely, not irrationally![43]

The notion that humankind is one family, with one set of ancestors for us all—ancestors who, at the headwaters of the human race

---

41. For discussion showing that this is the implication of this text, see my *Did Adam and Eve Really Exist?*, 70; see also my essays, "Adam and Eve in the Old Testament."

42. For a fine recent discussion, see Jay Sklar, *Sin, Impurity, Sacrifice, Atonement: The Priestly Conceptions* (Sheffield, UK: Sheffield Phoenix Press, 2005).

43. See discussion in my "Proverbs and the Levitical System," *Presbyterion* 35:1 (Spring 2009): 9–34, at 24, building on the work of Knut Heim, *Like Grapes of Gold Set in Silver: An Interpretation of Proverbial Clusters in Proverbs 10:1–22* (Berlin: Walter de Gruyter, 2001), 81–103.

brought sin and dysfunction into the world of human life—is behind all of these factors as an unwavering assumption. New Testament authors carry along this assumption. Certainly the apostle Paul spoke this way (e.g., Rom. 5:12–21; 1 Cor. 15:20–22, 44–49); but the most notable example of this assumption comes from Jesus himself in the *Gospels*.

For example, consider Matthew 19:3–9, where some Pharisees want to test Jesus, which probably means that they wanted to ensnare him into taking sides on a debate between their various schools of thought. So they asked him whether it is lawful for a man to divorce his wife "for any cause," and Jesus replied:

> "Have you not read that he who created them from the beginning *made them male and female*, and said, *'Therefore a man shall leave his father and his mother and hold fast to his wife, and the two shall become one flesh'*?" (Matt. 19:4–5).

Jesus' answer ties together Genesis 1:27 and 2:24 (see italics).[44] Since they are now one flesh, joined together by God, they should not be separated. The Pharisees then asked why Moses allowed divorce (Matt. 19:7, citing Deut. 24:1–4), and Jesus explains that it was a concession: "from the beginning it was not so" (Matt. 19:8).[45]

This conversation shows that Jesus viewed the creation account of Genesis 1–2 as setting the ideal for a properly functioning marriage for all human beings; that was how God intended things to be "from the beginning." The family legislation of Deuteronomy, on the other hand, does not set the ethical norm, but has another function—namely, that of preserving civility in Israel: a function that has become necessary by some change of circumstances since "the beginning."[46] The obvious

---

44. Matthew's Greek uses the Septuagint for Genesis 1:27, which is why it reads "made" (Greek) rather than "created" (Hebrew).

45. The "beginning" found in the expressions "from the beginning" (Matt. 19:4) and "from the beginning of creation" (Mark 10:6) is the beginning of human existence; see my discussion in *Science and Faith: Friends or Foes?*, 106–7, denying that this has a bearing on the presumed age of the earth. For a mid-nineteenth century source taking the same line as I do, see J. A. Alexander, *The Gospel According to Mark* (1858; reprint, Grand Rapids: Baker, 1980), 274.

46. For a good discussion of how this law functioned and its relation to the Bible's ethical ideals, see Christopher J. H. Wright, *Old Testament Ethics for the People of God*, 349–51; see also my *Genesis 1–4*, 144–45. For more background see Gordon Wenham, *Story as Torah: Reading Old Testament Narratives Ethically* (Grand Rapids: Baker, 2000), ch. 5.

candidate for making that change—really, the *only* candidate—is the sin of Adam and Eve, with its consequences for all human beings.

Jesus in the Gospels seems quite straightforwardly to have accepted the story in Genesis the way I am advocating. That story tells us where we come from and how we got to be the way we are; then in Genesis 3 God begins his program of redeeming his human creatures for the sake of his world. The last book of the Bible tells us where the whole story is headed; as we find in Revelation 22:1–5:

> Then the angel showed me the *river* of the water of life, bright as crystal, flowing from the throne of God and of the Lamb through the middle of the street of the city; also, on either side of the river, the *tree of life* with its twelve kinds of fruit, yielding its fruit each month. The leaves of the tree were for the healing of the nations. No longer will there be *anything accursed*, but the throne of God and of the Lamb will be in it, and his servants will worship him. They will see his face, and his name will be on their foreheads. And night will be no more. They will need no light of lamp or sun, for the Lord God will be their light, and they will reign forever and ever.

John's Revelation is of course filled with all manner of symbolism, and therefore I make no claim to know what the scene he describes will "actually" be like. But I can say this: John portrays it as Eden come to its full fruition: notice the *tree of life* and the *river*. The place is a sanctuary, which is how Genesis portrays the garden. And later in this chapter of Revelation (vv. 14–15) we read:

> Blessed are those who wash their robes, so that they may have the right to the tree of life and that they may enter the city by the gates. Outside are the dogs and sorcerers and the sexually immoral and murderers and idolaters, and everyone who loves and practices falsehood.

These people must "wash their robes" of the defilement that comes from sin, while those who persist in sin reap its consequences. They stay outside because they are *defiled*—defiled by something that does not belong in God's good world: evil. And evil came into God's world through the way that Satan deceived our first parents (see Rev. 12:9).

It is therefore quite a surprise to read in authors who think Adam and Eve are not historical the suggestions that the apostle Paul is really the only New Testament writer to make use of Genesis 3 and that the Gospels and Revelation do nothing with it![47]

In recent decades, specialists in the apostle Paul have realized how firmly he rooted his arguments in this overarching narrative of the Old Testament—just as Jesus did. From Romans 1:2–6, it is clear that Paul read the Old Testament as the early chapters of the biblical story, which tells of how God chose Abraham's family to be his fresh start on humankind, to restore what was damaged by sin, and which ends with the anticipation of a new era in which the Gentiles receive the light. He defines his key term "gospel" as the announcement that through the death, resurrection, and ascension of Jesus this new era has now begun (Rom. 1:2–6; Gal. 3:8–9; cf. Mark 1:15, see also Matt. 28:18–20).[48] As Paul tells us, Christian believers, both Jewish and Gentile, are those in whom God is renewing his image for proper human functioning in their individual and community lives (e.g., Col. 3:9–10; 2 Cor. 3:18), where the fractured family is once again united.

When it comes to the comparison of Adam and Jesus (Rom. 5:12–19; 1 Cor. 15:20–23, 42–49), Paul's argument likewise depends on a *narrative*. That is, someone did something (one man trespassed, Rom. 5:15), and as a result something happened (sin, death, and condemnation came into the world of human experience), and then Jesus came to deal with the consequences of it all (by his obedience to make the many righteous). The argument gains its coherence from its sequence of events; it is drastically inadequate to say that Paul is merely making a "comparison" here.[49] Further, consider the notion that people are "in Adam" or "in Christ": to be "in" someone is to be a member of that

---

47. E.g., Harlow claims, astonishingly (in "After Adam," 189), that Paul "is the only writer to appeal to the story of Adam, Eve, and the serpent," and thus he denies that the Gospels or Revelation appropriate the story. James Barr, *The Garden of Eden and the Hope of Immortality*, 4, is similar. These texts show differently. Further, examination of texts from Second Temple and Rabbinic Jewish authors shows that the Jewish mainstream held to Adam both as the first human and as the one through whom sin came into the world: for examination see my *Did Adam and Eve Really Exist?*, 72–76.

48. For discussion of this point, see my "Echoes of Aristotle in Romans 2:14–15: Or, Maybe Abimelech Was Not So Bad After All," *Journal of Markets and Morality* 13.1 (2010): 123–73, at 137.

49. James D. G. Dunn in his *Romans*, WBC (Dallas: Word, 1988), 289–90, makes just such a suggestion of a "comparison."

people for whom that someone is the representative. All the evidence we have indicates that only actual persons can function as representatives.[50]

Revelation continues this narrative focus: it portrays the final victory of God's purposes, using Edenic and sanctuary imagery to describe perfected human life in a cleansed creation.[51]

Hence, if we say that being prone to sin is inherent in being human with a free will (rather than a horrific aberration brought in at an early stage by someone's disobedience), then we must say the Bible writers were wrong in describing atonement the way they did, as addressing defilement as an intruder; and we must say that Jesus was wrong to describe his own death in these terms (e.g., Mark 10:45). Further, this approach makes nonsense of the joyful expectation of Christians that they will one day live in a glorified world from which sin and death have been banished (Rev. 21:1–8). Does anyone really want to imply that those who dwell in a glorified world will be less human because they no longer sin?

4. Is It Credible?

In sum, the story line of the Bible, to be coherent, leads us to expect that (1) humankind is actually one family, with one set of ancestors for us all; (2) God acted specially ("supernaturally") to form our first parents; and (3) our first ancestors, at the headwaters of the human race, brought sin and dysfunction into the world of human life. Bible believers have treasured the Adam and Eve story as the true and proper narrative that grounds these expectations. Certainly, without this front-end narrative it is hard to see how we can affirm these points—which means that we wind up telling a different Big Story than the one I have outlined here.[52] Christian theologians have differed in how they articulate the idea of "original sin," that is, in how Adam's disobedience transformed the moral condition of their descendants; but they have been united in beginning with these three affirmations.

Yet, how can we be responsible in believing that, when the sciences seem to be telling us otherwise? It is true that the biologists tell us that

---

50. For more detail on the Pauline material, see my *Did Adam and Eve Really Exist?*, 78–90; J. P. Versteeg, *Adam in the New Testament* (Phillipsburg, NJ: P&R Publishing, 2012).

51. For more on this point, see Beale, *The Temple and the Church's Mission*, 365–73.

52. It is theoretically possible, I suppose, that someone might affirm these three points and yet deny that *biblical* Adam and Eve are the characters in the actual events. This fails, though, because it cannot do justice to how the Genesis story underlies so much else in the Bible.

humans share important parts of our DNA with chimpanzees, for which they consider the best explanation to be that we and the chimps share a common ancestor. It is also true that in gradual evolution it is hard to speak of the first members of a species. I will say more about these in the next section; for now I would simply observe that in talking about the origin of the human kind (or of any kind), we are making a judgment or inference about a *historical* question, and our reasoning should follow the guidelines of good critical thinking. To the extent we base our inference entirely on, say, features of DNA, to the exclusion of other relevant kinds of evidence, we weaken the credibility of our inference. Hence, in addition to the DNA evidence, we must also include such things as the aspects of human existence that are *universally* human and that are *uniquely* human. Do these point toward a unified origin of humankind, an origin that goes beyond the powers of a purely natural process, and do they support the notion of sin as an alien invader? Again, for the sake of space, I will keep my list brief and suggestive and save a fuller apologetic for another venue.

Take, for example, our capacity for language. People have tried to teach language to the animals that are thought to be our nearest kin, namely chimps and gorillas; all of these attempts are failures. You can raise a chimp in your family, and try as you might, you will not be able to get it to talk. Take a human child, and you cannot *prevent* it from learning to talk — and repeating in public all the things you say at home! The differences between humans and other animals, as the linguists analyze them, are not simply of *degree* (as if we were simply more developed than the animals are) but of *kind* (human language is discontinuous with animal communication).[53]

But there is more: every human child is born ready to learn the language or languages to which he or she is exposed. Had my wife and

---

53. A notable example of such experiments was the chimpanzee Nim Chimpsky (so named to mock Noam Chomsky's insistence that language is uniquely human). For the outcome, see H. S. Terrace et al., "Can an Ape Create a Sentence?" *Science* n.s. 206.4421 (23 Nov. 1979), 891–902; Terrace, "How Nim Chimpsky Changed My Mind," *Psychology Today* (Nov. 1979), 65–91; and Jascha Hoffman, "The Interpreter: Q&A with Herbert Terrace," *Nature*, vol. 475 (14 July 2011), 175. Ernest Lucas, in his review of my *Did Adam and Eve Really Exist?* in *Evangelical Quarterly* 84:4 (2012): 374, mentions the FOX2P gene as having a "role in the ability to speak and process grammar." But this is a fundamental mistake: that there is a biological instrument for using language — which no one of note ever doubted — does not entail that language use, with its connection to reason and morality (which transcend our physical being), is fully explained by the genes. A better discussion appears in James Le Fanu, *Why Us? How Science Rediscovered the Mystery of Ourselves* (New York: Vintage, 2009), 50–58.

I taken our fair-skinned and blue-eyed children when they were babies and brought them to live in a Ugandan village, *we* would have had to struggle to learn the local languages; but *they* would have grown up speaking, not just the American English we use at home, but also the local languages, like natives, with no extra effort on the part of their parents or the villagers.

Take another example: art. No one knows for sure exactly when God bestowed his image on the first human beings; but we can find artifacts such that, when we see them, we have no doubt that the divine image is there.[54]

Think as well of the craving for a safe and just community — something we see all over the world, from ancient and modern cultures, whether or not they believe in the true God.

Aristotle (384 – 322 BC) observed that "the human being is by nature a political animal" — meaning an animal that lives in political communities, preferably a community organized by principles of justice. Our communities go beyond what you find in the beehive or the buffalo herd: we not only make noise, but "humankind alone among the animals possesses speech," and we use language to talk about what is right and wrong and about what is advantageous or disadvantageous.[55]

All human beings have experiences that make us feel that things are not the way they ought to be. We feel that conflicts between human beings divide us, when we should be able to live peacefully, enjoying each other's uniqueness. We yearn for some kind of healing of this breach. We experience loss of loved ones through death, which is often preceded by dreadful suffering. We see human brilliance diverted into pursuing fresh ways to wreak havoc and destruction.

In the same passage cited above, Aristotle goes on to argue:

> For as the human being is the best of animals when perfected [in a just community], so he is the worst of all animals when sundered from law and justice. For unrighteousness is most pernicious when possessed of weapons; and the human being is born possessing weapons for the use of wisdom and virtue, which it is possible to employ for entirely opposite ends.

---

54. For examples, see Le Fanu, *Why Us?* 24 – 31.
55. Aristotle, *Politics*, I.i.9 – 12; English is based on the Loeb edition.

Aristotle, speaking for all humankind, is describing aspects of what Christians call "the image of God."[56] Where does this come from, and why is its proper use so beautiful and its misuse so appalling? Poor Aristotle (bless him) lacked the story that would put this all into perspective; but surely Genesis gives us the best answer, as Ecclesiastes 7:29 summarizes it: "God made man upright, but they have sought out many schemes." That is, the story of Adam and Eve—who were created good, but who disobeyed and brought sin and misery into their lives and into ours—answers this exactly.

As Chesterton observed, the biblical story shows us "that happiness is not only a hope, but also in some strange manner a memory; and that we are all kings in exile."[57] Thus we have more than a diagnosis; we have grounds for optimism as well. If we have a good explanation for why things have gone wrong, then maybe the Christian hope that somehow God will put them right is a secure comfort also—a comfort that will help us to live fully human lives, as God's beloved people, even *now*.

5. Freedoms and Limitations

I say that Genesis 1–11 is "true history," because it gives us the true story of how the world began, how evil and suffering came into the world, and how God is still committed to the world he made.

Nevertheless the question remains, What would this look like in a scientific-historical description? How much room does this leave for free exploration? This is where an approach from Francis Schaeffer, dealing with "freedoms and limitations," is so helpful. According to

---

56. It often surprises people who are not exegetes that there is a great disagreement among Old Testament specialists regarding just what the "image of God" means. Traditionally it was held to refer to our unique capacities of reason, art, and morality that reflect God's own character; more common today is the view that it refers to our distinctive role of delegated dominion over God's world, or else to our relational nature. Part of the difficulty is that Genesis never defines the image, which means that we must infer it from the text. I would argue, on the basis of the linguistic features (the meanings of biblical words and the syntax of the relevant sentences) and literary requirements (depending on biblical narrators who favor indirect showing over explicit telling), together with the entirety of the biblical witness, that a combination of these options is best: the unique capacities make possible both the dominion and the relationships. I treat this at more length in *Did Adam and Eve Really Exist?*, 93–96, and elsewhere.

57. G. K. Chesterton, *As I Was Saying*, ed. Robert Knille (Grand Rapids: Eerdmans, 1985), 160. This is also a major theme in Blaise Pascal's *Pensées*; see Peter Kreeft, *Christianity for Modern Pagans: Pascal's Pensées Edited, Outlined, and Explained* (San Francisco: Ignatius, 1993), 51–72.

Schaeffer, there is a range of reasonable scenarios by which we may address the apparent conflicts between the Bible and the sciences, and yet there are limits to this range, limits set both by basic biblical concepts and by good human judgment.[58] This is wise, because far be it from an exegete or theologian to tell a geneticist what he or she may or may not find in the genome, or a paleontologist in the fossils! At the same time, when that geneticist or paleontologist wants to try to put those findings together into larger theories that tell the human story, then that person is reasoning as a human being, and his or her reasoning is subject to review for its compliance with good critical thinking.[59]

Schaeffer was willing to consider, among other freedoms, the possibility that Genesis 1 describes God creating a "grown up universe" (nowadays called the "appearance of age hypothesis"); or that God was reforming a creation that had been partially deformed by Satan's fall; or that the "days" refer to long ages. He concluded, sensibly and generously:

> I urge you again to remember that I am not saying that any of these positions are my own or that they will prove to be the case. I am simply stating theoretical possibilities as we consider the correlations between what the Bible sets forth about cosmogony and what we can study from general revelation.[60]

At the same time Schaeffer insisted on God's special *creative* activity at certain key places: at the original creation, then at the creation of conscious life, and finally at the creation of man, the result was discontinuous in some way from what had preceded.[61] He also thought it essential to say, for theological reasons, that Adam was the first man and that Eve was made from him. This left him with a careful view of what is called "theistic evolution": he saw no support for a *naturalistic*

---

58. Francis A. Schaeffer, *No Final Conflict* (London: Hodder and Stoughton/Downers Grove, IL: InterVarsity Press, 1975), ch. 3; see also *The Complete Works of Francis A. Schaeffer* (Westchester, IL: Crossway, 1982), vol. 2.

59. I have discussed this more fully in my *Science and Faith*, especially ch. 2.

60. Schaeffer, *No Final Conflict*, 33–34.

61. This is reminiscent of G. K. Chesterton's remark in *The Everlasting Man* (1925; reprint, Garden City: Doubleday, 1955), 27: "No philosopher denies that a mystery still attaches to the two great transitions: the origin of the universe itself and the origin of the principle of life itself. Most philosophers have the enlightenment to add that a third mystery attaches to the origin of man himself. In other words, a third bridge was built across a third abyss of the unthinkable when there came into the world what we call reason and what we call will."

molecule-to-man scenario, and he imagined that anyone who held to his limitations would not be an "evolutionist" in every sense of the word.

I commend Schaeffer's approach in a forthcoming essay:[62] He was motivated by a generosity of spirit and a desire for Christians to get along with one another. This approach also recognizes that a well-functioning Christian has a hierarchy of commitments: he or she will insist more strongly on the tenets of "basic" or "mere" Christianity—say, the Trinity, or the resurrection of Jesus—than on some other matters that are important, but not quite so vital—say, the number of sacraments and their exact effects. If we add into our consideration the literary features of Genesis 1–11, we conclude that the very nature of this biblical material leads to some sort of freedoms and limitations rubric, since the material both resists a strictly literalistic reading and invites recognition of its historical impulse. In practical terms this means that the author's main goal is to enable us to picture the events he recounts, without getting bogged down in details.

Let us fill this out some more. We start by considering how Genesis addressed the needs of the original audience. Since the first audience consisted mostly of agricultural workers,[63] we assume that they already knew full well that the way to get more sheep is by breeding sheep and the way to get barley is to plant barley seeds: that is, plants and animals reproduce "according to their kinds" (cf. Matt. 13:24–30 for a parable that depends on farmers knowing this principle). The question of what process God might or might not have used in getting to this point is certainly valid and interests us, but is irrelevant to the Genesis context. The crucial thing for the audience is that this is God's arrangement for *his* world, and thus they must follow his instructions for how to manage his stuff.

Similarly, I cannot envision any reasonable human, especially a farmer, unaware of *both* the similarities *and* the differences between humans and other animals. Hence an Israelite would be unsurprised

---

62. C. John Collins, "Freedoms and Limitations: C. S. Lewis and Francis Schaeffer as a Tag Team," to appear in the forthcoming *Firstfruits of a New Creation: Essays in Honor of Jerram Barrs* (Mark Ryan and J. E. Eubanks, eds.). A briefer treatment of these themes appears in my essay "A Peculiar Clarity: How C. S. Lewis Can Help Us Think about Faith and Science," in John G. West, ed., *The Magician's Twin: C. S. Lewis on Science, Scientism, and Society* (Seattle: Discovery Institute Press, 2012), 69–106.

63. This is true regardless of the date we assign to Genesis. If we take a traditional date, they were nomads; if we accept some form of composition criticism, we still are thinking of agricultural workers, albeit more settled in the Land.

at using the term "living creature" for them all; and portraying them all as being "formed" from the ground (Gen. 2:7, 19) corresponds to the "simple, obvious fact that the human body is made of the common elements of the soil."[64] Genesis gives a name to those features that distinguish human beings and assumes its readers can already recognize them: the image of God.

Most readers have (understandably) envisioned the event of forming Adam in fairly straightforward terms, with no animal intermediates between the dirt and Adam. Some today, aware of the significant overlap between human DNA and that of, say, a chimpanzee, would explain the overlap, not in terms of our shared genetic heritage, but from the perspective of overlapping functions: the DNA is similar because it does similar things.

Still, we can ask whether Genesis 2:7 is absolutely incompatible with some sort of process involving genetics to produce our first *human* father. Perhaps it is, but two reasons should make us hesitate to insist on this as the decisive question: First, as already discussed, we have the nature of the literature. Second, there is the way that Psalm 103:14 sings (with words from Gen. 2:7), "for he [God] knows how we are *formed*; he remembers that we are *dust*" (using ESV margin). Each of us is, ultimately, "formed of dust," even if the dust has gone through a few intermediate (genetic) steps![65]

But here is where it is easy to go astray. We must not confuse the possibility of intermediate steps in the forming process, with a purely naturalistic (or "ordinary providence") scenario for that process. It is simply unreasonable to suppose that one can arrive at human capacities without some "help" from outside; that is, good reasoning includes recognizing that God's creative activity is involved.[66] Hence, if a person

---

64. J. Oliver Buswell, *A Systematic Theology of the Christian Religion* (Grand Rapids: Zondervan, 1962–63), I:159.

65. For all humans as made from dust, see also Psalms 90:3; 104:29; Ecclesiastes 3:20; 12:7; Job 10:8–9. The verb "form," as Buswell observed (*Systematic Theology*, I:159), "gives no specifications as to the process by which the forming was accomplished. The result is all that is specified." Buswell himself, of course, provided arguments *against* any idea of a genetic process being involved, though he did not condemn those who might think otherwise.

66. C. S. Lewis is particularly clear and helpful on this, for all his openness to a kind of "evolution," as I discuss in the two essays I refer to above. Ernest Lucas, in his review of *Did Adam and Eve Really Exist?*, mistakenly brings up the "God-of-the-gaps" objection to such an argument, but shows no awareness of the actual case for discontinuity.

should want to suggest some level of intermediate process for Genesis 2:7, then rather than argue on *that* point I prefer to make sure that he can also acknowledge the event as a "special creation."[67]

Further, traditional readers of Genesis suppose that the original humans were just a pair, Adam and his wife. All other humans descend from them. However, many genetics researchers consider it out of the question for the initial human population to be only two. Surely more than two stretches beyond the limits of Genesis? It may well do so, but not necessarily. Derek Kidner proposed a scenario that deserves our attention, which might allow for a larger population than two at the start.[68] Kidner himself called it exploratory and tentative, and there are difficulties that we might not be able to solve.[69] One virtue of Kidner's proposal is that it arose from his reading of Genesis 4, which he took to imply that there were more people around at the time of Cain and Abel.[70]

At the same time, we should recognize that all scientific theorizing, including that about human genetics, should be open to review (although such review is not my purpose here, and I have not tied my conclusions to any outcome of that review).[71]

What, then, are the ground rules for sound reasoning about this subject? Here is my proposal for four principles:[72]

1. The origin of the human race goes beyond a merely natural process. This follows from how hard it is to get a human being or, theologically, how distinctive the image of God is.

---

67. This is the position of, say, Benjamin Warfield and James Orr. See Fred Zaspel, "B. B. Warfield on Creation and Evolution," *Themelios* 35:2 (July 2010): 198–211; W. Brian Aucker, "Hodge and Warfield on Evolution," *Presbyterion* 20:2 (1994): 131–42. Bruce Waltke is similar: see *An Old Testament Theology* (Grand Rapids: Zondervan, 2007), 202–3.

68. Derek Kidner, *Genesis*, Tyndale Old Testament Commentary (Downers Grove, IL: InterVarsity Press, 1967), 26–31.

69. See my discussion in *Did Adam and Eve Really Exist?*, 124–25. Denis Lamoureux, in his review of that book in *Perspectives on Science and Christian Faith* 63:4 (Dec. 2011): 277–78, mistakenly interprets me as favoring a kind of "concordism." Todd Wood, in "Who Were Adam and Eve? Scientific Reflections on Collins's *Did Adam and Eve Really Exist?*" in *Journal of Creation Theology and Science*, Series B: Biology 2 (2012): 29, recognizes that Lamoureux was mistaken in this interpretation.

70. But as Kidner himself acknowledged, this reading itself is uncertain: see my discussion in *Did Adam and Eve Really Exist?*, 112–13, 124–25.

71. See my discussion in *Did Adam and Eve Really Exist?*, 119–20.

72. My first three, as it turns out, are almost identical to Schaeffer's. The fourth expresses my respect for Kidner, without necessarily endorsing his proposal: it is how those who wish to consider a larger population can protect their sound thinking.

2. Adam and Eve are at the headwaters of the human race. This follows from the unified experience of humankind.

3. The "fall," in whatever form it took, was both *historical* (it happened) and *moral* (it involved disobeying God), and it occurred at the beginning of the human race. Our universal sense of loss makes no sense without this. Where else could this universality have come from?

4. If someone should become convinced that there were, in fact, more human beings than just Adam and Eve at the beginning of humankind, then in order to maintain good sense, he or she should envision these humans as a single tribe of closely related members. Adam would then be the chieftain of this tribe (produced before the others), and Eve would be his wife. This tribe "fell" under the leadership of Adam and Eve. This follows from the notion of solidarity in a representative. (Some may call this a form of "polygenesis," but this is quite distinct from the more conventional—and unacceptable—kind.)

I have not here given details on my own convictions about a number of topics, and I will say just a little more about two of them, namely, "evolution" and "biblical inerrancy," which I must first define.

Biological evolution can refer to the idea that animals change over time. It might go so far as to insist that the animals we know today are descended from the creatures we dig up in the fossils, and that changes have been introduced into the animals' genetic makeup in the process. It might go even farther and contend that all present-day animals descend from only a few ultimate ancestors, or even from just one.[73] In its strongest form, biological evolution asserts that the whole process is a purely natural one, with no "extra help" from God. If we say that the process is *God's* process, then we have "theistic evolution."

Sometimes Christians object to *all* kinds of evolution, and even to an old earth in general, because of how they involve animals dying, but I do not consider that a fatal objection. I argue elsewhere that *human*

---

73. I am here echoing the very words of Charles Darwin's conclusion to his classic, *The Origin of Species* (1872; reprint, New York: Collier, Harvard Classics, 1909), who imagines life as "having been originally breathed by the Creator into a few forms, or only one."

death is what the biblical authors have in view in places like Romans 5:12; animal death as such is *not* a theological problem and not a consequence of the fall.[74] Nevertheless, in agreement with Schaeffer, I find that the strongest form of theistic evolution is inadequate, both for the Bible and for historical science, since it fails to account for human distinctiveness.[75]

I described Genesis 1–11 as "true history," which leads me to comment on the Bible's truthfulness or "inerrancy." Although Benjamin Warfield (1851–1921) gets credit (or blame) for the popularity of the term "inerrancy of Scripture," the idea is part of the Christian tradition.[76] *The Chicago Statement on Biblical Inerrancy* (1978) sets out an evangelical approach to the idea, and a kindred statement from the Roman Catholic side comes in the encyclical *Divino Afflante Spiritu* (*Inspired by the Divine Spirit*, 1943).[77]

I will not now explore all the nuances of either statement, nor defend them; instead, I will take them as enough for our purposes. I do not have to settle here the question of how Genesis 1–11 came to be composed—whether from sources or by fresh composition or by what Henri Blocher has described as an inspired reconstruction, working backward from the present to the past.[78]

Both statements sagely recognize that we should adapt our expectations to the literary forms the sacred writers used—that is, we should not conflate inerrancy with a purely literalistic interpretation. This notion, according to *Divino Afflante Spiritu* (§37), goes back at least as far as Thomas Aquinas (1225–74). In fact, C. S. Lewis attributed to the church father Jerome (347–420) the opinion that Genesis tells of creation "after the manner of a popular poet" (though the actual words have been traced only as far back as John Colet, 1467–1519).[79] This

---

74. See, for example, my *Science and Faith*, ch. 10; "Did Adam and Eve Really Exist?," 115–16.

75. I have given further discussion on this topic in "A Peculiar Clarity."

76. The literature on the subject is vast. Helpful recent discussions include Michael D. Williams, "The Church, a Pillar of Truth: B. B. Warfield's Church Doctrine of Inspiration," *Presbyterion* 37/2 (2011): 65–84; Robert W. Yarbrough, "Inerrancy's Complexities: Grounds for Grace in the Debate," *idem*, 85–100.

77. Both of these statements are readily available online.

78. See Henri Blocher, *In the Beginning* (Downers Grove, IL: InterVarsity Press, 1984), 159.

79. See my discussion in "A Peculiar Clarity," 87–88.

manner or style in no way detracts from "historicity," so long as we define our terms carefully as *the text's ability to refer.*[80]

Within these guidelines, I cast the doctrine in light of the biblical narrative I have already described: "The Scriptures tell us the true story of the world and of God's people; and they show the members of God's people the right way to embrace that story, and to invite others to the embrace." The notion of inerrancy, then, aims at explaining why we take a disposition of trust and cooperation when we look for the Bible to speak from God to us.

We might enter into further discussions about faith and reason, about whether our trust in the Bible is a precondition for reading it properly or the result of our testing of the Bible. John Wenham helps us out of our difficulties:[81]

> The way out of this dilemma is to recognize that *belief in the Bible comes from faith in Christ, and not vice versa; and that it is possible to proceed from faith in Christ to a doctrine of Scripture without sorting out problems of criticism.*

Wenham argues that "Christ's view of Scripture can and should still be the Christian's view of Scripture."[82] Of course, this by itself does not settle just what view Jesus took of Genesis 1–11;[83] still less does it address what we should make of Paul. Further, as Wenham argues, "it is to the writings rather than to the writers that [Christ] ascribes authority."[84] Nevertheless, once we see that Jesus bases an ethical argument on the *narrative* of Genesis 1–2, and further, that the apostles are Jesus' authorized conveyers and interpreters of the story (e.g., John 14:26; 16:12–15), we find the motivation to read Genesis in the way I have argued. As a matter of fact, I have found

---

80. As Pope Pius XII said in his encyclical *Humani Generis* (1950), "The first eleven chapters of Genesis, although properly speaking not conforming to the historical method used by the best Greek and Latin writers or by competent authors of our time, do nevertheless pertain to history in a true sense" (§38). See also *The Chicago Statement*, art. XIII.

81. John Wenham, *Christ and the Bible* (Grand Rapids: Baker, 1994), 13 (his italics).

82. Ibid., 12.

83. Wenham himself, to be sure, sometimes—but not always—confuses historicity with a "literal" interpretation, and his brief mention of Matthew 19:3ff. (*Christ and the Bible*, 19) needs the development I have given it here.

84. Wenham, *Christ and the Bible*, 33.

that using modern literary and linguistic tools enables us to read Genesis very much as Paul did.[85]

I have no doubt that we could, and should, say more; but I trust I have said enough to show you why I think I can say with confidence, then, that the early chapters of Genesis provide the true and historical front end for the Big Story of the world.

DENIS O. LAMOUREUX

John Collins is a leading scholar within the evangelical science-religion community. I have learned much from his books and have been blessed by his friendship. One of the highlights of my career was sharing the podium with him in 2012 at a conference cosponsored by Westminster Theological Seminary and the Discovery Institute, where we presented our views on Adam. Although we have points of disagreement, I find that we have far more agreements, especially regarding the foundations of our Christian faith.

The Big Story of the Bible

A central theme throughout Collins's chapter is the notion that the Bible features an "overarching story line" (p. 145) or a "Big Story" (p. 158). He refers to this "story" or "grand narrative" some fifty times in various ways. Collins asserts that this story line

> deals with God's good creation invaded by sin, for which God has a redemptive plan; of Israel's calling to be a light to the nations; and of the church's prospect of successfully bringing God's light to the whole world. That story concerns the unique role and dignity of the human race, which is a matter of daily experience for everyone: All people yearn for God and need him, must depend on him to deal with their sinfulness, and crave a wholesome community for their lives to flourish (p. 143).

I embrace this "Big Story of the world" (p. 158) without any reservation whatsoever. But does it require a historical Adam? My answer is "no." I do not believe Adam ever existed, yet I cling to the Scripture's "basic story line" (p. 157) in my heart of hearts.

Later in his chapter Collins adds three more tenets to "the story line of the Bible": "(1) humankind is actually one family, with one set of ancestors for us all; (2) God acted specially ('supernaturally') to form our first parents; and (3) our first ancestors, at the headwaters of the human race, brought sin and dysfunction into the world of human life" (p. 164).

I accept Collins's tenets (1) and (3). As I mentioned in my chapter, "humans descended from a group of about 10,000 individuals," and the entrance of sin into the world "coincides with the appearance of behaviorally modern humans about 50,000 years ago" (p. 64). However, tenet (2) is the key to Collins's position, and it is the critical difference between us. According to Collins, God created humans through a supernatural event. But why is this divine act included in "the story line of the Bible"?

Scientific Concordism and God-of-the-Gaps

The answer to this question is that Collins embraces scientific concordism and the God-of-the-gaps. Remarkably, he protests, "Lamoureux ... mistakenly interprets me as favoring a kind of 'concordism'" (p. 171, fn. 69). He also complains that "Ernest Lucas ... mistakenly brings up the 'God-of-the-gaps' objection to such an argument [i.e., the need for "some 'help' from outside" to create humans], but shows no awareness of the actual case for discontinuity" (p. 170, fn. 66).

It is necessary to emphasize that *in principle* I am not opposed to either scientific concordism or the God-of-the-gaps. As I stated, "Scientific concordism is a reasonable assumption" and also "a logical expectation"; but I asked the questions, "Is scientific concordism true? And is it an inerrant feature of the Word of God?" (p. 45). Similarly, God can intervene into "gaps" or "discontinuities" in nature to introduce new species or add/modify body parts or genes of already existing species. After all, He is God! But the question is whether the Lord actually intervened this way in origins.

First, let's consider statements by Collins to see if he is a scientific concordist. In his abstract he asserts that "the biblical material along with good critical thinking provides certain freedoms and limitations for *connecting* the Bible's creation account to a scientific and historical account of human origins" (p. 143, my italics). "Connecting" Scripture to science is scientific concordism.

Later Collins proclaims, "This means that how long those days were [of Gen. 1], or how they *relate* to time as we know it—let alone how they might *match* what we find in the fossils—is not important for Genesis" (p. 145, my italics). Any attempt to "relate" time or "match" the fossil record with the days of Genesis 1 is scientific concordism.

Finally, Collins quotes Francis Schaeffer's booklet *No Final Conflict* and claims that his conclusions are "sensibl[e]" (p. 168). Writes Schaeffer, "I am simply stating theoretical possibilities as we consider the *correlations* between what the Bible sets forth about cosmology and what we can study from general revelation [i.e., science]" (p. 168, my italics).[86] Any "correlations" made between Scripture and general revelation is scientific concordism. In sum, Collins is a scientific concordist.

Second, let's see if Collins embraces the God-of-the-gaps. He includes in "the story line of the Bible" that "God acted *specially* ('*supernaturally*') to form our first parents" (p. 164, my italics). Any divine being who acts "specially" and "supernaturally" in human origins is a God-of-the-gaps.

Collins proclaims, "It is simply unreasonable to suppose that one can arrive at human capacities without some '*help' from outside*; that is, good reasoning includes recognizing that God's creative activity is involved" (p. 170, my italics). A Creator "help[ing] from outside" is a God-of-the-gaps.

Again appealing to Schaeffer's *No Final Conflict*, Collins writes,

> At the same time Schaeffer insisted on *God's special creative activity at certain key places*: [1] at the original creation, [2] then at the creation of conscious life, and finally [3] at the creation of man, the result was discontinuous in some way from what had preceded. He also thought it essential to say, for theological reasons, that [3a] Adam was the first man and that [3b] Eve was made from him (p. 168, my italics).

Any "special creative activity" at "key places" in origins is a God-of-the-gaps. In sum, Collins accepts the God-of-the-gaps.

What I found surprising is that Collins would even cite Schaeffer as an authority on origins. Only two paragraphs earlier he stated, "[F]ar be

---

86. Francis A. Schaeffer, *No Final Conflict* (Downers Grove, IL: InterVarsity Press, 1975), 24.

it for an exegete or theologian to tell a geneticist what he or she may or may not find in the genome, or a paleontologist in the fossils!" (p. 168).

Schaeffer was a fine pastor who founded a wonderful Christian ministry, the L'Abri Community. However, he had no training in science. This is painfully evident in *No Final Conflict* (1975). For example, Schaeffer asserts, "I am not at all convinced it has been proven that the dinosaurs became extinct prior to the advent of man."[87] But most know that dinosaurs went extinct 65 million years ago and that behaviorally modern humans appeared only 50,000 years ago. Moreover, Schaeffer's forty-eight-page, pocket-size booklet without any citations was published nearly forty years ago. There has been a massive revolution in biology since that time, especially with advances in evolutionary genetics. Additionally, numerous pre-human fossils have since been discovered. To use Collins's terminology, appealing to Francis Schaeffer about origins is not exactly "good critical thinking" (pp. 143, 165, 168).

The problem with scientific concordism is that it fails. The Bible includes ancient science (e.g., the 3-tier universe), and therefore it's *impossible* to align Scripture with modern science. Collins's belief in the historicity of Adam is ultimately rooted in an ancient understanding of human origins — *de novo* (quick and complete) creation.

De novo creation is also behind Collins's God-of-the-gaps intervention to create Adam. However, history reveals the problem with this view of divine activity. Every time someone has proclaimed a point of divine intervention, it has later been shown to be not a gap in nature, but a gap in that individual's knowledge of nature.

Consider so-called "irreducible complexity" with the bacterial flagellum as its *cause célèbre*. There is no need to posit a divine intervention for its creation, because nearly all of the roughly forty components were already present in the bacterial cell membrane performing other functions. The evolutionary mechanism of recruitment easily explains the origin of the flagellum.

This is exactly the problem with Collins's "case for discontinuity" (p. 170). He claims, "The origin of the human race goes beyond a merely natural process. This follows from how hard it is to get a human being" (p. 171). Collins argues that language, art, and craving for a just

---

87. Ibid., 27.

community (pp. 165–66) are evidence that "at the creation of man, the result was discontinuous in some way from what had preceded" (p. 168). However, any introductory textbook on evolutionary psychology offers explanations for Collins's purported discontinuities, which reflect gaps in his knowledge, not gaps in nature.

"True and Historical," But Not "Too Literalistic"

Collins's scientific concordism and God-of-the-gaps undergird his method for interpreting Genesis 1–11. He asserts that "the early chapters of Genesis provide the true and historical front end for the Big Story of the world" (p. 175), but he cautions us from being "too literalistic" (p. 143).

> If we add into our consideration the literary features of Genesis 1–11, we conclude that the very nature of this biblical material leads to some sort of freedoms and limitations rubric, since the material both resists a strict literalistic reading and invites recognition of its historical impulse. In practical terms, this means that the author's main goal is to enable us to picture the events he recounts, *without getting bogged down in the details* (p. 169, my italics).

Earlier in his chapter Collins offers a commendable definition of the term "history." He states that history "is a way of referring, of talking about events in the real world" (p. 147). But the problem immediately arises: how do we differentiate between parts of Genesis 1–11 that are "true and historical" and those which are inconsequential "details"?

It appears to me that Collins's interpretive method is arbitrary and *ad hoc*. Take for example his understanding of the first chapter of Scripture.

> Genesis 1 presents God as if he were a workman, going through his week, so that we can celebrate the creation as a magnificent achievement. This means that how long those days were, or how they relate to times as we know it—let alone how they might match what we find in the fossils—*is not important to Genesis* (p. 145, my italics).

With one fell swoop Collins writes off the length of the creation days as irrelevant. But what are his criteria for doing so? He never mentions them. Collins arbitrarily proclaims this issue "is not important to

Genesis." I disagree. The days in Genesis 1 are significant. This chapter reflects the Sabbath commandment (Exod. 20:8–11), and the length of each creation day is clear. They are regular twenty-four-hour days. Each ends with "There was evening, and there was morning—the [nth] day." Why does Collins dismiss the length of creation days as irrelevant? It's because he "do[es] not object to the standard theories of cosmology and geology" (p. 145). Collins knows that the universe is billions of years old and that it is impossible to align Genesis 1 to the time frames of cosmology and geology.

The *ad hoc* character of Collins's method of interpretation appears in another passage dealing with Genesis 1.

> Since the first audience consisted mostly of agricultural workers, we assume that they already knew full well that the way to get more sheep is by breeding sheep and the way to get barley is to plant barley seeds: that is, plants and animals reproduce "according to their kinds." ... The question of what [creative] process God might or might not have used in getting to this point is certainly valid and interests us, *but is irrelevant to the Genesis context* (p. 169, my italics).

Again Collins writes off parts of Genesis as "irrelevant." Once more there is no mention of his criteria for doing so. This passage is an arbitrary proclamation, not an argument.

Collins's inconsistency is evident. He claims that the "process God might or might not have used" in the creation of plants and animals is "irrelevant." Yet, when it comes to the creation of humans, he *insists* that "God acted specially ('supernaturally') to form our first parents" and that this is part of "the story line of the Bible" (p. 164). But why is this divine creative act deemed "true and historical," while the other supernatural events in Genesis 1 dealing with the origin of plants and animals or the heavens and earth are seen as "irrelevant"?

Part of the answer is that Collins accepts modern cosmology/geology and realizes that the heavens and earth originated *entirely* through natural processes. So on the one hand, Collins rejects divine interventions in cosmological/geological origins because of his science and thus rejects what Genesis 1 clearly states. But on the other hand, he dismisses human evolution because of his scientific concordist reading of Scripture. This arbitrary and *ad hoc* method not only is inconsistent, but also creates an unjustified and false dichotomy between the science of evolutionary biology and the sciences of cosmology and geology.

Parallels with Mesopotamia

Collins correctly states, "We gain a great deal when we notice that Genesis really *does* have parallels with the stories that come from other ancient Near Eastern cultures" (p. 155, italics original). He is also right in claiming that Genesis 1–11 is similar to ancient Mesopotamian literature (p. 155). However, he and I use this pagan material in completely different ways.

Collins argues that because Mesopotamian authors believed they were writing history in their accounts of origins, it only stands to reason that the author(s) of Genesis 1–11 did so as well. He notes, "Mesopotamians aimed to accomplish their purpose by founding their [front-end] stories on what they thought were *actual events*" (p. 151, italics original). Collins asserts that since there is "a historical core" in these pagan accounts (p. 153), this is also the case with Genesis 1–11. Appealing to pagan myths to justify the historicity of Genesis 1–11 must strike most Christians as rather odd.

Here is the problem with Collins's argument: the Mesopotamians "thought" that their stories referred to real events. Well, maybe they thought incorrectly. And maybe the authors of Genesis 1–11 were also incorrect in their thinking about the beginning of human history. I raised this issue in my review of Collins's book *Did Adam and Eve Really Exist?* I noted that he missed a possible scenario

> whereby "the [biblical] author was talking about what he thought were actual events," but in fact these events never actually happened, because the author was reconstructing history from *an ancient phenomenological perspective*. In other words, this would be an ancient understanding of history similar to an ancient understanding of science[88].

Collins's affirmation of Mesopotamian parallels to Genesis 1–11 aligns well with my view that the inspired authors employed not only ancient science, but also an ancient conceptualization of early human

88. Denis O. Lamoureux, Reviews of John C. Collins, *Did Adam and Eve Really Exist?* (2011), in *Perspectives on Science and Christian Faith* 63:4 (2011):277.

history. In the chart on page 150, Collins identifies a pattern within both Genesis 1–11 and the Mesopotamian accounts of origins: Creation—Alienation—Flood—New Start—Modern Times. Indeed, these were the scientific and historical paradigms-of-the-day in the ancient Near East. But they are *ancient* paradigms. From my perspective, they are incidental vessels used by the Holy Spirit in the revelatory process to deliver inerrant spiritual truths in Genesis 1–11.

JOHN H. WALTON

John Collins makes many clear and reasoned statements about the need for a historical Adam, both textually and theologically. One of the mainstays of his position is the need for a historical event that brought sin into the world. I agree with him on these points. He is less insistent on the implications of historical Adam and historical fall for the scientific questions such as material continuity/discontinuity and whether Adam was the first or only human. I applaud his caution on these issues and share it. How, then, do our positions differ?

One difference is the way that we employ our methods. For example, I found it interesting that Collins spent time assessing how different people today might think about historiography. I agree that people use the word differently today, but I am more concerned to discern how the ancient world thought about the representation of events. Nevertheless, I appreciate the distinction that he draws between "historical" and "literal" as well as his careful treatment of the referential nature of historical writing. I agree that it is important to see this literature as referring to real events and real people in a real past.

Another methodological issue concerns how Collins handles the ancient Near Eastern literature. I believe that he unnecessarily focuses on Mesopotamia (Egypt has much important material) and too narrowly focuses on cosmological texts. While cosmological texts certainly should receive our careful attention, in the end we don't just want to become informed about how close or distant the biblical cosmological literature is to the Mesopotamian cosmological literature. We want to absorb the wide expanse of ancient literature to understand how people at that time generally thought about the world around them.

He is right to move beyond superficial similarities between Genesis and the ANE cosmologies to see the deep and highly significant differences. But in the end we are not only interested in comparing pieces of literature; we also need to see the similarities and differences in the larger cognitive environment.

Nevertheless, I am a bit baffled by what Collins cites as his conclusion about comparative studies:

> The point to take away is this: We have gained a great deal when we notice that Genesis really *does* have parallels with the stories that come from other ancient Near Eastern cultures. One of these gains is to realize that "history" is an appropriate category for such a tale; another is to recognize that no one expected the stories to be read in a thoroughly literalistic fashion (p. 155).

It is not at all clear *why* this should be considered history or *why* they should not be read as literalistic.

Occasionally Collins uses subjective terminology, which by its nature weakens his case. "Genesis appears to trace all humankind back to a common source. That is, the genealogies of Genesis 5 and 10 present Adam and Eve as the ancestors of a wide range of 'families of the earth'—in fact, *all* the families so far as the audience is concerned" (p. 154, emphasis added). Notice his use of "appears"—a significant concession. For example, one could say that in the example he used earlier, Psalm 105 "appears" to say that there were only eight plagues. But we have to be more concerned with actual claims than with appearances. Does the Bible *claim* that all humankind traces its origins back to a single source? Christian belief does not depend on a conviction that we have all descended from Adam to "foster a respect for common human dignity" (p. 154); instead, it is the fact that all people are made in the image of God no matter how or from whom they descended.

Collins spends several pages arguing for the rhetorical unity of Genesis 1–11. While there are many scholars who might dispute that, none of the contributors to this volume would. I am not convinced however, that parallels to the Mesopotamian literature help substantiate that claim (he admittedly makes less of this in his argument). Likewise, none of us would disagree that there is a grand biblical narrative.

In these sections Collins is arguing against someone else, and these points are irrelevant to the internal discussion in this book. But of course, he has a point to make in bringing it up, which becomes evident as he concludes: "I am confident that texts from the Old Testament, the

New Testament, and Second Temple Judaism consistently testify to a unified origin of humankind in Adam and Eve" (p. 159). Confidence is a wonderful thing, but what is the evidential basis for this confidence?

As he unfolds his evidence, it does not in fact pertain to "unified origin" but to the universal impact of sin. The two have *traditionally* been interrelated, but we must ask whether they are *necessarily* related. Collins shows his path to relating the two ideas when he says:

> The notion that humankind is one family, with one set of ances-
> tors for us all—ancestors who, at the headwaters of the human
> race brought sin and dysfunction into the world of human life—is
> behind all of these factors as an unwavering assumption. New Tes-
> tament authors carry along this assumption. Certainly the apostle
> Paul spoke this way (e.g., Rom. 5:12–21; 1 Cor. 15:20–22, 44–49);
> but the most notable example of this assumption comes from Jesus
> himself in the Gospels (p. 161).

The question to ask is whether Adam and Eve can be at the headwaters in relation to sin without being at the headwaters genetically. One
could question whether Jesus is discussing genetics.

Here again Collins resorts to what *seems* to be the case: "Jesus in
the Gospels seems quite straightforwardly to have accepted the story in
Genesis the way I am advocating" (p. 162). What something *seems* to be
does not stand as an explicit claim.

In the end, Collins makes a strong case for the historicity of the fall,
with which I agree, but he barely addresses the issues of material human
origins from the text. Does he assume that if Adam and Eve are historical and the fall is historical, therefore the Bible also teaches material
discontinuity in human origins and common genetic ancestry in Adam
and Eve? These issues have been traditionally bundled together, but are
they necessarily bundled together? By maintaining a historical Adam
and Eve and a historical fall, is the Bible *claiming* material discontinuity
or that all humans are descendants of Adam and Eve?

When Collins sums up (on p. 164), he says, "In sum, the story line of
the Bible, to be coherent, leads us to expect that (1) humankind is actually one family, with one set of ancestors for us all; (2) God acted specially ('supernaturally') to form our first parents." Yet, in reality he has
said little about these and certainly did not seek to prove these points.

It seems that he has assumed that if one proves the historical fall and the universal reach of sin, then the other points are inevitable. I would disagree that those points all are bundled as one. Historical Adam and Eve and a historical fall do not necessarily entail discontinuity in material human origins or necessitate that Adam and Eve were the first or the only humans.

Over and over Collins returns to the concept of sin, which leads backward to a historical sinner. I have no objections to that and am in agreement with him. But to take the path farther back into the scientific questions becomes more complicated, and he really doesn't deal with that path.

When he talks about "freedom and limitations" then, Collins assumes that if Adam and the fall are theological and historical realities, then material discontinuity and genetic ancestry from a single pair (monogenesis) are also historical and theological essentials. But these latter do not necessarily follow from the former. Does the Bible claim material discontinuity and monogenesis as historical and/or theological realities?

In the end Collins steps away from a specific statement about material human origins and the question of continuity or discontinuity (p. 168) and is content to say that all that is necessary is that God is involved in the process, evolutionary though it be. He also leaves room for a more complex genetic history for human beings. At that point it is difficult to see how his view is very different from mine. I can affirm all four points he enumerates on pages 171–72.

So I can agree with his conclusion: "I can say with confidence, then, that the early chapters of Genesis provide the true and historical front end for the Big Story of the world." Yet we still have to work out what historical claims the text is making.

WILLIAM D. BARRICK

Since the view represented by John Collins reflects many of the same biblical arguments that the young-earth view presents against the evolutionary creation view of Denis Lamoureux and the archetypal creation view of John Walton, our differences revolve primarily around the matter of dating creation. Two aspects of the old-earth view reveal similarities to the views of Lamoureux and Walton: (1) rejection of the traditional Judeo-Christian interpretation of the opening chapters of Genesis, and (2) acceptance of the modern scientific community's interpretation of physical evidence to place the origins of the earth and mankind millions of years ago.

The accuracy of the details within a history makes the original writer's viewpoint "far more effective than that based on sheer invention" (p. 151). Without such accuracy in detail, any polemical intent suffers from an inherent weakness that invites the counterattack of adherents to the pagan worldviews dominating the ancient Near East. I agree with Collins's definition of "historical" as the author's intent that his audience "believe the events really happened" (p. 147). I would add, however, that the author's intent also involved his audience's belief that those events not only happened in actuality, but that they happened exactly as described by the biblical text in every detail—including the evenings and mornings identifying each of the first six days in Genesis 1 as actual days.

As Collins himself points out, history does matter in the biblical text, because it is "a narrative of God's great works of creation and redemption, and not simply a list of 'timeless' principles" (p. 158). The very significance would indicate the necessity of a narrative including references to time. Just as there was a specific time frame for the plagues on Egypt, the crossing of the Red Sea, the crossing of the Jordan, and the events around the death of Christ, so too the creation events possess a time frame of seven actual days (cf. Exod. 20:11 and the use of the same time frame for the Sabbath observance).

Contrary to the actual days that the detailed chronological reference to evenings and mornings seems to support, Collins adopts a workman analogy or metaphor for the seven "days" in the Genesis 1 account of creation. He asserts that the workman analogy alone indicates that the Bible does not specify a time line (p. 145). This allows him to reject any biblical time line and to adopt the current geological and cosmological positions of secular scientists. Elsewhere, Collins opts to understand the seventh day as an ongoing creation Sabbath that did not end in the record the way the previous six days ended—with an evening and morning formula.[89] Since he does not see the formula as significant when present, how can he argue for some significance for its absence—especially when he takes the six days as referring to long periods of time, just like his view of the seventh day?

Collins's appeal to readers' intuition for distinguishing the transition between Genesis 1–11 and Genesis 12–50 can be a risky business. First, it makes the interpretation quite subjective. Second, it leaves the door open for too many unacceptable options (e.g., taking the first eleven chapters as nonhistorical). The inherent differences between the two major sections of Genesis do not reside in some difference in literary type or function, but in the content and purpose of the two sections. Genesis 1–11 presents primeval history according to a universal scope involving all mankind, while Genesis 12–50 narrows the focus to the history of one specific line of human descent and its divine election as a specific people of God through whom he will accomplish his redemptive purposes.

According to Collins, the intuitive understanding regarding the nonhistorical nature of Genesis 1–11 finds confirmation in the ancient Near Eastern stories—especially those from Mesopotamia. He admits that the ancient Mesopotamian story writers purposed to found their accounts "on what they thought were *actual events*, albeit told with a great deal of imagery and symbolism" (p. 151).

If the Mesopotamian stories refer to real events, so must the Hebrew account. However, the Hebrews' worldview does not give them the freedom to mythologize history the way the Mesopotamians did. In

---

89. C. John Collins, *Genesis 1 – – 4: A Linguistic, Literary, and Theological Commentary* (Phillipsburg, NJ: P&R Publishing, 2006), 74–75, 92–93, 125.

place of the imaginative and fantastic elements characteristic of the Mesopotamian stories, Genesis 1–11 set out to record events exactly as they happened, with the Creator, not the human author, endowing the aspects and elements of the creation accounts with symbolic value and function.

That is why the Genesis 1 account of creation repeatedly states that "it was so" (vv. 7, 9, 11, 15, 24, 30). The same phrase is found elsewhere in the Old Testament, as at 2 Kings 15:12: "This is the word of the LORD which He spoke to Jehu, saying, 'Your sons to the fourth generation shall sit on the throne of Israel.' *And so it was*" (NASB, emphasis mine). In other words, the force of this phrase is that the events happened just exactly as described. In Genesis 1 this included the time elements of consecutive normal days comprised of evening and mornings defined by the Creator as time markers for earth dwellers.

With an appeal to similarities in the DNA of chimpanzees and humans, Collins seeks some compatibility between the biblical account and the modern evolutionists' theory of the origin of life and the variety of living species. Does not the existence of the same Designer better explain the similarities? God, the Creator, has left his imprint on all life forms by means of the common factors for life and the common characteristics of life forms. These include such things as the meiosis of cells and the role of DNA, as well as the seeming replication of physical characteristics found between phyla even in embryonic development.

Although Collins rightly reminds us that Romans 5:12 deals with human death, not animal death, the biblical evidence does not consist only of that verse. Romans 8:19–22 must also be considered, with its specification that the entire created universe was affected by decay (v. 21). The Creator's curse on account of Adam's disobedience extends to the ground itself (Gen. 3:17; 5:29). The first recorded animal death in Genesis comes with the description of Abel's sacrifice (Gen. 4:4). Granted, absence of other mention might be due to the focus on mankind. Genesis 1 describes the pre-fall creation as "good" (vv. 4, 10, 12, 18, 21, 25) and "very good" (v. 31).

A "very good" creation does not seem at all consistent with millions of years of death and disease (e.g., known cancer tumors in dinosaurs). As far as the eating of plants is concerned (vv. 29–30), plants are not "living creatures" (*nepeš ayyâ*) like humans, animals, and birds, so biblical death as part of the curse does not apply to plant life. Elsewhere in the Old Testament, the disobedience of human beings brought death and destruction to animal life (e.g., Gen. 6:17; 7:4; 8:21–22; Deut. 28:15–45).

In conclusion, the old-earth view that Collins presents supports the historicity of Adam, but displays major differences with the traditional young-earth view. The old-earth view yields to the opinions of evolutionary scientists about the age of the earth and about the process of evolution—just like the views presented by Lamoureux and Walton. It boils down to the acceptance of an authority outside the Bible—a dominantly secular authority often very antagonistic to the biblical record—to force the account in Genesis 1–11 to conform to that external authority. The young-earth view does not accept reinterpreting the Scriptures to force it into the evolutionary mold.

A REJOINDER

C. JOHN COLLINS

I am grateful to Denis Lamoureux, John Walton, and William Barrick for these helpful interactions. We who write for publication have both the privilege and the responsibility to continue our education in public and to conduct ourselves in a civil manner, while at the same time exploring our differences and arguing earnestly.

My role was to support an "old-earth creation view," so I offered a statement that covers a wider range of views than my specific preferences, contending for "mere-historical-Adam-and-Eve-ism" within the boundaries of "mere Christianity." Accordingly, I address the larger conversation currently going on, not just my present interlocutors.

Here I will clarify and sharpen the chief points of contention that arise from my colleagues' comments (albeit briefly!).

Lamoureux finds me to err in being a "scientific concordist" who relies on "God-of-the-gaps" arguments. I respond by noting, as discussed in my book *Did Adam and Eve Really Exist?*,[90] that there are different kinds of concordism. "Scientific concordism"—e.g., coordinating Genesis 1 with geological ages—is mistaken because it improperly treats the biblical material as if it were scientific discourse. On the other hand, everyone who is a Christian in any traditional sense follows *historical* concordism: We think that the accounts of Jesus' life and ministry and resurrection in Palestine refer to actual events. Further, most of us think that the Exodus account also corresponds to an actual event, and we try to correlate the biblical materials with sources from ancient Near Eastern history as well as from geological and geographical studies.[91]

---

90. C. John Collins, *Did Adam and Eve Really Exist? Who They Were and Why You Should Care* (Wheaton, IL: Crossway, 2011), 106–11.

91. For careful and responsible efforts at historical concordism, see the studies by James Hoffmeier: *Israel in Egypt: The Evidence for the Authenticity of the Exodus Tradition* (Oxford: Oxford University Press, 1997), and *Ancient Israel in Sinai: The Evidence for the Authenticity of the Wilderness Tradition* (Oxford: Oxford University Press, 2005).

Such studies often do not settle every single question, but they can usefully lead to plausible scenarios by which we can envision the biblical events. That is, we try to comply with both the text's referentiality and its literary features. The danger is that we might unreasonably tie our confidence to our cleverness in constructing our scenarios. But: abuse does not nullify proper use.

When it comes to Genesis 1–11, we must decide what kinds of sources to interact with, including "scientific" theories—a decision based on our judgment of the text's genre. I have given literary reasons for rejecting Lamoureux's approach to Genesis; quite simply, to see it as "science," ancient or otherwise, is a colossal mistake.

Similarly with "God-of-the-gaps": there are different kinds of gaps, as I have argued elsewhere.[92] Not all gaps are simply gaps in our knowledge, at least as Christians have normally construed things; some gaps we judge to be unbridgeable in principle, except by "outside help." Does anyone know otherwise? We do not expect physiologists to uncover a hitherto unknown *natural* pathway by which Jesus might have risen from the dead. This is not properly called God-of-the-gaps reasoning, since it (1) applies to a unique and epochal event in the world's story rather than to ordinary processes; and (2) does not rely on gaps due to our ignorance.

Like Benjamin Warfield, I do not find either the possibility of animal intermediates or a material process that involves descent between the "dust" and human beings as necessarily a theological problem. But also like Warfield, C. S. Lewis, Alvin Plantinga, Francis Collins, and evolutionary biologists I have spoken with, I find the notion of a strictly *natural* and *material* path from molecule to mankind to fall foul of serious philosophical problems.[93] The assertions of *some* biologists that purely natural processes are adequate should themselves come up for evaluation and do not merit our consent.[94] As Lewis observed,

---

92. See C. John Collins, "Miracles, Intelligent Design, and God-of-the-Gaps," *Perspectives on Science and Christian Faith* 55:1 (2003): 22–29, and also my earlier comments on Lamoureux. The Canadian philosopher Robert Larmer has also explored this matter in several publications.

93. I have discussed Lewis in Collins, "A Peculiar Clarity: How C. S. Lewis Can Help Us Think about Faith and Science," in *The Magician's Twin: C. S. Lewis on Science, Scientism, and Society*, ed. John G. West (Seattle: Discovery Institute Press, 2012), 69–106, as mentioned in my comments on Lamoureux.

94. I contend that such assertions indicate inadequate *scientific* reasoning: they ignore relevant evidence (e.g., from linguistics), and their logic fails to distinguish between "I can imagine this progression" and "this progression is possible," let alone "this progression is probable"—in many cases because of a prior commitment to an exclusively natural progression.

They ask me at the same moment to accept a conclusion and to discredit the only testimony on which the conclusion can be based. The difficulty is to me a fatal one; and the fact that when you put it to many scientists, far from having an answer, they seem not even to understand what the difficulty is, assures me that I have not found a mare's nest but detected a radical disease in their whole mode of thought from the very beginning.[95]

That is, all reasoning, scientific and otherwise, must involve good critical thinking, and I judge that failure to grasp the chasm between us and our nearest animal "kin" undermines the conclusions. As a person with a scientific education and experience, I know that scientists are human beings, with epistemic obligations like everyone else.

We gain nothing by deriding Francis Schaeffer's scientific or philosophical qualifications. He aimed to set out guidelines, based on his understanding of sound critical thinking. It is no shame to acknowledge one's intellectual debts and at the same time to refine and update the guidelines, which is what I have done—arguing that Schaeffer's instinctive approach gains support from more developed literary notions.[96] I have not taken him as any kind of "authority on origins," or on Genesis for that matter—a move that Schaeffer would have thought absurd.

Both Lamoureux and Barrick claim that the reason I hold my views on Genesis 1 is that I am under the influence of "modern science": for Lamoureux a compliment, while for Barrick a reproach. This leads us nowhere; the only thing open to public inspection is the rationale I have advanced, and I like to think that the reason I continue to think the way I do about Genesis is that I find the arguments satisfying[97]—arguments that I have detailed elsewhere and have left out due to space.[98] In these arguments I hardly ignore the refrain about the

95. C. S. Lewis, "Is Theology Poetry?" in *The Weight of Glory,* ed. Walter Hooper (1980; New York: Simon & Schuster, 1996), at 103; cf. "Funeral of a Great Myth," in *Christian Reflections,* ed. Walter Hooper (Grand Rapids: Eerdmans, 1967), 89.

96. I develop this in Collins, "Freedoms and Limitations: C. S. Lewis and Francis Schaeffer as a Tag Team," to appear in *Firstfruits of a New Creation: Essays in Honor of Jerram Barrs,* ed. Mark Ryan and J. E. Eubanks.

97. On the matter of attributing "causes" to a person's beliefs rather than attending to the "reasons" he or she offers, see C. S. Lewis, "Bulverism," in *God in the Dock: Essays on Theology and Ethics,* ed. Walter Hooper (Grand Rapids: Eerdmans, 1970), 271–77.

98. See, for example, Collins, *Science and Faith: Friends or Foes?* (Wheaton, IL: Crossway, 2003); *Genesis 1–4: A Linguistic, Literary, and Theological Commentary* (Phillipsburg, NJ: P&R

evening and the morning (which both Lamoureux and Barrick imply), since I spend some time showing why it (and the order of events: evening *followed by* morning) factors into my view!

Both Lamoureux and Barrick do what in my main essay I say their positions do — namely, identify historicity with strong literalism in interpretation. Barrick even goes so far as to infer that I take Genesis 1–11 to be "nonhistorical," which mystifies me. But I leave my main essay and my comments to speak for themselves.

Walton's comments are very gentle with me. The chief disagreement here is whether Adam and Eve belong at the genetic headwaters of humankind, and in my comments I have criticized his negative answer and thus supported a more traditional answer to the question.

Walton also remarks on my occasional "subjective terminology," which "weakens his case." In the specific instance that he cites, "Genesis *appears* to trace all humankind back to a common source," I abbreviated for the sake of space: Genesis is widely thought to do so, and we should seek reasons to support or undermine this widely accepted reading. I then aimed to supply the required reasons. If I failed to be clear, this is a *literary* blemish, but not a *logical* one. I pray that all readers will overlook such blemishes and attend to the logic.

Publishing, 2006); and most recently, "Reading Genesis 1–2 with the Grain: Analogical Days," in *Reading Genesis 1–2: An Evangelical Conversation*, ed. J. Daryl Charles (Peabody, MA: Hendrickson, 2013), 73–92.

A HISTORICAL ADAM:
YOUNG-EARTH CREATION VIEW

WILLIAM D. BARRICK

In my view Adam is the originating head of the entire human race. Adam's historicity is foundational to a number of biblical doctrines and is related to the inspiration and inerrancy of Scripture. This traditional view of Adam rejects accommodation to evolutionary science, upholding instead that the Holy Spirit superintended the author of Genesis so that he wrote an objective description of God's creative activities in six consecutive literal days.

The biblical account represents Adam as a single individual rather than an archetype or the product of biological evolution, and a number of New Testament texts rely on Adam's historicity. More importantly, without a historical first Adam there is no need for Jesus, the second Adam, to undo the first Adam's sin and its results. Evangelicals should uphold and defend the uniqueness of the Genesis record and give it priority over ancient Near Eastern materials and modern science in all discussions of primeval history and the historicity of Adam and Eve.

Introduction

The Importance of the Topic

Was Adam the first of the human race or just the head of a particular clan, tribe, or nation? Or did he exist at all? Was Eve the mother of the human race or merely the woman who was married to Adam? Or was Eve even a historical person? These are questions demanding careful evaluation. The traditional Christian and Jewish view answers these questions with a resounding affirmation that Adam was and is not only a historical person, but also the originating head (not merely the representative head or an archetypal reference) of the entire human race, and that God created Eve out of a portion of Adam's side. As the first woman, Eve was and is the mother of all mankind, not just a representative woman.

John Walton, on the other hand, believes that we should not view the clay and the man's side as actual material ingredients. Instead, the materials serve only to define the class of human being. "It is indicative of human destiny and mortality, and therefore is a functional comment, not a material one."[1] Walton does not deny the historical or biological reality of Adam's existence,[2] but he does reject the straightforward sense of the biblical account regarding the creation of both the man and the woman. In other words, Adam and Eve do not need to be the very first humans, nor the only humans in existence at the time, since they merely represent all humanity.

Hermeneutically, to read Genesis 1 and 2 as presenting Adam as humanity's archetype without reference to his material formation resembles allegorical interpretations of the text.[3] The non-allegorical interpretation understands that the text presents a historical Adam as the first and only head of the human race. Without Adam's historicity many of the teachings of Scripture will look very different from common evangelical theological concepts or fail the test of logical consistency.

In his *Christianity Today* article on the topic of Adam's historicity, Richard Ostling specifies the potential of the debate over a historical Adam:

> The emerging science could be seen to challenge not only what Genesis records about the creation of humanity but the species's unique status as bearing the "image of God," Christian doctrine on original sin and the Fall, the genealogy of Jesus in the Gospel of Luke, ... Paul's teaching that links the historical Adam with

---

1. John H. Walton, *The Lost World of Genesis One: Ancient Cosmology and the Origins Debate* (Downers Grove, IL: InterVarsity Press, 2009), 70.

2. Ibid., 179.

3. Adrian Cunningham, "Type and Archetype in the Eden Story," in *About a Walk in the Garden: Biblical, Iconographical and Literary Images of Eden*, JSOTSup 136 (Sheffield, UK: Sheffield Academic Press, 1992), 290.

redemption through Christ (Rom. 5:12–19; 1 Cor. 15:20–23, 42–49; and his speech in Acts 17).[4]

Indeed, a brief summary of the theological aspects effectively shaped by the historicity of Adam and Eve as the original parents of the entire human race reveals the topic's importance. A historical Adam as the original man from whom all human beings descended is

- foundational to a biblical understanding of God's creative activity,
- foundational to a biblical understanding of the history of the human race,
- foundational to a biblical understanding of the nature of mankind,
- foundational to a biblical understanding of the origin and nature of sin,
- foundational to a biblical understanding of the existence and nature of death,
- foundational to a biblical understanding of the reality of salvation from sin,
- foundational to the progressive account of the historical events recorded in the book of Genesis,
- and perhaps most importantly, foundational to a biblical understanding of Scripture's authority, inspiration, and inerrancy.[5]

The Assumptions of the Traditional View

The traditional view is associated in the title of this essay with young-earth creationism because the two aspects are integrally related. The traditional view rejects an old-earth view that accommodates itself to the millions and billions of years proposed by modern evolutionary science.[6] A number of assumptions define this viewpoint.

First, the traditional view commonly affirms that God gave the Genesis account of creation to Moses by special revelation. Thus the

---

4. Richard N. Ostling, "The Search for the Historical Adam," *Christianity Today* 55, no. 6 (June 2011): 24.

5. "Inerrancy means that when all facts are known, the Scriptures in their original autographs and properly interpreted will be shown to be wholly true in everything that they affirm, whether that has to do with doctrine or morality or with social, physical, or life sciences." Paul D. Feinberg, "The Meaning of Inerrancy," in *Inerrancy*, ed. Norman L. Geisler (Grand Rapids: Zondervan, 1980), 294.

6. An earth at even 100,000 years would still be "young" by comparison to the current scientific opinion, but most young-earth proponents would place earth's age at 6,000–25,000 years old.

narrator is both omniscient and reliable,[7] because the ultimate author is God himself.[8] After all, if Adam was truly the first human being, there were no human eyewitnesses to his creation. Additionally, Adam could not have described the making of the woman, because he was in a deep sleep throughout the divine procedure. The only witnesses are God and the angels. The only alternative to divine revelation would be an unlikely angelic report. The absence of eyewitnesses plagues any account, biblical or extrabiblical, of original creation. Along these lines of divine inspiration, the traditional view does not rely upon or adopt the documentary hypothesis and its theory of J, E, D, and P documents to explain the composition of Genesis or the Pentateuch.[9]

Second, traditionalists take the position that the declarations of Genesis bear the stamp of divine truth, historical fact, and historiographical accuracy. The accuracy of Scripture's account of creation does not depend on confirmation of its events through extrabiblical sources. The traditional approach applies the same uniform hermeneutical methodology to Genesis 1–11 as to the remainder of the book.[10] This approach differs profoundly from the view that biblical inerrancy does not extend to "incidental statements" in the biblical record about the origins of the universe, the earth, and mankind.[11]

---

7. A point conceded by C. John Collins in *Did Adam and Eve Really Exist? Who They Were and Why You Should Care* (Wheaton, IL: Crossway, 2011), 24; see, also, *idem, Genesis 1–4: A Linguistic, Literary, and Theological Commentary* (Phillipsburg, NJ: P&R Publishing, 2006), 11.

8. This statement should not be taken as a denial of the participation of human writers. As correctly defined by Clark H. Pinnock, *A Defense of Biblical Infallibility* (Philadelphia: Presbyterian & Reformed, 1967), 1, the Bible as the Word of God displays an inspiration that is "'confluent' (product of two free agents, human and divine)." As James McKeown, in *Genesis*, THOTC (Grand Rapids: Eerdmans, 2008), 7, reminds us, "Emphasis on divine authorship should not blind us to the human dimension of Scripture because God used human beings to write down the words."

9. For a brief presentation of the documentary approach and its impact on interpreting Genesis 1–2, see Donald E. Gowan, *From Eden to Babel: A Commentary on the Book of Genesis 1–11*, ITC (Grand Rapids: Eerdmans, 1988), 33–37. A more detailed explanation can be found in Martin Noth, *A History of Pentateuchal Traditions* (Englewood Cliffs, NJ: Prentice Hall, 1971). For critiques and conservative responses to the documentary approach, see U[mberto] Cassuto, *The Documentary Hypothesis and the Composition of the Pentateuch*, trans. by Israel Abrahams (1961; reprint, Jerusalem: Magnes Press, 1972), and Gleason L. Archer, *Survey of Old Testament Introduction*, 3rd ed. (Chicago: Moody Press, 1994), 89–172.

10. See Michael A. Grisanti, "The Book of Genesis," in *The World and the Word: An Introduction to the Old Testament*, by tr. Eugene H. Merrill, Mark F. Rooker, and Michael A. Grisanti (Nashville: B&H Academic, 2011), 176.

11. Denis O. Lamoureux, "Lessons from the Heavens: On Scripture, Science and Inerrancy," *Journal of the American Scientific Affiliation* 60 (June 2008): 13.

Third, the Genesis record does not limit its scope to one ethnic or national group. From its very beginning it addresses mankind universally. The judgment at Babel accounts for the dispersion of the human race across the face of the whole earth. The genealogy in Genesis 5 lists the actual physical ancestors of all mankind. Noah becomes like a new Adam by being the progenitor of all post-flood human beings.[12] The scattering of the peoples closes the universal message of the early chapters of Genesis, but "the fragmentation of humanity is a positive step forward, because the divine plan of redemption requires a particularized instrument."[13] Thus, Genesis 10 and 11 account for the origins of all peoples of sociopolitical significance to the descendants of Abraham, the one through whom the Redeemer would come.[14] Genesis 1–11 records "the origins of the universe and God's plan to relate to it, and especially to humans,"[15] while Genesis 12–50 deals with the origins of Israel.

Fourth, biblical writers in both testaments appear to take for granted a common origin of all human beings in Adam whenever they touch on topics related to Genesis 1–11 (e.g., Mal. 2:10 and Rom. 5:12–14).

Interestingly, some scholars admit that what the Bible declares is actually what the writers did indeed believe and intend to say. However, they do so not in support of the traditional view, but to attribute erroneous, pre-scientific views to the biblical authors. Modern interpreters of the Bible often think of the biblical record as the viewpoint of pre-scientific humanity. The findings of modern paleontology and the theory of evolution cause Bible readers to question the biblical chronology, pushing it back farther than the text itself seems to permit.[16] For example, Peter Enns writes that the biblical writers "assumed that the earth is flat, was made by God in relatively recent history (about 4,000 years before

12. Bruce K. Waltke with Cathi J. Fredricks, *Genesis: A Commentary* (Grand Rapids: Zondervan, 2001), 296.

13. R. R. Reno, *Genesis*, BTCB (Grand Rapids: Brazos Press, 2010), 134.

14. Bill Cooper, in *After the Flood: The Early Post-Flood History of Europe* (Chichester, UK: New Wine Press, 1995), traces the ancestors of a number of European nations all the way back to Japheth. This demonstrates that the genealogies in Genesis 10–11 do extend beyond the ancient Near East's immediate environs.

15. Bill T. Arnold, *Genesis*, NCBC (Cambridge, UK: Cambridge University Press, 2009), 7. Also, John H. Walton, *Genesis*, NIVAC (Grand Rapids: Zondervan, 2001), 37.

16. Daniel P. Fuller, in "The Importance of a Unity of the Bible," in *Studies in Old Testament Theology*, ed. by Robert L. Hubbard Jr., Robert K. Johnston, and Robert P. Meye (Dallas: Word, 1992), 72, summed up the issue in this very fashion.

Jesus) just as it looks now, and that it is the fixed point in the cosmos over which the sun actually rises and sets."[17] Enns' characterization of Israelite beliefs (e.g., a flat earth) consists of overstatement and misinterpretation that denigrate both true believers in ancient Israel and the current biblical text.[18] Beyond that, his characterization of the ancient Near Eastern conceptual world as riddled with pre-scientific error that God himself adopted in inspired Scripture impugns God's moral integrity.[19]

Ignoring the possibility that Enns has misinterpreted what the writers are truly saying, we see that his point still amounts to admitting that the Bible accurately conveys the intent of its writers regarding creation, the monogenesis of mankind, and a global flood. So, if that is the intent of the biblical writers, why should we not also believe what they apparently believed?

Biblical Evidence for the Traditional View
Genesis 1:1-25

Why did the writer of Genesis 1 choose to narrate the creation story according to an orderly sequence of six days? David Cotter's approach offers one potentially significant insight regarding the reasons for the orderly sequence of days: "This storyteller must convince the reader that this account can be trusted; to achieve this, the storyteller creates the impression that everything is being told, that nothing is being held back. Therefore the narrator has to be omniscient."[20] In other words, by taking a detailed, step-by-step, objective tone the author reveals everything just as it actually happened.

---

17. Peter Enns, *The Evolution of Adam: What the Bible Does and Doesn't Say about Human Origins* (Grand Rapids: Brazos Press, 2012), xiii.

18. See the detailed and documented response to the fallacies in this approach in Walter C. Kaiser Jr., "The Literary Form of Genesis 1–11," in *New Perspectives on the Old Testament*, ed. J. Barton Payne (Waco, TX: Word, 1970), 55–58. Cf. Jonathan F. Henry, "Uniformitarianism in Old Testament Studies," *Journal of Dispensational Theology* 13 (Aug 2009): 25–28; Jeffrey Burton Russell, *Inventing the Flat Earth: Columbus and Modern Historians* (New York: Praeger, 1991), ix; and Lesley B. Cormack, "Myth 3: That Medieval Christians Taught That the Earth Was Flat," in *Galileo Goes to Jail and Other Myths about Science and Religion*, ed. Ronald L. Numbers (Cambridge, MA: Harvard University Press, 2009), 178–86.

19. James W. Scott, "The Inspiration and Interpretation of God's Word, with Special Reference to Peter Enns—Part I: Inspiration and Its Implications," *WTJ* 71 (Spring 2009): 155–58.

20. David W. Cotter, *Genesis*, Berit Olam Studies in Hebrew Narrative and Poetry (Collegeville, MN: Liturgical Press, 2003), 8.

In his Genesis commentary, Waltke states that the "narrator's inspiration from God, who cannot lie, is sufficient to guarantee its truthfulness without other historical corroboration."[21] He then argues that the Genesis narrative presents "an essentially coherent chronological succession of events"[22] by means of the narrative verb form, validation by time and space location, use of genealogies, and citing sources. However, Waltke later separates the creation account from that history for the reason that no human was present to write a normal history. Waltke offers evidence of dischronologization, similarities to other ancient Near Eastern materials, and contemporary science as reasons to read the creation narrative differently from the rest of Genesis.[23] Many evangelicals likewise claim on the one hand that God's inspiration is sufficient in and of itself to make Scripture trustworthy and inerrant, but on the other hand, like Waltke, exclude Genesis 1–2 (or even Gen. 1–11) from that concept regarding the sufficiency and accuracy of God's Scripture. In their approach, science and ancient Near Eastern texts trump simple acceptance of the sufficiency and historical accuracy of those early chapters of Genesis.

In the minds of many scholars the historicity of Genesis 1–11 stands separated from the matter of the historicity of Genesis 12–50. After all, most evangelicals readily acknowledge the presence of considerable evidence supporting the historical accuracy, integrity, and authenticity of the latter text unit.[24] It seems fairly clear that Genesis 12–50 builds on

---

21. Waltke, *Genesis*, 29.

22. Ibid.

23. Ibid., 75–77. Responses to Waltke's three basic types of evidence (dischronologization, ancient Near Eastern similarities, and contemporary science) have been presented in a wide range of books and journal articles. Following are a few of the more significant books: Larry Vardiman, Andrew A. Snelling, and Eugene F. Chaffin, eds., *Radioisotopes and the Age of the Earth: Results of a Young-Earth Creationist Research Initiative* (El Cajon, CA: Institute for Creation Research, 2005); Terry Mortenson and Thane H. Ury, eds., *Coming to Grips with Genesis: Biblical Authority and the Age of the Earth* (Green Forest, AR: Master Books, 2008); Andrew A. Snelling, *Earth's Catastrophic Past: Geology, Creation & the Flood*, 2 vols. (Dallas: Institute for Creation Research, 2009); and Andrew S. Kulikovsky, *Creation, Fall, Restoration: A Biblical Theology of Creation*, (Fearn, UK: Mentor, 2009).

24. E.g., see Victor P. Hamilton, *The Book of Genesis Chapters 1–17*, NICOT (Grand Rapids: Eerdmans, 1990), 59–67; John H. Sailhamer, *The Pentateuch as Narrative: A Biblical-Theological Commentary*, LBI (Grand Rapids: Zondervan, 1992), 23–24; and Kenneth A. Kitchen, *On the Reliability of the Old Testament* (Grand Rapids: Eerdmans, 2003), 313–72. A collection of essays in A. R. Millard and D. J. Wiseman, eds., *Essays on the Patriarchal Narratives* (Winona Lake, IN: Eisenbrauns, 1980), tackled this issue and supported the historicity of the patriarchal records in Genesis.

the themes of blessing and curse already introduced in Genesis 1–11.[25] So, can the patriarchs expect the continuation of blessing and curse in their real experience if the recipients and events in which blessing and curse occurred prior to the Noahic flood are nothing but a theological construct in the minds of later Israelites writing about both periods? If the persons and events of the earlier text truly existed, then the reality of blessing and curse clearly carry over to the later persons and events. As John Goldingay so insightfully observes, if a latter text grounds its faith in earlier events and realities that did not take place, "the grounds of faith are removed."[26] Sidney Greidanus makes a similar point, but with direct application to Genesis 1–3: "For redemptive-historical narratives, the lack of historical foundations is fatal, for the factuality that God acted in history is part and parcel of their message."[27]

From its opening line ("In the beginning God created the heavens and the earth"), Genesis possesses a universal focus rather than a national or ethnic focus, even if it is preparatory for the narratives that narrow the focus toward Israel in Genesis 12–50. From this broad inclusive reference, the second verse narrows the focus to planet Earth.[28] Having noted this narrowing focus, the reader of the text must not assume that the true center or focus of the text is upon Earth or upon human beings.

One of the major characteristics of Genesis 1–11 consists of the theocentricity of the biblical writer's intent.[29] A theocentric or theological emphasis in the text, however, does not mean that the record lacks historicity (viz., factual reality for the events and persons). Consider the relative silence in extrabiblical materials about the existence, deeds, and death of Jesus. Arguments used to deny the historicity of the first Adam can be equally applied to the historicity of the second Adam. The

25. John Goldingay, "The Patriarchs in Scripture and History," in *Essays on the Patriarchal Narratives*, 18–19. Cf. Walton, *Genesis*, NIVAC, 37: "Chapters 1–11 establish the need for the covenant."
26. Ibid., 29. Goldingay is discussing the exodus-conquest narrative and its dependence on the reality of the patriarchal narratives.
27. Sidney Greidanus, *Preaching Christ from Genesis: Foundations for Expository Sermons* (Grand Rapids: Eerdmans, 2007), 32. So also Collins, *Genesis 1–4*, 17.
28. The anadiplosis (see the definition in footnote 38) reinforces the focus on Earth by placing *hāʾāreṣ* ("the earth") at the end of verse 1 back-to-back with *wĕhāʾāreṣ* at the start of verse 2.
29. See Walton, *Genesis*, NIVAC, 152.

potential of that type of consistent rationale that ends up denying the historicity of both Adam and Jesus heightens the urgency of the first of these two matters.

The following verses (Gen. 1:2–31) all deal with the preparation of the planet for sustaining the life forms and the Creator's actions to populate it. The text implies that the account identifies the origin of all life on Earth. Thus every man, woman, and child at any subsequent time can look back to this as the beginning of terrestrial life and the start of the human race. God's program in creation, as in redemption, targets all mankind, not just one segment.[30] Significant to the rest of the creation account, these first twenty-five verses mention "seed" (*zera'*) six times — all with reference to plants. The significance of the concept of "seed" consists of the fact that each plant produces its own kind — a fruit can be traced back to the parent.

The next occurrence of "seed" comes in 3:15 (NIV, "offspring"). No other usage of "seed" occurs in the report regarding days three, four, and five. For plants, "seed" indicates the means of plant reproduction and their spread over the surface of the earth. The absence of a further mention of "seed" throughout the creation of man raises a question: how will mankind fill the earth? Will they produce after their kind? The answer waits until a fuller description of humankind appears in the record. When "seed" does appear with regard to mankind, it sets a story line for the remainder of Genesis: God has chosen a line of descendants to fulfill his program of redemption. The seed of fallen Adam is like him, fallen and disobedient. The paradox that Scripture unfolds is that the ultimate descendant of blessing cannot be like fallen Adam, but can still be traced back to Adam.[31]

The six-day narrative in 1:1–2:4 includes a conceptualization of how God provides for making Earth a viable habitat for sustaining plant, animal, and human life. The basics appear in order of his creating them: water, light, land, and plants. "Day" in the creation account refers primarily to actual days in accord with the following observations: (1) each

---

30. C. John Collins, in "Adam and Eve in the Old Testament," *SBJT* 15 (Spring 2011): 6: "The shape of this biblical story assumes that all human beings have a common origin, a common predicament, and a common need to know God and have God's image restored in them."

31. For an introduction to the significance of "seed" in Genesis, see McKeown, *Genesis*, THOTC, 197–219.

"day" is made up of evening and morning; (2) numerical adjectives modify "day"; (3) "day" occurs in company with "seasons" and years in Genesis 1:14; and (4) Exodus 20:8 – 11, which patterns the human work week with the days of creation, requires the literal understanding of "day" in the creation account on which the legal analogy was established.[32]

In the first three days of creation God provides the basics for life while he forms the earth into a habitat ready for animal and human life. During days four through six, the Creator begins to fill the earth with the life forms for which he has made preparation. Interestingly, he chooses to make the sun, moon, and stars at this point. I suggest that he did so because he wanted to make an environment that would be pleasurable, interesting, and utilitarian for both animal and human life. Light alone can maintain life, but light alone does not provide seasons, navigational aids, or chronological markers. The earth did not yet require solar light. The plants on day three do not need anything more than a light source to survive their first full day of existence. Moreover, they are not the focus of God's creative purposes. The metanarrative now moves to a focus on the multiplication of human beings and the divine design for accomplishing it.

Genesis 1:26 – 2:3

The first description of the origin of mankind recites the general picture minus all of the details. The text mentions the human female, but gives no account of how the male or the female came into existence. The metanarrative focuses on God as the creator of all life (including human beings) and on mankind being made in the image of God. Divine image bearers manifest that image, at least in part, by acting as God's vice-regents on earth. The divine mandate to "be fruitful and increase in number; fill the earth" (v. 28) occupies the revelatory focus without explaining how that might take place. The authoritative command of God remains at center stage. The second section of the creation

---

32. Trevor Craigen, "Can Deep Time Be Embedded in Genesis?" in *Coming to Grips with Genesis: Biblical Authority and the Age of the Earth*, ed. Terry Mortenson and Thane H. Ury (Green Forest, AR: Master Books, 2008), 194. See also Gerhard Hasel, "The 'Days' of Creation in Genesis 1: Literal 'Days' or Figurative 'Periods/Epoch' of Time?" *Origins* 21 (1994): 5 – 38; and J. Ligon Duncan III and David W. Hall, "The 24-Hour View," in *The Genesis Debate: Three Views on the Days of Creation*, ed. David G. Hagopian (Mission Viejo, CA: Crux Press, 2001), 21 – 66.

account (2:5–24) reveals the means by which mankind will fulfill that command.

Two first-person plurals punctuate the accounts of the creation and the fall of mankind in the Genesis account (1:26 and 3:22). Whether these plurals are taken as plurals of majesty, plurals of self-address (deliberation[33]), Trinitarian plurals, or references to a council of spirit beings, the references draw attention to the significance of the events with which the text associates them.[34] The account indicates that the creation and fall of mankind comprise notable events pertinent to a proper theological understanding of who God is, what deeds God has performed (both in creation and in setting about to redeem fallen mankind), who man is, and what man has caused by his disobedience to his Creator. Together with the global setting depicted by Genesis 1, such attention seems more fitting with regard to Adam being the progenitor of the human race than with a view that limits the account to the origin of the nation of Israel.[35] One of the biggest hurdles for this latter view to overcome involves the absence of any reference to Israel as a people until Genesis 32:32.

Genesis 2:4-24

The inspired record of creation does not close after its description of the world and humankind, but proceeds to focus solely on humanity

---

33. William David Reyburn and Euan McG. Fry in *A Handbook on Genesis*, UBS Handbook Series (New York: United Bible Societies, 1998), 50, explain that this involves a speaker "conferring or consulting with himself."

34. S. R. Driver, in *The Book of Genesis, with Introduction and Notes* (New York: Edwin S. Gorham, 1904), 14, remarks that God adopts "this unusual and significant mode of expression" in order to introduce the account of man's creation with solemnity. Arnold, in *Genesis*, NCBC, 44, agrees that the "lofty words of v. 26 make this event distinctive." John Peter Lange—in *Genesis, or the First Book of Moses*, translated by Tayler Lewis and A. Gosman, Commentary on the Holy Scriptures, electronic ed. (1864; reprint, Bellingham, WA: Logos Bible Software, 2008), 173—lists five different ways to understand these first-person plurals, but concludes that the carrying of the plural into "our image" might more accurately point to "a distinction in the divine personality."

Hebraists point out that the so-called "plural of majesty" applies primarily to nouns and that it is uncertain whether that applies also to plural verbs or pronouns—cf. McKeown, *Genesis*, THOTC, 26; and Paul Joüon, *A Grammar of Biblical Hebrew*, trans. and rev. by T. Muraoka, 2 vols., Subsidia Biblica 14/I–II (Rome: Pontifical Biblical Institute, 1993), 2:376 (§114e n. 1).

35. Cf. Enns, *The Evolution of Adam*, 66: "If the Adam story is not really a story of the beginning of humanity but of one segment of humanity, at least some of the tensions between Genesis and evolution are lessened."

to set the stage for a far grander story. As C. John Collins observes, the worldview story should not be treated "simply as the husk, which we can then discard once we have discovered the (perhaps timeless) concepts."[36] The second description of mankind's origin pays attention to the details purposely not included in 1:26–2:4.[37] An envelope figure brackets the entire creation account with 1:1–2 and 2:4. The chiasm in 2:4 reflects the content of 1:1–2 and complements those two verses' anadiplosis[38] focusing on "the earth" (see Figure 1). The fact that 2:4 actually introduces the second segment of the book of Genesis, rather than concluding the first segment, does not hinder its use in the inclusio. Collins suggests that the chiasm of 2:4 "invites us to read the two passages in union."[39]

1:1–2	2:4
In the beginning God created	This is the account of
the heavens	**a** the heavens
and the earth	**b** and the earth
	c *when they were created*[40]
	c *when*[41] the LORD God made
And the earth	**b** the earth
	a and the heavens

Figure 1. The Structural Inclusio Bracketing Genesis 1:1–2:4

---

36. Collins, *Did Adam and Eve Really Exist?*, 27.

37. McKeown, *Genesis*, THOTC, 30: "Chapter 1 is a majestic overview, while ch. 2 selects certain aspects of creation and deals with them in more detail."

38. Anadiplosis refers to the rhetorical repetition of a word or phrase in both ending one statement (or verse) and beginning the next statement (or verse).

39. Collins, "Adam and Eve in the Old Testament," 9. According to McKeown in *Genesis*, THOTC, 30, "By inverting the usual order, this phrase prepares the reader for the detailed accounts of the first human beings and the earth that they inhabit."

40. The divine passive (Nifal infinitive construct) avoids naming the agent directly, and then the following parallel line specifies him by name. As though to draw attention to the Creator alone, the closing references to the objects of creation lack the definite article.

41. Literally, "in (the) day." Reyburn and Fry, in *A Handbook on Genesis*, 59, identify this phrase as a Hebrew idiom meaning "when, at the time when." See also Umberto Cassuto, *A Commentary on the Book of Genesis — Part I: From Adam to Noah, Genesis I–VI*, trans. Israel Abrahams (1961; reprint, Jerusalem: Magnes Press, 1998), 99.

The writer commences the first *toledot* (2:4–4:26) with a specific goal in mind: to reveal how mankind will be able to multiply and fill the earth as God had commanded. The Hebrew noun *'ādām* ("man," "mankind," "Adam") occurs twice in Genesis 1. The definite article is absent in the first occurrence (1:26), since this key noun is making its initial appearance in the narrative. The next verse (1:27) uses the article as a matter of previous reference ("the previously mentioned man"). Likewise, the first occurrence in Genesis 2 (v. 5) is also anarthrous (that is, without an article), and each reference after that includes the definite article (2:7 twice, 8, 15, 16, 18, 19 twice, 20a). However, 2:20b refers to "Adam" (without the definite article)[42] in a context of naming the animals—a significant context in which to employ initially the proper name[43] for the first human.

The anarthrous form does not appear again until 3:17 and 21. Fittingly, the anarthrous form makes its appearance in the genealogy of chapter 5 (vv. 1–2). The ambiguity of *'ādām* in Genesis 1–2 leads some scholars to conclude that Genesis does not refer to a God-created man as first or even "one in a definite series."[44] Claus Westermann reasons that primeval history "lies beyond history that can be experienced and documented. The contention is that humanity (meaning every individual) owes its existence to God—no more and no less."[45] These details regarding the use or nonuse of the article with *'ādām*, however, should not cause the reader to miss the fact that the first *toledot* repeatedly presents the man as a single individual:

- God forms a single individual (designated "the man," or "human"[46])—not a clan, tribe, or people—from the dust (or

---

42. Cf. Herbert E. Ryle, *The Book of Genesis in the Revised Version with Introduction and Notes*, Cambridge Bible for Schools and Colleges (Cambridge, UK: Cambridge University Press, 1921), 29. Driver, in *The Book of Genesis*, 42, observes that the Masoretes indicated the proper name, "Adam," by the absence of the definite article. However, in 2:20 Driver prefers to add the definite article.

43. Contra David J. A. Clines, "אדם, the Hebrew for 'Human, Humanity': A Response to James Barr," *VT* 53, no. 3 (2003): 303 n. 12; R. S. Hess, "Adam," *Dictionary of the Old Testament: Pentateuch*, ed. T. Desmond Alexander and David W. Baker (Downers Grove, IL: InterVarsity Press, 2003), 18–21; Victor P. Hamilton, "אדם," in *New International Dictionary of Old Testament Theology & Exegesis*, 5 vols., ed. by Willem A. VanGemeren (Grand Rapids: Zondervan, 1997), 1:263–64.

44. Claus Westermann, "אדם," in *Theological Lexicon of the Old Testament*, 3 vols., ed. by Ernst Jenni and Claus Westermann, trans. Mark E. Biddle (Peabody, MA: Hendrickson Publishers, 1997), 1:35.

45. Ibid.

46. See Clines, "אדם, the Hebrew for 'Human, Humanity'," 297–310 (esp. 302–4).

clay) of the ground (2:7a). This fact alone rules out any form of evolution (theistic or otherwise).

- God breathes the "breath of life" into that individual's nostrils (2:7b)—not into the nostrils of hundreds or thousands of humans.
- The text designates this individual as a "living being" (or "living soul," 2:7c).
- God places this individual in a specially designed "garden" (2:8).
- God assigns to this individual the care and protection of the garden (2:15).
- To this individual God gives a command concerning what he could and what he could not eat (2:16–17).
- This individual is "alone," a condition the Creator considers "not good" (2:18a). How could "alone" refer to a clan, tribe, or people? A group of people would not face the situation Adam faces "alone." The implication is that he cannot reproduce and fulfill the divine mandate ("be fruitful and increase in number; fill the earth," 1:28 ESV).[47] For evolutionists, this presents another problem. If it takes countless years to produce one such individual, how will he survive long enough while another similarly developed individual evolves who is his compatible opposite in gender for the human race to begin?
- God declares that he will make an appropriate counterpart for that individual human (2:18b)—apparently not a reference to another clan, tribe, or people. The wording, "a helper suitable for him," refers to complementarity as opposed to identity.[48] This second individual, like the man, will be a special creation by God himself.
- The individual whom God had placed in the garden names the animals, but finds no individual like himself (2:19–20).[49]

---

47. See Laurence A. Turner, *Announcements of Plot in Genesis*, JSOTSup 96 (Sheffield, UK: Sheffield Academic Press, 1990), 21–49, who systematically develops the implications of the blessing announcement through Genesis 2–11.

48. Gordon J. Wenham, *Genesis 1–15*, WBC 1 (Waco, TX: Word Books, 1987), 68.

49. Collins, in *Genesis 1–4*, 134, solves the apparent dischronological nature of 2:19 as compared to Genesis 1 by taking the verb as a pluperfect (God "had *already* formed" the animals from the ground). See also C. John Collins, "The *Wayyiqtol* as 'Pluperfect': When and Why," *Tyndale Bulletin* 46 (1995): 135–40.

- God causes the individual to enter into a deep sleep and he takes a portion of flesh and bone from the man's side (2:21)—not out of multiple sides belonging to multiple individuals. The creation of the woman cannot be taken as archetypal, because it cannot be experienced again and again in such a way that we recognize ourselves in it.[50] No woman originates from a man in the way Eve came into existence from Adam. God made a woman from a portion of a man's flesh only once. Nor can she be the product of thousands or millions of years of evolution. Human characteristics and DNA must be passed on prior to the death of the first human, or the first of the species dies and the evolutionary process must begin all over again.[51]
- To this one individual God brings one woman, whom he had formed out of the material he had taken from the man (2:22).
- The man (Adam) reacts to this presentation of the woman with a declaration that the woman (not multiple women) is related to him, because her origin is from him (2:23). In the Hebrew a threefold "this one" (zōʾt) emphatically[52] identifies this woman as one of a kind—all eyes are on her.[53] Among other things, Adam's speech and Eve's understanding it do not fit any evolutionary model, since evolution requires innumerable stages of slow and minute development over thousands of years even for an individual to acquire such powers of speech with such sophistication.[54]

The references to one individual man (Adam) and his one wife throughout the subsequent context (e.g., 2:24, 25; 3:1, 4, 6, 7) demonstrate that the biblical writer intends the reader to understand that these two are the parents of the entire human race and there are no others like them until they themselves have borne children

50. Gowan, *From Eden to Babel*, 47.

51. Michael Behe, in *Darwin's Black Box* (New York: Free Press, 1996), argues this point quite effectively by describing multiple examples of irreducible complexity whereby biological organisms cannot accumulate any gradual changes or adaptations because they are virtually a dead end.

52. Cassuto, *A Commentary on the Book of Genesis—Part I*, 135.

53. Wenham, *Genesis 1–15*, WBC, 70.

54. See Jack Barentsen, "The Validity of Human Language: A Vehicle for Divine Truth," *GTJ* 9 (Spring 1988): 37–38.

(4:1–2).[55] Furthermore, these first individuals cannot be the product of an evolutionary process. Such organisms (human beings) "cannot be understood except as the products of a directly acting, purposeful intelligence."[56] The example of the first pair's commitment to one another becomes the paradigm for all future monogamous marital relationships (2:24; cf. Matt. 19:4–6). God provides marriage as a pattern for all mankind, not just for Israel.

Genesis 3

Gordon Wenham identifies seven features indicating that the narrative of Genesis 2–3 is more historical than paradigmatic:[57]

- The account's heading (2:4, "This is the account of") links the record with subsequent histories of Noah, Abraham, Jacob, and Joseph.
- The immediately following story of Cain and Abel (Gen. 4) ties the events of Genesis 2–3 to real historical outcomes.
- Chapter 5 links Adam with Noah, indicating that the writer associates the earliest events with real people.
- God's curse on the serpent results in the serpent crawling on the ground—not something that can be applied to every person who might sin subsequently.
- Subsequent people inherit pain, toil, and death because of the first pair's disobedience.
- God expels Adam and Eve from the garden—an event not repeated with later people who disobey him.
- In the light of God's declaration that everything is "very good" (1:31), chapters 2–3 provide explanation for why that is not true today.

---

55. Cf. Donald MacDonald, *Creation and Fall: A Defence and Exposition of the First Three Chapters of Genesis* (Edinburgh: Thomas Constable and Co., 1856), 372: "Nothing can be plainer than the testimony of this narrative, that Adam and Eve were the only human dwellers on this earth until the birth of their children. The whole tenor of the history is opposed to any other previous or subsequent creation of human beings." See also, Collins, *Genesis 1–4*, 254.

56. Paul Nelson and John Mark Reynolds, "Young Earth Creationism," in *Three Views on Creation and Evolution*, ed. Paul Nelson, Robert C. Newman, and Howard J. Van Till, Counterpoints (Grand Rapids: Zondervan, 1999).

57. Wenham, *Genesis 1–15*, WBC, 91. He concludes that Genesis 2–3 is "both paradigmatic and protohistorical" (ibid.).

The disobedience and fall of mankind take the metanarrative to a new level. The writer has specified the mechanism for the propagation of human beings on the earth. Now the text must introduce God's ultimate purpose. The *protoevangelium* in Genesis 3:15 contains that concept by its attention to the "seed" (NIV, "offspring") of the woman.

The introduction of soteriological thought does not eliminate the historicity of the original pair, nor does it do away with the two being the literal first parents of all of earth's peoples. The entire human race descends from Adam and Eve and is, therefore, Adamic. There are no pre- or extra-Adamic people(s). Adam, as the seminal (physical) head of the human race, presides also as the federal (legally representative) head of the human race. Even the first woman came from Adam — she possesses his DNA as altered by God at the time he formed her.

According to the biblical record, the fall stands as a historical event rather than something imaginary or mythological. The biblical record discloses that the first human beings disobeyed God's command. The time of this disobedience was very early — at the beginning of the history of the human race on planet Earth, before the newly created man and woman could begin to produce children with which to populate the world.

How significant is the early entrance of sin into the created order? Paul House responds to that question by answering, "In a very real sense, the rest of Scripture deals with the solution to the sin problem."[58] The disobedience results in the entrance of death, as God himself indicates in the statement of his prohibition in Genesis 2:17. That death must refer either (1) to the initiation of the process of aging and dying, or (2) to the entrance of spiritual death, or (3) to both of these kinds of death. The last seems more consistent with the immediate, as well as the remote, context.

In the midst of divine judgment for Adam's disobedience, God extends his mercy to the man and the woman. Immediate physical death would have put an end to God's program for Adam and Eve. Instead, God allows the pair to continue living so that they might produce offspring (seed) that eventually will triumph over the serpent. Without that extension, the Restorer cannot come. Without that extension, no

---

58. Paul R. House, *Old Testament Theology* (Downers Grove, IL: InterVarsity Press, 1998), 67.

remedy can be applied. Thus God reveals his character in both the justice he administers and the grace-filled mercy he applies—all with an eschatological end in mind.

The same kind of merciful extension of life for the sake of continuing the seed and accomplishing God's ultimate purpose occurs again at the time of the golden calf incident, when he allows the first generation of Israelites to live until a second generation has been prepared to enter the land of promise (Exod. 32:1–34:28).[59] Noting this revelation of God's character, James Hamilton identifies death in Genesis 2–3 as alienation from the life of God, which replaces freedom and innocence with shame and fear.[60]

The announcement that the man will "return to the ground" (Gen. 3:19) cannot be understood as anything but physical death. That contrasts starkly with the potential that would have been there for the human pair had God allowed them to continue eating from the tree of life (3:22). Thus, death is a new reality arising out of the disobedience of man. As far as that disobedience is concerned, the second masculine singular grammatical forms (verbs, pronouns, and pronominal suffixes) throughout Genesis 3 make it clear that the Creator holds Adam accountable. As Eve's husband, Adam is head of his family and responsible for both Eve's and his actions leading to sin's entrance into the world.[61]

As Collins argues, in order for mankind to be accountable for sin, there needs to be a common origin of all mankind in a state of goodness interrupted by voluntary rebellion.[62] If this scenario does not represent historical fact, then God himself can be blamed for the existence of sin. Genesis 1–3 reveals that (1) God creates Adam and Eve directly—he does not select them out of any existing group of hominids; (2) God

---

59. For a more detailed handling of Exodus 32, see William D. Barrick, "The Openness of God: Does Prayer Change God?," *Master's Seminary Journal* 12 (Fall 2001): 156–65.

60. James M. Hamilton Jr., *God's Glory in Salvation through Judgment: A Biblical Theology* (Wheaton, IL: Crossway, 2010), 78.

61. God singles out the man when he asks, "Where are you?" (Gen. 3:9). That is a second masculine singular, not a plural. God is not asking where the two of them are. The context specifies the man's accountability again and again—as an individual, not as a clan, a tribe, a people, or a race. For an exposition on this topic, see Thomas R. Schreiner, "*Sermon:* From Adam to Christ: The Grace that Conquers all our Sin (Romans 5:12–19)," *SBJT* 15 (Spring 2011): 80–90.

62. Collins, *Did Adam and Eve Really Exist?*, 134.

does not add the image of God to Adam and Eve—it is a unique component involved in their creation; (3) God creates Adam and Eve for dominion over the animals and the earth; (4) God creates Adam and Eve so that they possess a totally righteous nature and character; (5) God prepares the garden of Eden for Adam and Eve; (6) God gives a direct command to Adam and Eve not to eat fruit from the tree of the knowledge of good and evil; (7) Satan, through the instrumentality of the serpent, tempts Adam and Eve to defy that specific divine prohibition; (8) Adam chooses to disobey God's directly revealed prohibition; (9) God banishes Adam and Eve from the garden of Eden, following their willful disobedience; and (10) Adam and Eve produce children bearing their image as rebels against a holy God.[63]

Genesis 4

Sin's history continues as the writer reveals that mankind's rebellion against God makes its presence known even in the act of worship and within the close relationships of the first family. Cain, an actual person from the primeval past, offers an unacceptable sacrifice and then murders his brother Abel. Adam's failure to protect the garden from the incursion of evil now results in Cain's failure to rightly care for his own brother.

The occasion confronts the reader with the first physical death. Abel's death does not come as the direct and immediate application of the "you will surely die" declaration in Genesis 2:17. Yet, his death is a result of Adamic disobedience. Adam's disobedience to God's spoken word results in his son's willful destruction of one who, like him, bears the image of God. Cain learns that "life without God or his blessing [is] a dangerous life without protection."[64] Human beings become self-centered and violent. Something has gone terribly wrong—and it is all due to what Adam had done. Because of his disobedience sin and death enter the world. Yet, hope still exists, because the theme of human "seed" makes its second appearance in 4:25 (Seth).

---

63. See John W. Mahoney, "Why an Historical Adam Matters for a Biblical Doctrine of Sin," *SBJT* 15 (Spring 2011): 75–76, for a slightly different listing containing all of these aspects.

64. Allen P. Ross, *Creation and Blessing: A Guide to the Study and Exposition of Genesis* (1988; reprint, Grand Rapids: Baker, 1996), 153.

Genesis 5

The first of the *toledots* to include the name of an individual in the heading is the second *toledot* (Gen. 5:1, "This is the book of the generations of Adam" [NASB]). First, the statement identifies a single individual as the one whom God has created in his likeness. Second, the text reveals that this single individual lives for 130 years, then sires a son, whom he names "Seth" (5:3). Such personal details, repeated throughout the genealogy, signal to the reader that "these were real human people made in God's image who lived before the flood."[65] Third, the "image" and "likeness" that Seth receives "were transferred to Seth because of the fact that Adam had fathered him."[66] Could it be that parentage also transmits the Adamic sin?—more specifically, the male parent? Parentage being the clear connection in the transfer of the image of God lends itself to the concept of seminal headship rather than federal headship. According to John A. Witmer,

> The natural headship view ... recognizes that the entire human race was seminally and physically in Adam, the first man. As a result God considered all people as participating in the act of sin which Adam committed and as receiving the penalty he received. Even adherents of the federal headship view must admit that Adam is the natural head of the human race physically; the issue is the relationship spiritually.[67]

The genealogy commencing with Adam assumes that the image of God marks every individual as human. It indicates that all humans descend from one original pair. In staccato-like fashion, "then he died" reminds the reader again and again that death is in the world to stay. The genealogy presents Enoch (5:21–24) as the sole exception, demonstrating that it is yet possible for a person to obey and worship God as the Creator intended. Abel is the first to attempt to live a worshipful life, and his brother kills him. Enoch appears as the second individual

65. Wenham, *Genesis 1–15*, WBC, 146.
66. C. L. Crouch, "Genesis 1:26–7 as a Statement of Humanity's Divine Parentage," *JTS* NS 61 (April 2010): 10.
67. John A. Witmer, "Romans," in *The Bible Knowledge Commentary: An Exposition of the Scriptures*, 2 vols., ed. John F. Walvoord, Roy B. Zuck, and Dallas Theological Seminary (Wheaton, IL: Victor Books, 1985), 2:458.

to live for God, rather than self, and God removes him from Earth to abide with him. The contrast discloses both the reality of life in a fallen world and the hope that involves abiding with God outside this world.

Witnesses in the Rest of the Old Testament

Throughout the Hebrew Bible writers speak of creation, marriage, the Sabbath, and the fall by referring to those original events. Exodus 20:11 provides a key example with its direct reference to the six days of creation as the pattern for Israel's Sabbath observance. Later in the Pentateuch, Deuteronomy 4:32 speaks of God's creation (*bārāʾ*) of human beings (a use of *ʾādām* without the definite article), using the vocabulary of Genesis 1:27. Among the prophets, Isaiah 42:5 not only employs *bārāʾ*, but also describes the Creator as the one who "gives breath" (cp. Gen. 2:7) to the earth's peoples.

Mention of the garden in Eden appears in Ezekiel 28:11–19. Genesis 2:24 apparently forms the backdrop for Malachi 2:15. A number of English translations prefer the personal name "Adam" in Hosea 6:7 (ASV, NASB–updated 1995, ESV, HCSB, NLT, NIV–1984; cp. "at Adam" in NRSV, NIV–2011, TNIV, NET).[68] Duane Garrett offers a potential interpretation allowing both a geographical and a theological association with Adam: "The prophet has made a pun on the name of the town and the name of the original transgressor. His meaning is, 'Like Adam (the man) they break covenants; they are faithless to me there (in the town of Adam).'"[69]

Additional references back to Genesis 1–11 in the remainder of the Hebrew Bible could fill the space allotted for this essay (e.g., Deut. 32:8; Isa. 45:12, 18; Mal. 2:10; Eccl. 3:20; 7:20, 29; 12:7; Job 31:33; Prov. 3:18; 11:30; 13:12; etc.). All of these references indicate an acceptance of the historical reality of events recorded in the early chapters of Genesis.

A noteworthy reference to Adam occurs at the start of 1 Chronicles, the final book of the Hebrew Bible. Genealogies commencing with Adam both open the Hebrew Bible (Gen. 1:26–27 and, especially, 5:1)

---

68. See Collins, *Genesis 1–4*, 113. Francis I. Andersen and David Noel Freedman, in *Hosea: A New Translation with Introduction and Commentary*, AYBS 24 (New Haven: Yale University Press, 2008), 437–39, provide detailed argumentation contrary to "like Adam."
69. Duane A. Garrett, *Hosea, Joel*, NAC (Nashville: Broadman & Holman, 1997), 163.

and close the Hebrew Bible (1 Chron. 1:1). The final compiler evidently observes this element contributing to the overall structure of the biblical record. Jesus himself also takes note of this bracketing of the Hebrew Bible by distinct parallels when he refers to the death of Abel and the death of Zechariah (Luke 11:50–51). Jesus even identifies the Hebrew Bible as having preserved an accurate historical record of the killing of prophets "since the beginning of the world" (a reference to the proximity of creation to the first murder in the early chapters of Genesis). As Eugene Merrill points out, the reason Genesis and 1 Chronicles make the connection of Adam to Israel is that "Israel could arrive at an accurate self-perception only by understanding its place in relationship to the first parents and, indeed, to creation itself."[70]

New Testament Evidence

Under the heading "The New Testament Appropriation," Victor Hamilton examines the impact of Genesis 1–11 on numerous New Testament texts, noting again and again the New Testament writers' theological dependence on those early events.[71]

Consider the manner in which the gospel of Matthew commences with a genealogy and a heading saying essentially, "the book/record of the generations of Jesus Christ" (1:1; *biblos geneseōs 'Iēsou Christou*). That is exactly as the first Adam's genealogy begins in Genesis 5:1 (NASB): "This is the book [record] of the generations of Adam" (*zeh sēper tōlĕdōt 'ādām*). No other *toledot* formula in Genesis contains a reference to "book," and that *toledot* relates most intimately to creation and the first man. Since Matthew makes such connections, it should be no surprise that Paul identifies Jesus as the "last Adam" (1 Cor. 15:45). Luke 3:38 also refers to Adam by name in the genealogy of Christ that concludes, "the son of Enosh, the son of Seth, the son of Adam, the son of God." There is no reason to take the name of Adam any differently from any other name in the entire genealogy as being anything but a real person (including God himself).

---

70. Eugene H. Merrill, *Everlasting Dominion: A Theology of the Old Testament* (Nashville: B&H Publishing Group, 2006), 167.

71. Hamilton, *The Book of Genesis Chapters 1–17*, NICOT, 144–50, 182–85, and 212–18 with regard to Genesis 1–3 alone.

Paul's message on Mars Hill specifies that God created all mankind over the entire surface of the planet from but one man (Acts 17:26). Denial of the truth of Paul's declaration places suspicion on all that Paul says and on the foundation for his preaching in regard to universal sin and God's program of redemption.[72] The historical individuality of Adam as the parent of the race forms the basis of New Testament theology. A mere archetype[73] cannot fulfill the same textually and theologically significant role.

As Hamilton observes, Romans 5:12–21 and 1 Corinthians 15:21–22, 45–49 make "an unmistakable connection between Adam and Christ."[74] Paul's argumentation appears to be consistently historical in nature. In other words, he appeals to historical facts as he reads them in the book of Genesis. Donald MacDonald expresses the traditional understanding of New Testament argumentation:

> But it is not as a bare historical fact that the New Testament views the unity of mankind; it is the very foundation of the cardinal doctrine of Christianity—the atonement through Christ. It is on the assumption that all men are descended from the first Adam and are involved in his guilt that the atonement proceeds and that the offers addressed to sinners of the blessings are procured by the second Adam, the new head of *humanity* (Rom. 5:14, 19). The denial of this doctrine, then, involves more than the rejection of so-called Hebrew myths. It is practically a rejection of Christianity and, in

---

72. A reader might argue that Paul spoke of Noah instead of Adam. After all, all post-flood nations did arise from him, not Adam. However, the vast array of commentators overwhelmingly understand it as a reference to Adam, because (1) Paul begins with the creation of the world and all that is in it (Acts 17:24); (2) the apostle speaks of God as the one who "gives everyone life and breath" (v. 25; cf. Gen. 2:7); (3) on "the whole earth" (v. 26) represents the Hebrew used in Genesis 2:6 and 11:8; (4) God ordered the seasons and the zones of the planet that are habitable by mankind (v. 26; cf. Gen. 1:14); and (5) "since we are God's offspring [*genos*]" (v. 29) finds a close conceptual parallel in Luke's genealogy ("the son of Adam, the son of God," Luke 3:38).

Paul's address proposes that God is the Maker of all nations because "they are one in their common ancestry and in their relationship to their Creator"—John B. Polhill, *Acts*, NAC 26 (Nashville: Broadman & Holman, 1995), 374. See also Joseph A. Fitzmyer, *The Acts of the Apostles: A New Translation with Introduction and Commentary*, AYBS 31 (New Haven: Yale University Press, 2008), 607–11.

73. The view of John H. Walton, "Genesis," in *ZIBBC*, 5 vols., ed. by John H. Walton (Grand Rapids: Zondervan, 2009), 1:27, regarding the Genesis 2–3 references to Adam and Eve.

74. Hamilton, *The Book of Genesis Chapters 1–17*, NICOT, 212.

a personal point of view, raises doubts that on this theory are from their nature incapable of solution. For, if there be any tribe not descended from Adam, how can any individuals assure himself or those around them of this connexion [sic!], and so of any title to participate in the blessings of the gospel?[75]

The issue in Romans 5 involves the biblical concepts of sin and death. Before going further, we must define what we mean (or, what the Bible means) by sin. According to a brief analysis of biblical terms for sin, it consists of "lawlessness" (*anomia*, 1 John 3:4), "unrighteousness" (*adikia*, Rom. 3:5), "ungodliness" or "godlessness" (*asebeia*, Rom. 11:26), willful "ignorance" (*agnoia*, Eph. 4:18), "missing the mark" or "sin" (*hamartia*, Rom. 3:23), "trespass" (*paraptoma*, Rom. 5:15), "transgression" (*parabasis*, Rom. 4:15), and "disobedience" (*parakoē*, Rom. 5:19). Note the employment of the alpha-privative as part of the formation of the first four terms (*anomia*, *adikia*, *asebeia*, and *agnoia*). These four terms focus on the contrastive nature of sin when held up to the nature and will of a holy God. Sin is inherently unlike God and anti-God. The use of the preposition *para* with the final three terms emphasizes the aspect of contrary behavior that willfully passes over the moral boundary marked out by God and His Word. Sin is rebellion against the clearly understood command of God. Scripture teaches[76] the following:

• Sin is a failure to glorify God.
• Sin consists of active rebellion against God's established standards.
• Sin is both a state of being and an act of the human will.
• Sin is moral evil.
• Sin can only be defined in the context of the God of the Bible and his character.
• Sin is not an inherent aspect of the created order.

Sin and its consequences (including spiritual, physical, and eternal death) enter the created order through the willful transgression of Adam (Rom. 5:12). As such, *the biblical description of sin depends entirely on the*

---

75. Donald MacDonald, *Creation and Fall: A Defence and Exposition of the First Three Chapters of Genesis* (Edinburgh: Thomas Constable and Co., 1856), 373.

76. The bullet points that follow are adapted from Mahoney, "Why an Historical Adam Matters for a Biblical Doctrine of Sin," 61–64.

historicity of Adam. He must be a real individual who rebels against a clear divine directive at a specific moment in real time in a real place.

Some scholars, to the contrary, argue that Paul's view of Adam depended on "the assumptions and conventions held by other Jewish interpreters at that time."[77] As the argument goes, the influence of Jewish tradition on Paul's interpretation of the Old Testament compares well with the way modern Christians receive a traditional telling of the Christmas story that inserts elements not actually found in the biblical account.[78] However, this approach fails to give adequate attention to the role of the Holy Spirit in superintending the writing of the biblical books, preserving them from just such error.

The fact is that Paul actually proclaimed a message that was obviously unacceptable to the Jewish rabbis of his day; otherwise they would not have sought to silence him. Paul was not colored by the erroneous rabbinic teachings of his day. Like Jesus,[79] he spoke of the accuracy and integrity of the biblical account of creation and the messianic prophecies, unlike first-century Judaism.

Moreover, Adam must be a completely righteous person, bearing the image of God, who succumbs to a specific temptation from outside his own person and who represents the entire human race.[80] This representation consists of something more than viewing the events and people of Genesis 1–3 as archetypal, as solely theological lessons for us.[81] Many Christians claim that it makes no difference whether Adam and Eve were historical persons or mere archetypes, because they believe the theological outcome is the same.[82] Perhaps the doctrine of man remains

---

77. Enns, *The Evolution of Adam*, 95.

78. Ibid., 114.

79. Some scholars might object and say that the gospel writers present their accounts as men living in a pre-scientific world equally influenced by contemporary Jewish thought. If the Evangelists wrongly believed that Adam was the original head of the human race, why is there any reason to trust anything they report with regard to Jesus? That places in doubt their reporting on Jesus' genealogy, his miracles, his teaching, and his resurrection. Science denies the miraculous and supernatural, so the entire biblical history of Jesus becomes suspicious and in need of demythologization.

80. See Mahoney, "Why an Historical Adam Matters for a Biblical Doctrine of Sin," 71–75, for a superbly detailed discussion of these matters as they relate to the historicity of Adam.

81. According to Gowan, in *From Eden to Babel*, 36, the author/composer of the J (Yahwist) document may have held an archetypal view of Genesis 2–3.

82. E.g., Gareth Weldon Icenogle, *Biblical Foundations for Small Group Ministry: An Integrative Approach* (Downers Grove, IL: InterVarsity Press, 1993), 276.

the same, but this approach has serious implications for the doctrine of Scripture and the doctrine of Christ.

Since God promises in his Word to restore the descendants of the first Adam through the substitutionary sacrifice of the second Adam (Jesus Christ), the issue of the historicity of Adam has soteriological implications. According to the apostle Paul,

> Therefore, just as sin entered the world through one man, and death through sin, and in this way death came to all people, because all sinned—
>
> To be sure, sin was in the world before the law was given, but sin is not charged against anyone's account where there is no law. Nevertheless, death reigned from the time of Adam to the time of Moses, even over those who did not sin by breaking a command, as did Adam, who is a pattern of the one to come.
>
> But the gift is not like the trespass. For if the many died by the trespass of the one man, how much more did God's grace and the gift that came by the grace of the one man, Jesus Christ, overflow to the many! (Rom. 5:12–15

John Mahoney articulates the matter in the following way: "If the first man is not historical and the fall into sin is not historical, then one begins to wonder why there is a need for our Lord to come and undo the work of the first man."[83] *That makes the historicity of Adam a gospel issue.* Many scholars also dispute the bodily resurrection of Jesus from the dead, making basically the same arguments employed against a historical Adam. They claim that resurrection is scientifically impossible and that rational people cannot accept such a religious concept. Listen to what Paul had to say about rejecting the resurrection of Christ:

> And if Christ has not been raised, our preaching is useless and so is your faith. More than that, we are then found to be false witnesses about God, for we have testified about God that he raised Christ from the dead. But he did not raise him if in fact the dead are not raised. For if the dead are not raised, then Christ has not been raised either. And if Christ has not been raised, your faith is futile; you are still in your sins. Then those also who have fallen asleep in

---

83. Mahoney, "Why an Historical Adam Matters for a Biblical Doctrine of Sin," 76.

Christ are lost. If only for this life we have hope in Christ, we are of all people most to be pitied. (1 Cor. 15:14–19)

It is no accident or mere coincidence that Paul addresses the issue of Adam in the same context (1 Cor. 15:21–22, 45–49). The implication is inescapable: *Denial of the historicity of Adam, like denial of the historicity of Christ's resurrection, destroys the foundations of the Christian faith.*

Concluding Thoughts

Why do some students of Scripture abandon a traditional view of Adam and refuse to accept the biblical text's testimony as historically accurate? In one word, evolution—the scientific theory of evolution for both the origins of the material universe and the forms of life that inhabit our planet.[84] In Enns' words, "If evolution is correct, one can no longer accept, in any true sense of the word 'historical,' the instantaneous and special creation of humanity described in Genesis, specifically 1:26–31 and 2:7, 22."[85]

Another reason some propose for abandoning the biblical record of mankind's origins resides in the scholarly preference for identifying the ancient Near Eastern myths (such as Enuma Elish) as the prototype

---

84. According to Enns, in *The Evolution of Adam*, xiv: "Evolution, however, is a game changer. The general science-and-faith rapprochement is not adequate because evolution uniquely strikes at central issues of the Christian faith." Rather than take Enns's position ("evolution requires us to revisit how the Bible thinks of human origins"; ibid., 82), I would argue that it is the Bible that requires that we rethink evolution. The difference rests upon a different priority. In spite of his occasional attempt at a disclaimer, Enns comes across as holding to the priority of modern science.

The issue is one of *primary* authority. The undergirding antagonism of young-earth creationists to the *theory* (something rarely remembered today) of evolution arises from a high view of Scripture. Our theological reasoning runs thus: God is true, therefore God's Words are true; God is trustworthy, therefore God's Words are trustworthy; God is without error, therefore God's Words are without error.

And what of science? (1) Methods don't make truth claims; human beings using the methods are the ones making truth claims, and interpreters can be mistaken. (2) Origin science differs from operation science. Origin science functions like forensic science used in criminal investigations, when one must properly interpret circumstantial evidence. (3) Uniformitarian assumptions heavily influence secular geologists, who interpret the evidence through anti-biblical and pro-evolution lenses. (4) Science changes; it is not constant, but dynamic. The science of today is not the science of your great-grandfather, and the science of your great-grandchild will not be the science you know today. The Bible, on the other hand, presents the unchanging testimony of the only eyewitness to creation, the Creator himself. Only God's view is objectively true and perfect.

85. Ibid.

for Israel's creation account.[86] However, those scholars assume that the biblical account originated with Moses, and they often summarily reject any concept of Moses' employment of older records[87] unrelated to the Mesopotamian myths. What if Genesis 1–3 represents the original account that the later Mesopotamian materials skewed and spun to their own particular purposes, rewriting the factual record?[88]

Similarities between the Israelite and the Mesopotamian materials need not require Israelite dependence on the Mesopotamian. Past and present scholars sometimes overstate the similarities while understating the differences. Genesis 1 does not offer a specific or direct ideological polemic. The biblical account of creation contains no description of God at war in any cosmic conflict among the gods, nor any victory enthronement motif, as one sees with these ancient Near Eastern myths.[89] With these absent elements in mind, Bill T. Arnold concludes that "Israel's God has no rivals.... There can be no enthronement portrait here because God has not *become* sovereign; he has simply never been *less than* sovereign."[90] With regard to the historicity of the biblical Adam, the Genesis account distinguishes itself from the ancient Near Eastern stories by the clear declaration that God created only one human pair (monogenesis) as compared to the polygenistic beliefs of other ancient peoples in the region.[91] Evangelicals should uphold and defend that

---

86. Ibid., 39.

87. Nahum M. Sarna, in *Genesis*, JPS Torah Commentary (Philadelphia: Jewish Publication Society, 1989), 41, and Ross, in *Creation and Blessing*, 35, both deem it reasonable that the writer (Ross specifies Moses) used ancient records.

88. Walton, in *Genesis*, NIVAC, 319, makes a similar point regarding the extrabiblical flood stories: "Yet the possibility cannot be ruled out that the Genesis account is a pristine record of the event as passed down from Noah, which suffered corruption when transmitted in the hands of other cultures."

89. The characteristics that make the ancient Near Eastern accounts of creation mythological as opposed to the characteristics of the biblical account are as follows: (1) polytheism versus monotheism, (2) representation of the gods by means of physical images versus iconoclasm, (3) the existence of eternal matter versus Spirit as the first principle, (4) a low view of the gods versus a high view of God, (5) the everlasting conflict between the forces of chaos and the forces of construction versus an absence of conflict in the original creation, (6) a low view of humanity versus a high view of humanity, and (7) lack of a uniform standard of ethics versus expectation of ethical obedience to a uniform standard. These are an adaptation and summary of some of the distinguishing characteristics presented by John N. Oswalt, *The Bible among the Myths* (Grand Rapids: Zondervan, 2009), 57–84.

90. Arnold, *Genesis*, NCBC, 32. Collins, in *Did Adam and Eve Really Exist?*, 153–57, discusses this issue at some length. See also Kitchen, *On the Reliability of the Old Testament*, 424–25.

91. Walton, "Genesis," in *ZIBBC*, 1:26.

uniqueness as one of the key indicators that the Genesis record should have priority in all discussions of primeval history.

Why persist in identifying the apparent similarities between biblical and extrabiblical materials as some sort of literary borrowing? Why continue to associate the biblical account so closely with the conceptual milieu of the Mesopotamian culture?[92] Might the similarities provide evidence of a shared historical memory based on a shared (originally singular) revelation? If so, then the Mesopotamian cultural myths might derive their core concepts from divine revelation.[93] As Enns notes, the differences between the extrabiblical myths and the biblical accounts of both creation and the flood do, indeed, reflect theological differences.[94] However, the chief theological disharmony involves the concept of direct divine revelation and the conviction of the biblical writers that God's supernatural revelation preserves his own witness to the events for which there were no human eyewitnesses.[95] One of the reasons that the God of Israel is greater than the gods of the nations rests with his ability to supernaturally reveal historical truth from the far distant past and from the distant future—both unknown to the human recipient of the revelation (cf. Isa. 45:12, 18–19; 46:10–11; 48:3–8, 12–16).[96]

Walton notes that extant extrabiblical materials offer no help in either defending or contradicting the historicity of Adam and Eve,[97]

---

92. E.g., Enns, *The Evolution of Adam*, 40–41.

93. Jeffrey J. Niehaus, in *Ancient Near Eastern Themes in Biblical Theology* (Grand Rapids: Kregel Academic & Professional, 2008), 21–33, argues that both the ancient Near Eastern and biblical accounts of creation and flood flow from a common source.

94. Enns, *The Evolution of Adam*, 50.

95. Those who reject this focus on God's eyewitness account through special revelation possess a different worldview founded upon a more mechanistic approach to natural or physical laws. The traditional young-earth creationist worldview holds to a personal God who is superior to the regularities that scientists investigate and who governs the world in such a manner that he can choose to intervene in natural processes or to contravene the natural order in his own personal wisdom. See the discussion of worldview conflicts between science and the Bible by Vern Sheridan Poythress, in *Inerrancy and Worldview: Answering Modern Challenges to the Bible* (Wheaton, IL: Crossway, 2012), 34–42.

96. Of course, scholars who question this understanding point to their opinion that Isaiah did not write these words, so the later writer's prophecies develop after the fact (*vaticinia ex eventu*). A lower view of divine omnipotence and omniscience becomes entangled with the reinterpretation of Isaiah's prophecies as well as of the contents of Genesis 1–11. Scholars who still uphold the integrity of true prophetic revelation of future events might argue, however, that the statements in Isaiah smack of hyperbole and exaggeration that ought not to be taken literally.

97. Walton, *Genesis*, NIVAC, 47.

so it does little good to appeal to those materials in regard to the issue at hand. In other words, the full gamut of viewpoints contradicting the traditional view of a historical Adam are nothing more than speculation in the interest of seeking a way to harmonize the Bible and the evolutionary views held by the majority of scientists.

When the reader of the Bible accepts extrabiblical evidence (whether from ancient Near Eastern documentation or from modern scientists' interpretation of circumstantial evidence) over the biblical record, that denigrates the biblical record and treats it with skepticism rather than as *prima facie* evidence. In other words, we err when we assume that any major interpretive problem is due to a lack of accuracy within the text itself. We should assume that the Scriptures are accurate until proven otherwise by equally accurate, equally authentic, and equally ancient evidence.

Does the issue of genre have an impact on the historicity of the Genesis account regarding the creation of mankind? Enns rightly reminds his readers that "narrative is not an automatic indication of historical veracity, either in the Bible or any other literature, ancient or modern."[98] In similar fashion, we might say that poetry provides no automatic confirmation of a lack of historical veracity. Collins goes so far as to declare that the presence of anachronism within any account does not prevent the text from referring to actual events in history.[99]

Nonbiblical examples of narrative prose literature without historical veracity include works of fiction. Poetry that conveys accurate historical descriptions of true events include biblical poems such as Exodus 15 (the "Song of Moses") and Judges 5 (the "Song of Deborah"), among others. Without argument, Psalm 104 contains poetic descriptions of creation events. The imagery and metaphors of such poetry must be understood for being just that—no one takes a figurative expression such as "He walks upon the wings of the wind" (Ps. 104:3 NASB) to mean that God has legs and the wind actually has wings. Properly interpreting such wording requires recognition of the figures of speech.

Catalysts for these historical poems arise out of the actual historical events themselves. Even the ancient myths carry a seed of historical truth; one or more historical events often provide the basis for their

---

98. Enns, *The Evolution of Adam*, 53.
99. Collins, *Did Adam and Eve Really Exist?*, 113–14.

composition. Myths, however, skew the original events and revise them according to the fallen imagination of fallen human beings. Speaking God-given truth sets the biblical record apart from the pagan myths.

With all these observations in mind, the issue of genre actually acts as a red herring in this discussion. Whether Genesis 1 is poetry or narrative, the text conveys accurate historical truth, and an actual historical event comprises the basis for the record. Of course, some traditionalists would argue that genre definitions and identifications tend to be subjective and often directed by secular motives.[100] However, we need not jettison legitimate literary analysis and recognition of different types of literature in order to reach the conclusion that Adam is a real, historical figure—the first human being and father of all mankind.

The traditional viewpoint regarding the historicity of Adam chooses to stick primarily to the testimony of the biblical text. However, due to the argumentation used by those who adapt their interpretation of the text to current scientific opinion, we believe it necessary to respond in kind. If the opposition to the traditional view appeals to science, then the traditionalists must also deal with the issues thus raised—in the realm of science. We must remember that declarations by scientists represent their interpretation of the evidence, not the evidence itself. Science changes, the Scripture does not. But that is a matter for another essay or volume.

Walton provides the best words with which to bring this essay to a close: "We need to defend the teaching of the text, not a scientific reconstruction of the text or statements that are read between the lines of the text."[101]

---

100. E.g., Jeremiah Loubet, "Genre Override in Genesis 1–2," *Journal of Dispensational Theology* 15 (Dec. 2011): 79.

101. Cf. Walton, *Genesis*, NIVAC, 100. I realize that this maxim cuts two ways—including the science of both old-earth and young-earth creationists.

DENIS O. LAMOUREUX

I have not had the pleasure of meeting William Barrick, but I look forward to it someday. In reading his chapter I found his love for the Lord and Scripture to be palpable. He also reminded me of my young-earth creationist years when I used roughly 90 percent of his arguments. Of course, my position has since changed, but it was not because of an "accommodation to evolutionary science" (p. 197). When I rejected young-earth creation, I remained a staunch anti-evolutionist. In my book *Evolutionary Creation* I revealed, "Ironically, the evidence in Scripture undermined my vision of becoming a creation scientist. After three years of focusing on Genesis 1–11 [at seminary], I concluded that young earth creation is un-biblical."[102]

Sin without a Historical Adam

Barrick offers an excellent summary of the reality and meaning of sin. He lists:

- Sin is a failure to glorify God.
- Sin consists of active rebellion against God's established standards.
- Sin is both a state of being and an act of the human will.
- Sin is moral evil.
- Sin can only be defined in the context of the God of the Bible and his character.
- Sin is not an inherent aspect of the created order (p. 220).

Barrick concludes, "Sin and its consequences (including spiritual, physical, and eternal death) enter the created order through the willful

---

102. *Evolutionary Creation: A Christian Approach to Evolution* (Eugene, OR: Wipf & Stock, 2008), 351.

transgression of Adam (Rom. 5:12). As such, *the biblical description of sin depends entirely on the historicity of Adam*" (p. 220–21, italics original).

But does the reality of sin "*depend entirely*" on a historical Adam? My answer is "no." In fact, notice that there is no mention of Adam in Barrick's list above. As I stated in my chapter, I suspect the entrance of sin "coincides with the appearance of behaviorally modern humans about 50,000 years ago" (p. 64). In other words, I believe in the reality of sin and that it entered the world, but not through Adam.

Barrick also contends that "without a historical first Adam there is no need for Jesus" (p. 197). He then concludes, "*That makes the historicity of Adam a gospel issue* ... The implication is inescapable: "*Denial of the historicity of Adam, like denial of the historicity of Christ's resurrection, destroys the foundations of the Christian faith*" (p. 223, italics original).

Most readers will have identified Barrick's strategy. He attempts to conflate "the historicity of Adam" with "the historicity of Christ's resurrection." However, these are two entirely separate issues. In my chapter I wrote, "Do the Gospels report eyewitness accounts of actual historical events, including the Lord's teaching and miracles, and especially His physical resurrection from the dead? *Absolutely yes!* Even though I do not believe that Adam was historical, I thoroughly believe in the historicity of Jesus and the biblical testimonies of His life" (p. 44).

Barrick magnifies his conflation by telling his readers, "Listen to what Paul had to say about rejecting the resurrection of Christ: ..." (p. 222). He then cites 1 Corinthians 15:14–19. But if Barrick had "listen[ed] to what Paul had to say" regarding what constitutes the gospel in that very same chapter, he would recognize that the historicity of Adam is *not* a gospel issue. Paul writes, "I want to remind you of the *gospel* ... that Christ died for our sins according to the Scriptures, that he was buried, that he was raised on the third day according to the Scriptures, and that he appeared to Peter, and then to the Twelve" (1 Cor. 15:1, 3–5, my italics).

The gospel is about Jesus Christ, not Adam. The gospel is about the reality of sin, not how sin entered the world. The gospel is about Jesus dying on the cross for our sins, not specifically Adam's sin. And it is because of the gospel that we are called "Christ-ians" and not "Adam-ites."

230 FOUR VIEWS ON THE HISTORICAL ADAM

"An Objective Description" of Origins

According to Barrick, "[T]he Holy Spirit superintended the author of Genesis so that he wrote an *objective* description of God's creative activities in six consecutive literal days.... In other words, by taking a detailed, step-by-step, *objective* tone the author reveals everything just as it actually happened" (pp. 197, 202, my italics). Clearly, Barrick is a scientific concordist, and for him the Bible is a book of science.

However, it is not possible to align Scripture with modern scientific facts for one simple reason: The Bible has an ancient understanding of science. The best example is the creation of the heavens on the second and fourth days of creation in Genesis 1. Scripture states that God created the firmament to separate the heavenly sea from the earthly sea (day two), and then He placed the sun, moon, and stars in the firmament (day four). Of course, no one today believes this is how the universe is structured. Therefore, this biblical passage is not "an objective description of God's creative activities" in forming the heavens.

Barrick makes no mention of the divine creative events on creation days two and four. Nor does he deal directly with the very words in the Word of God referring to the firmament or the heavenly sea. Barrick cites my paper on this topic and brushes it off in one sentence (p. 200, fn. 11). His pointed criticism of Peter Enns is in effect a criticism of my views.

> Enns's characterization of Israelite beliefs (e.g., a flat earth) consists of *overstatement* and *misinterpretation* that *denigrate* both true believers in ancient Israel and the current biblical text. Beyond that, his characterization of the ancient Near Eastern conceptual world as riddled with pre-scientific error that God himself adopted in inspired Scripture *impugns God's moral integrity* (p. 202, my italics).

Comments such as these do not encourage respectful dialogue. This is not a logical argument, but an emotional outburst. If the Holy Spirit descended to the level of the biblical writers and used their ancient science as an incidental vessel to deliver inerrant spiritual truths, then that was the Lord's decision, whether we like it or not. This accommodation does not "denigrate" Scripture or ancient believers, nor does it "impugn God's moral integrity." Instead, divine accommodation reveals the Creator's amazing grace in communicating to finite sinful creatures.

The Fossil Pattern Prediction of Young-Earth Creation

Science involves formulating theories and testing them against the facts. Since Barrick contends that Genesis 1 is "an objective description" of origins, we can compare the fossil pattern predicted by his view of origins to the actual fossil pattern in the geological record. This test does not require any assumptions about the age of the earth. It merely uses the sequential order in which different fossils appear in the crust of the earth.

Figure 1 (top) presents the fossil pattern prediction of young-earth creation. This position asserts that the universe and life were created in one week. Soon afterward, sin entered the world and with it physical death for humans and all other living organisms. Therefore, at the bottom of the geological record there should be remains of every creature, including all extinct animals. Notably, dinosaurs and humans should appear together at the base of the fossil record. Young-earth creation predicts a Creation Basal Layer.

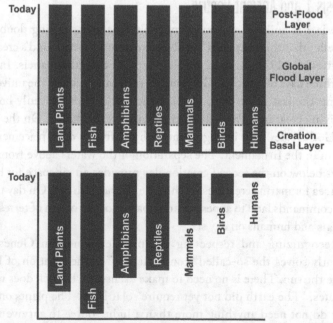

Figure 1. Fossil pattern prediction of young-earth creation (top) and the fossil record (bottom).

Young-earth creationists believe Noah's flood was worldwide. Consequently, this position predicts a Global Flood Layer in the middle of the geological record with the mixing together of every animal and plant ever created.

After the flood, God called Noah's family and all the animals to "be fruitful" and "multiply on earth" (Gen. 8:17). Note that God does not say to the dinosaurs, "Leave the ark and go extinct." In other words, dinosaurs should be here with us today. And since death is still in the world, young-earth creation predicts the accumulation of the bones of every creature ever created in a Post-Flood Layer.

Figure 1 (bottom) presents the actual pattern of fossils in the crust of the earth. The fossil pattern prediction of young-earth creation does not come close to the scientific facts. In fact, the geological record presents an evolutionary sequence with the appearance of fish, then amphibians, followed by reptiles (from which birds descend), and then mammals with humans last.

Genesis 1 and Ancient Poetry

Genesis 1 is built on an ancient poetic framework, casting doubt on the belief that this chapter is "an objective description of God's creative activities" (p. 197). Figure 2 displays a pair of parallel panels. In the first three days of creation, God defines the boundaries of the universe. During the last three days, He fills the world with heavenly bodies and living creatures. Parallels emerge between the panels. On the first day, God creates light in alignment with the fourth day's placement of the sun in the firmament. The separation of the waters above from the waters below on the second creation day provides an air space for birds and a sea for marine creatures, both made on the fifth day. On day three God commands land to appear in anticipation of the origin of terrestrial animals and humans on day six.

Recognizing and respecting the parallel panels in Genesis 1 instantly solves the so-called "contradiction" of the creation of light before the sun. There is no need to make excuses as Barrick does when he states, "The earth did not yet require solar light. The plants on day three do not need anything more than a light source to survive their first full day of existence" (p. 206). The parallel panels in Genesis 1 are

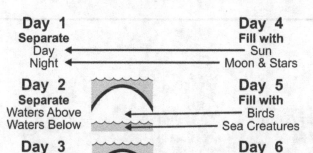

Figure 2. Genesis 1 parallel panels.

evidence *within Scripture itself* of poetic license, and they indicate that the biblical author never intended to offer a list of divine creative acts in a chronological sequence, as Barrick proposes.

Christian Tradition Is *Not* Inerrant

Barrick repeatedly points out that the "traditional" Christian view upholds a historical Adam. I value Christian tradition, but tradition is not inerrant. Only Scripture is inerrant.

Let me offer an example. Protestant Reformer Martin Luther played an important role in the later development of evangelical Christianity. He was a young-earth creationist who stated, "We know from Moses that the world was not in existence before 6000 years ago.... [it] was created in six days."[103] Luther's 1534 Bible translation features a diagram of the universe across from Genesis 1. Figure 3 reveals that he accepted a spherical earth at the center of the universe (geocentricity); a spherical firmament embedded with the sun, moon, and stars; and a heavenly sea above the firmament.

Luther definitely believed that this was the actual structure of the universe. He argued,

> Scripture ... simply says that the moon, the sun, and the stars were placed ... in the firmament of the heaven (below and above which

---

103. Martin Luther, *Luther's Works: Lectures on Genesis*, ed. and trans. J. Pelikan (1536; St. Louis: Concordia, 1958), 3, 5.

Figure 3. Martin Luther's universe.

are the waters).... The bodies of the stars, like that of the sun, are
round, and they are fastened to the firmament like globes of fire....
We Christians must, therefore, be different from the philosophers
in the way we think about the causes of things. And if some are
beyond our comprehension (like those before us concerning the
waters above the heavens), we must believe them ... rather than
wickedly deny them or *presumptuously* interpret them in conformity
with our understanding.[104]

Are Christians today "wicked" or "presumptuous" for not believing in a heavenly sea? The *traditional* Christian position regarding the
structure of the heavens for more than 1,500 years accepted a firmament and a heavenly sea above it. If Barrick wants to appeal to tradition
regarding Adam, then to be consistent he should also believe in this
ancient astronomy.

But if we recognize that Christian tradition is similar to Scripture
in that it includes ancient science, then we can separate the inerrant
spiritual truths from their incidental ancient vessels. In this way we will
no longer conflate the historical Adam of Christian tradition with the
biblical revelations that God created us in His Image and that we are all
sinners in need of a Savior—the Lord Jesus Christ.

---

104. Ibid., 30, 42–3; my italics.

JOHN H. WALTON

I found myself in agreement with many of the points that William Barrick has made. I affirm that Adam and Eve were real people in a real past and that the fall was a historical event. I strongly support inerrancy as well as all the other aspects of a robust evangelical doctrine of Scripture. I give the text priority over both science and literature from the ancient Near East. But of course, our responses are designed to discuss further the things that differentiate us, and I now turn to that task.

The objections that I have to Barrick's treatment concern his methods and his rhetoric. I will deal with these in ten categories.

1. Barrick spent more time refuting others rather than offering the evidence to advance his own case.

In many cases the positions that he was refuting were not those held in this book, so it did not advance the conversation taking place here. This is particularly unfortunate when he appears to include everyone who disagrees with him together, even when it would be questionable whether anyone in this book is characterized by the thinking that he is denigrating. For example, most of us in this book do not "accommodate to evolutionary theory," and none of us deny the role of the Holy Spirit—both items identifying his distinct position in the opening summary of his position.

In this category, his arguments against the documentary hypothesis (p. 200) accomplish nothing in the discussion of this book, for none of us are depending on that theory of composition. As another example, his second description of traditionalism states that "accuracy of Scripture's account of creation does not depend on confirmation of its events through extrabiblical sources" (p. 200). None of us is suggesting that such confirmation is needed. We might expect that at places the biblical cognitive environment may reflect that of the ancient world, but in that case we are identifying how they coincide. That is nothing close to the way that Barrick makes his case. On page 203 Barrick states, "In their approach, science and ancient Near Eastern texts trump simple acceptance of the sufficiency and historical accuracy of those early chapters of Genesis." This is a misrepresentation. Certainly there are some out there for whom science or ANE can trump the biblical text. But that is not the only kind of thinking that might lead people to arrive at a different conclusion than Barrick. It is simply too facile to claim that everyone who disagrees with him has prioritized science or ANE over Scripture.

Barrick spends a lot of time arguing against Peter Enns and others more radical than him. All of us have arguments we might make against all sorts of positions out there. But it would be wrong for readers to assume that Barrick's arguments against Enns carry any weight in the discussion of this book. It would have been preferable for him to spend his time offering evidence for his own position.

It is most unfortunate when his arguments against other positions shows misunderstanding of the position that he is refuting. For example, his discussion of Evolution and Evolutionary Creation (pp. 210 ff.) show serious misunderstanding of what those positions hold. Effective refutation is not possible if the position is misunderstood or caricatured.

2. Barrick consistently misunderstood or misrepresented the concept of archetype.

The misunderstanding and misrepresentation is most evident in the way that he interacts with my "archetype" view. On page 198 he equates "archetypal" with "allegorical," a significant misrepresentation. Allegorical interpretation intentionally neglects what the *human* author of Scripture intended in favor of what the interpreter's imagination says about what *God* intended. In contrast, my archetypal approach only has validity if this is how the biblical author understood it, and I have sought to demonstrate that indeed the author does. The psalmist and Paul both insist that we are all formed from dust. Thus the biblical authors propose the archetype, not me. And, of course, I do not use "archetypal" as an alternative to "historical" Adam and Eve. There is nothing allegorical about this.

At another point, Barrick believes he is refuting an archetypal view by suggesting events in the narrative that do not happen to everyone (p. 222). The nature of archetypal connection doesn't suggest that something *happens* to everyone; rather, it describes the *nature* of everyone: we are gendered; halves of an original whole. By his numeration of all the things that must refer to individuals rather than to all human beings, he demonstrates his lack of understanding of the archetypal position. Specifically, the position I present identifies the "forming" accounts as archetypal—not everything in the chapter.

The way we determine what is archetypal and what is not is by asking the question whether it does or does not refer to everyone. If it does not refer to everyone, it is not archetypal. In this case his arguments accomplish nothing. But all people are formed from dust—the Bible says this (Ps. 103:14; 1 Cor. 15:48). Genesis 2:24 clearly articulates an archetypal application in its wording.

When Barrick states that "A mere archetype cannot fulfill the same textually and theologically significant role" (p. 219), this again misrepresents my position. I never claim Adam to be a "mere" archetype; instead, I suggest that certain aspects are archetypal. Paul does no differently, for when he speaks of the "first Adam," he is treating him archetypally as he represents all of us.

By the time he gets to page 221 Barrick is suggesting that an archetypal interpretation offers "solely theological lessons for us." He has not comprehended that the archetypal issues are ontological in nature and, as such, are more than theological lessons. When he continues that "Many Christians claim that it makes no difference whether Adam and Eve were historical persons or mere archetypes, because they believe the theological outcome is the same," he does not represent what I mean by archetype. Archetypal treatment is not mutually exclusive with historicity. If one wishes to refute an argument, one must be careful not to misrepresent it.

3. Barrick at times resorted to slippery slope scare tactics.

I will say little about this one, but the suggestion that "if you accept X, then X will inevitably lead to Y and eventually to Z" can easily be oversimplification. Often there are many obstacles and methodological distinctions that would prevent the whole chain from unfolding. It is an overstatement to claim that if you believe X, you will soon reject the resurrection or you cannot be called a Christian. Academic debate should not resort to such scare tactics and defamation.

4. Barrick tended just to state his conclusion as if it were the only possibility and obvious to anyone, yet did not offer evidence.

I believe that this is the most obvious and troubling shortcoming of his essay. One of the ways that this manifests itself is in the use of subjective language ("seems" or "appears"). In academic dialogue, it is not enough to indicate what seems right or accurate; one is obligated to demonstrate why others should be able to agree with what the speaker subjectively feels. In short, evidence is required.

Example #1: Barrick states that "Together with the global setting depicted by Genesis 1, such attention seems more fitting with regard to Adam being the progenitor of the human race" (p. 207). But where is his evidence? Genesis 2 has nothing to say about reproduction. He assumes that the problem of Adam being alone is that he cannot reproduce (p. 210). That is unlikely, not least because Adam and God first seek to resolve the problem by presenting the animals to him. We cannot therefore imagine that he is seeking a reproduction partner. When we take the context seriously, we see in verse 15 that Adam has been given a task—caring for sacred space. He needs an ally for this task. What "seems fitting" to Barrick can be refuted by evidence in the chapter.

Example #2: "The references to one individual man (Adam) and his one wife throughout the subsequent context (e.g., 2:24, 25; 3:1, 4, 6, 7) demonstrate that the biblical writer intends the reader to understand that these two are the parents of the entire human race and there are no others like them until they themselves have borne children (4:1–2). Furthermore, these first individuals cannot be the product of an evolutionary process. Such organisms (human beings) 'cannot be understood except as the products of a directly acting, purposeful intelligence'" (p. 212). In this case his conclusion does not flow logically from his "evidence." Beyond that he is just stating people's opinions as if they must be accepted as fact.

Example #3: In some cases we find Barrick just making claims without offering evidence: "The entire human race descends from Adam and Eve and is, therefore, Adamic. There are no pre- or extra-Adamic people(s). Adam, as the seminal (physical) head of the human race, presides also as the federal (legally representative) head of the human race. Even the first woman came from Adam—she possesses his DNA as altered by God at the time he formed her" (p. 213). He offers no evidence that the Bible actually makes the claims that he asserts.

Example #4: Barrick again just cites someone's opinion as if the stating of it makes it right: "As Collins argues, in order for mankind to be accountable for sin, there needs to be a common origin of all mankind in a state of goodness interrupted by voluntary rebellion" (p. 214). What about Paul's statement that "without the law there is no sin"? Maybe he has a way to mitigate that, but he should offer that instead of just relying on someone's statement. This is no way to construct an argument.

Example #5: Finally in this category, on pages 214–15, Barrick lists ten points that he believes Genesis 1–3 reveal. While I agree with many of these, one cannot think that simply by stating one's opinions you have proven them to be true. Others come to different conclusions with careful biblical exegesis and orthodox theology in place. Pontification does not constitute successful argumentation.

5. Barrick occasionally reflects unnuanced readings of some of the areas of investigation.

Here I will cite only one example that is evident in the way that Barrick refers to the evidence from the ancient Near East. He asserts that ANE material should not take precedence over the biblical material (e.g., on p. 223), and I agree. But that does not mean that the ANE literature has no role in understanding the biblical text. The question is not whether the biblical text is accurate (of course it is) — the question is whether we are reading the biblical text through our own modern (and therefore anachronistic) grid. Overall, Barrick talks as if anyone dealing with the ANE is doing so at the expense of the Bible. Barrick shows no recognition of the fact that nuanced use of the ANE is not interested in literary dependency.

6. Barrick bundles together issues that are not necessarily connected logically or that make logical jumps that ignore important alternatives.

He bundles together the historicity of Adam and Eve and the historicity of the fall with the questions of genetic ancestry and human material discontinuity. The issues do not necessarily all stand or fall together. The historicity of Adam and the fall may be foundational in all the areas he lists on page 199, but that all human beings are descended from Adam is not foundational to all of them.

Similarly, on pages 199 ff. Barrick assumes that an old-earth view can result only from accommodating Scripture to science. But there is a prior question: does Scripture claim that the earth is young? Likewise, when he deals with Eve's role in the temptation and fall, he immediately jumps to the issue of gender hierarchy (p. 214). It is difficult to derive the entire structure of society and ontological relationship of men and women from the incidental detail that God called out to Adam. This sort of jumping to far-reaching conclusions based on small and questionable observations shows a methodological flaw that is manifested too frequently in Barrick's argumentation.

As with many of the points Barrick makes about the historical Adam (e.g., p. 205), I would not disagree that Paul makes a connection between Adam and Jesus that supports a historical Adam. The question is whether anything that Paul says in the epistles claims material discontinuity or indicates that Adam was the first or only human. I am not suggesting Adam was *not* the first and only, nor am I arguing for material continuity; I am simply asking the question about what claims Paul is making or is not making. I am not interested in what Paul may or may not believe; I want to know what he is claiming with divinely given authority. The complexity of these issues demands that we build our case carefully. It is not sound argumentation just to quote someone who happens to agree with you (e.g., the MacDonald quote on p. 219).

7. Barrick is guilty of repeated logical non sequiturs.

Example #1: By his logic on page 212 that the relationship between man and woman applies only to Adam and Eve, one could easily end up with the idea that Adam and Eve must therefore have parents (Gen. 2:24) — since this supposedly refers only to them. If, in contrast, this verse refers to everyone, it demonstrates the archetypal nature of the account.

Example #2: Barrick suggests that the "image" and "likeness" that Seth receives "were transferred to Seth because of the fact that Adam had fathered him" (p. 216). That indeed has textual support. He then continues, "Could it be that parentage also transmits the Adamic sin? — more specifically, the male parent? Parentage being the clear connection in the transfer of the image of God lends itself to the concept of seminal headship rather than federal headship." This is very weak argumentation, as it depends first on a rhetorical question and then on a logical jump through speculation.

Example #3: "The genealogy commencing with Adam assumes that the image of God marks every individual as human. It indicates that all humans descend from one original pair" (p. 216). Yes, the image of God marks all human beings. The genealogies reinforce this, but Genesis 1 proves it. Nevertheless, the genealogy does not indicate that all people descended from Adam; it indicates that Adam's descendants descended from Adam.

Example #4: Finally in this category, he takes a statement that I make in previous works but then misapplies it. "Walton notes that extant extrabiblical materials offer no help in either defending or contradicting the historicity of Adam and Eve, so it does little good to appeal to those materials in regard to the issue at hand. In other words, the full gamut of viewpoints contradicting the traditional view of a historical Adam are nothing more than speculation in the interest of seeking a way to harmonize the Bible and the evolutionary views held by the majority of scientists" (p. 226). When he says "in other words," he draws illegitimate conclusions from the statement that he quotes me as making—a form of non sequitur.

8. Barrick makes some hermeneutical missteps.

In this category I would include his comments about genre and about the relationship of incidentals to the doctrine of inerrancy. It sounds as if he rejects the possibility of incidentals in inerrancy, but no one believes that Scripture's inerrancy applies to incidentals in the text. The biblical spelling of Nebuchadnezzar is an incidental and not addressed by biblical inerrancy (which is a good thing, because in Jeremiah it is spelled Nebuchadrezzar). Everyone believes there are incidentals; the question pertains to what we identify as incidentals. Our hermeneutic is always the same: we use every tool at our disposal to determine as best we can what the author intended to communicate.

When Barrick discusses genre, he talks as if the genre question and continuity between Genesis 1–11 and Genesis 12–50 solves all the problems (p. 203). The point I would make is that genre labels work on the premise of common features in form and function of pieces of literature. "Historicity" is not a genre—it expresses a belief in the reality of what has been presented. But of course, reality can take many literary forms.

9. Barrick uses vague, subjective formulations

Barrick writes on page 201: "Fourth, biblical writers in both testaments appear to take for granted a common origin of all human beings in Adam whenever they touch on topics related to Genesis 1–11 (e.g., Mal. 2:10 and Rom. 5:12–14)." I am not interested in what it "appears" to be—appearances can be misleading. We need to determine what specific claims the biblical text is making in its authority. It "appears" that the Bible takes for granted that the earth is the center of the universe; fortunately that is not its authoritative claim. We do not commit to believing what the biblical writers believe; we commit to believing what the affirmations of the biblical text are.

10. Barrick neglects important evidence for interpretation. I will forego discussion for reasons of space.

In conclusion, my objections to Barrick's positions derive largely from how he conducts his argumentation and the absence of evidence for the details of the position that he maintains.

RESPONSE FROM THE OLD-EARTH VIEW

C. JOHN COLLINS

William Barrick wants particularly to argue that we must read the account of Genesis 1–2 as telling us of historical events. He considers this the natural consequence of the relation of Genesis 1–11 to the rest of Genesis, and he is quite clear that New Testament writers refer to events in these stories as actual happenings. In that light he insists that we must take Adam and Eve as real historical figures, the progenitors of the entire human race. Among his virtues is his attention to detail, of which his treatment of the definite article in Genesis 1:27 (and elsewhere) is a good example that satisfies the grammarian in me.

Of course, this is quite similar to my own position; in fact, he has cited me several times with approval! Therefore, if this were all he had contended for, my comments would consist entirely of nods of assent and affirmation.

However, Barrick's general argument has a few wrinkles in it that I must address. Since this book is set up to highlight differences, I must attend to such differences in these comments; but I hope that some points of agreement will be clear even so.

It appears to me that, fundamentally, Barrick assumes a tight connection between historicity and a "literal" hermeneutic, every bit as much as Lamoureux does; and I contend that this assumption is drastically oversimplified. He has also tied this literalism to his notion of "inerrancy" and further added a few comments about "science" that require more nuance.

Barrick represents the young-earth creationist approach, and he briefly offers reasons for holding it. Since I have given my reasons for *not* holding that position elsewhere, I pass it by in these comments.[105]

---

105. See, for example, Collins, *Science and Faith: Friends or Foes?* (Wheaton, IL: Crossway, 2003), chs. 5–7, 15; *Genesis 1–4: A Linguistic, Literary, and Theological Commentary* (Phillipsburg, NJ: P&R Publishing, 2006), 122–29; "Reading Genesis 1–2 with the Grain: Analogi-

Let me begin with the matter of the Bible's truthfulness, or "inerrancy." One difficulty is to discern what characterization of inerrancy we intend to use. The definition that Barrick cites, from Paul Feinberg, suffers from some serious defects:

> Inerrancy means that when all facts are known, the Scriptures in their original autographs and properly interpreted will be shown to be wholly true in everything that they affirm, whether that has to do with doctrine or morality or with social, physical, or life sciences.

I cannot see any point to including human verification of biblical claims in the definition; and this definition limits itself to "facts," saying little about the affective shaping that is a rhetorical goal of the biblical materials. Thankfully the *Chicago Statement on Biblical Inerrancy* does not suffer from these defects.[106] In its summary statement we find this helpful way of putting it:

> Being wholly and verbally God-given, Scripture is without error or fault in all its teaching, no less in what it states about God's acts in creation, about the events of world history, and about its own literary origins under God, than in its witness to God's saving grace in individual lives.

As I mentioned in the footnotes to my essay, in Article 13 the *Chicago Statement* wisely recognized, "We deny that it is proper to evaluate Scripture according to standards of truth and error that are alien to its usage or purpose." In its Article 18, it insists on "taking account of its literary forms and devices."

None of this is surprising about the *Chicago Statement*, given that its framers aimed at a unifying document. And since these framers happily included "old-earth" creationists, and some who tended closer to a form of "theistic evolution," one simply cannot imagine that its declarations

---

cal days," in J. Daryl Charles, ed., *Reading Genesis 1–2: An Evangelical Conversation* (Peabody: Hendrickson, 2013), 73–92.

106. I consider the Statement satisfactory so far as it goes, though I might want to say a thing or two differently. As is clear from my essay, I would lay greater stress on the narrative and on the affective shaping functions, but the Statement is broad enough to include my concerns.

were intended to make the young-earth model more consistent with its overall doctrine.

Since Benjamin Warfield is typically credited with bringing the term *inerrancy* into general use among evangelicals, I think we should let his voice have a say in how we think about the notion. Warfield was by no means a young-earth creationist and was willing to consider that God might have used a genetic process to create our first parents. Commenting on the Genesis genealogies, he observed:[107]

> These genealogies must be esteemed trustworthy *for the purpose for which they are recorded;* but they cannot be safely pressed into use for other purposes *for which they were not intended, and for which they are not adapted.*

This same Warfield allowed the possibility that the formation of the first man involved some intermediate genetic steps, although the final result, the first human, must come from a supernatural addition to whatever process God used (what Warfield called "mediate creation"):[108]

> The difference between the modern [evolutionary] speculator and the biblicist cannot be conciliated at this point until and unless the speculator is willing to allow the intrusion into the course of evolution — if it be deemed actual in this case — of a purely supernatural act productive of something absolutely new which enters into the composite effect as a new feature. But there seems no reason why the speculator should not admit this, unless he occupies a position which is dogmatically antisupernaturalistic.

Just to be clear: I am not at all suggesting that everyone who accepts an old earth takes the same view of evolution as Warfield did. Rather, I want to show, first, that appeal to inerrancy will not decide the case; and second, that Warfield exemplifies the freedoms and limitations approach that I have advocated.

---

107. Benjamin Warfield, "On the Antiquity and Unity of the Human Race," in Warfield, *Biblical and Theological Studies;* ed. Samuel Craig (Philadelphia: Presbyterian and Reformed, 1968), 240 [orig. *Princeton Theological Review* 9 (1911)]; my italics.

108. Benjamin Warfield, *Evolution, Scripture, and Science: Selected Writings;* ed. Mark Noll and David Livingstone (Grand Rapids: Baker, 2000), 216 [orig. *The Bible Student* n.s. 8:5 (November 1903)]. See further Fred Zaspel, "B. B. Warfield on Creation and Evolution," *Themelios* 35:2 (July 2010), 198–211.

It is controversial, even among those who hold to a view of inerrancy, just how one should invoke that doctrine in deciding theological disputes; it is not clear to me that this is the best way to use the doctrine. Better to say, with J. I. Packer:[109]

> Believers will view the Spirit's teaching role as, first and foremost, one of keeping our minds humbly and eagerly attuned to Scripture, the divine textbook, so that we are *willing to have Scripture change our minds where it finds us wrong.*

Or with Warfield,[110]

> Let it suffice to say that to a plenarily inspired Bible, humbly trusted as such, we actually, and as a matter of fact, owe all that has blessed our lives with hopes of an immortality of bliss, and with the present fruition of the love of God in Christ ... It is actually to the Bible that you and I owe it that we have a Christ, — a Christ to love, to trust and to follow, a Christ without us the ground of our salvation, a Christ within us the hope of glory.

In other words, we cannot raise the matter of "inerrancy" in order to circumvent the hermeneutical discussion. Hence we turn to the question of history and interpretive literalism. As I have discussed the sense of the word "historical" in my essay, I take the word to imply that the account is about *real people* and *actual events*. It does not denote a literary genre, and thus it says nothing about the details of a hermeneutic; rather, it is about whether a text of any type can refer to things in the real world. That means that the proper contrast is not between *literal-historical* and *figurative*, but instead between *historically referential* and *nonreferential*. In the case of a referential text, we must discern from the text, including its historical context, genre, and stylistic features, how to cooperate with what the author is saying about his referents.

Barrick notes — and I agree — that all of Genesis 1–11, including chapter 1, comes to us in narrative, with its standardized usage of the *wayyiqtol* tense for the main story line; I do not see how we can take

---

109. J. I. Packer, *Truth and Power: The Place of Scripture in the Christian Life* (Downers Grove, IL: InterVarsity Press, 1996), 27.

110. Cited in Michael D. Williams, "The Church, a Pillar of Truth: B. B. Warfield's Church Doctrine of Inspiration," *Presbyterion* 37/2 (2011): 65–84, at 83.

seriously anyone who disputes this. Nevertheless, that does not entail that everything in the whole of Genesis is of the same sort. For example, I agree that there is no discernible *grammatical* break between Genesis 1–11 and 12–50. At the same time, the literary feel of the text requires that we notice some distinction: if for no other reason, at least because of the way the narrator slows down in the Abraham story.

But it turns out that there *is* another reason, namely the parallels between Genesis 1–11 and what the Assyriologists call "pre-history" and "proto-history" from Mesopotamia. Barrick may have a valid objection to the *misuse* of ancient Near Eastern parallels; but that does not in itself negate the possible *proper use*, namely, of helping us to perceive the literary and rhetorical conventions that the first audience would likely have been accustomed to (which he does not seem to consider).[111]

Looked at this way, the well-grounded parallels actually help us to cooperate with authorial intent, and we should welcome the help. These conventions indicate that the texts intend to make historical assertions and that the texts should not be taken literalistically (as in the lengths of the reigns of the Sumerian kings).

Further, I for one think it plain that Genesis 1 has its own distinctive stylistic features, as I have argued in calling it "exalted prose narrative," a designation that I arrived at under the influence of the linguist Robert Longacre.[112] (Some earlier scholars had misleadingly called the pericope "poetic," referring not to the form but to these stylistic features.) The narration beginning in Genesis 2:5 is more "ordinary," although it still has its own special features due to the distance between the first readers and the events recorded—a distance that allows for some degree of idealization and of anachronism, since the historian did not write with what we might call "antiquarian" aims.[113]

The predominant use of narrative in the Hebrew Bible is indeed for reporting actual events; but the best works in biblical historiography

---

111. Further, in saying, "the Genesis account distinguishes itself from the ancient Near Eastern stories by the clear declaration that God created only one human pair," Barrick implicitly acknowledges that Genesis is over against these other accounts and therefore that what they say is relevant.

112. Cf. my *Genesis 1–4*, 44.

113. On the literary role of anachronisms here, see Collins, *Did Adam and Eve Really Exist? Who They Were and Why You Should Care* (Wheaton, IL: Crossway, 2011), 113–14 (to which Barrick refers, apparently with agreement).

recognize that even in the "ordinary" narratives we do not always have a straightforward relation between the referent and the author's representation—that is, they employ literary technique.[114] That hardly detracts from their historicity, under my definition of that word. These concerns apply more acutely in the case of Genesis 1–11, and especially to chapter 1. (For more on this, I refer the reader to my use of C. S. Lewis, "The Language of Religion," in my comments on Lamoureux's essay.)

Barrick rightly points to the literary phenomenon of the "omniscient narrator," although I am not certain that he is using it as the literary theorists do. The idea is that of "the biblical narrator's access to privileged knowledge—the distant past, private scenes, the thoughts of the dramatis personae, from God down."[115] We take the narrator as "reliable" as well: his perspective represents God's.[116] The focus is on the narration as such, rather than on the narrator as a human being. Under no circumstances does it imply that a narration must be exhaustive in detail, or strictly sequential, or free from rhetorical and poetical devices. In this light, Barrick's frequent use of the qualifier "accurate" is potentially misleading, unless we are careful to insist, with the *Chicago Statement*, on attention to the genre conventions. Hence, to describe the narration style in Genesis 1 as Barrick does, as "a detailed, step-by-step, objective tone" does not follow at all from the literary requirements—and seems out of step with the celebratory tone of the passage.

This is consistent with how the rest of the Bible alludes to the events and persons in these chapters of Genesis. As N. T. Wright observed about Paul's reference to Adam in Romans 5,[117]

> Paul clearly believed that there had been a single first pair, whose male, Adam, had been given a commandment and had broken it. Paul was, we may be sure, aware of what we would call mythical or metaphorical dimensions to the story, but he would not have

---

114. See, for example, Long's chapter 4 in Iain Provan, V. Philips Long, and Tremper Longman III, *A Biblical History of Israel* (Louisville: Westminster John Knox, 2003).

115. Meir Sternberg, *The Poetics of Biblical Narrative: Ideological Literature and the Drama of Reading* (Bloomington: Indiana University Press, 1985), 12.

116. An example of an unreliable narrator is Oswald Bastable in E. Nesbit's stories: the attentive reader learns to doubt that Oswald's perspective is always the best.

117. N. T. Wright, "Romans," in Leander Keck et al., eds., *New Interpreter's Bible, Volume X* (Nashville: Abingdon, 2002), 524ab.

regarded these as throwing doubt on the existence, and primal sin, of the first historical pair.... What "sin" would have looked like in the early dawn of the human race it is impossible to say; but the turning away from open and obedient relationship with the loving creator, and the turning toward that which, though beautiful and enticing, is not God, is such a many-sided phenomenon that it is not hard to envisage it at any stage of anthropoid development.

Barrick worries that accepting "extrabiblical evidence (whether from ancient Near Eastern documentation or from modern scientists' interpretation of circumstantial evidence)" necessarily "denigrates the biblical record and treats it with skepticism rather than as *prima facie* evidence." This is astonishing. When it comes to whether we *should* compare the material we find in the Bible to the materials we find from the surrounding cultures, it seems almost obvious that of course we should. The biblical writers spoke into a specific context and regularly had to warn their audiences against the blandishments of the competing worldviews. Whether it be an Old Testament prophet inveighing against idolatry and syncretism, or a New Testament apostle reminding people about Greco-Roman depravity, these warnings are common stuff. Surely a sane interpreter will do what he or she can to discover what these dangers were. The right stance, as I have already argued, is that we must make every effort to make a good and wise use of this extra material.

Barrick agrees with Peter Enns that "evolution" is incompatible with attributing historicity to the biblical creation story. But neither Barrick nor Enns is clear as to what he means by "evolution," which undermines this strong claim. As for Enns, I cannot tell whether he has a particular notion of what "evolution" is, or if it is a general term for "the results of the modern sciences regarding the antiquity of the cosmos and earth, and the development of life over a long period," or some combination. I cannot tell whether he even recognizes this as a meaningful question. Further, Enns makes the strong identification between historicity and literalism that I consider so unwarranted.

In the same vein, I cannot tell whether Barrick allows any nuance in the sense of "evolution," or if he follows the common young-earth practice of characterizing all non-young-earth views as evolutionary. I would urge more attention to such distinctions.

Further, Barrick surprisingly claims (in a footnote) that "Science denies the miraculous and supernatural, so the entire biblical history of Jesus becomes suspicious and in need of demythologization." This reflects a view of science and scientists that should be highly controversial. Since I have addressed some of these matters elsewhere, I will not delve into more detail here.[118] I will instead take the opportunity to commend again the relationship of the sciences and Christian faith that I have articulated:

> Far be it from an exegete or theologian to tell a geneticist what he or she may or may not find in the genome, or a paleontologist in the fossils! At the same time, when that geneticist or paleontologist wants to try to put those findings together into larger theories that tell the human story, then that person is reasoning as a human being, and his or her reasoning is subject to review for its compliance with good critical thinking.

I believe this does the most justice to the nature of the biblical material, to the overarching biblical story, and to the proper place of the historical sciences in God's providence.

---

118. E.g., see Collins, *Science and Faith*, chs. 2–3.

A REJOINDER

A measure of grace goes a long way when discussing a significant issue like the historicity of Adam with strongly differing viewpoints. Hopefully, my respondents will forgive me for any unintentional misrepresentation of their viewpoints. Likewise, I will try to be equally forgiving when one of them criticizes my view—such as assuming my position on the fossil record when my essay does not even mention fossils (see pp. 23–32). No over-simplified caricature of the young-earth interpretation of the fossil record can accurately represent my own viewpoint.

I want to focus this final response on the greatest contrast between the old-earth and young-earth views regarding the historicity of Adam. That contrast appears in the variety of ways by which some biblical scholars choose to reduce or minimize the historical accuracy of the biblical text. Minimalists rely more heavily on human authority as the lynch-pin for their argumentation than on the divine authority of Scripture. For example, Lamoureux employs a subtle form of this argumentation when he says, "Of course, no one today believes this is how the universe is structured" (p. 230). Walton makes a similar statement addressing the issue more directly: "no one believes that Scripture's inerrancy applies to incidentals in the text" (p. 242). Their statements indicate that the yardstick for determining biblical truth resides with the most current scientific beliefs, not the objective biblical revelation itself. In addition, these two statements attempt to isolate and demean the maximalist position of young-earth proponents regarding the total historical accuracy of the Bible.

Some old-earth proponents like Lamoureux argue that the presence of human misconceptions and errant ancient science in Scripture manifests God's grace (see p. 230). This approach to biblical inerrancy treats such biblical statements as incidental to the Bible's spiritual truths. Incidentals for Walton include the fact that Old Testament writers use two different spellings for Nebuchadnezzar (see p. 242). His example reveals the divide between young-earth convictions and most old-earth viewpoints. Robert Dick Wilson, the eminent Princeton scholar, long ago demonstrated that both spellings of Nebuchadnezzar are legitimate and accurate rather than arbitrary or erroneous.[119] Biblical writers use the spelling (Nebuchadnezzar or Nebuchadrezzar) that best fits each text's context and content. The spellings provide evidence supporting total biblical inerrancy.

If the Bible is totally inerrant, then we *cannot* "separate the inerrant spiritual truths from their incidental ancient vessels" (p. 235). Minimalist interpreters select which biblical statements and concepts to identify as inerrant. That results in partial inerrancy and leaves the reader with the idea that God's Word contains error. Young-earth adherents do not practice this method of biblical interpretation that doubts the historical accuracy of the text and depends on the biblical writers' acceptance and intentional propagation of errant ancient science.

Young-earth evidence for the historicity of Adam comes from Scripture itself and its own direct statements. Such biblical evidence does not require confirmation from any external scientific, historical, or sociological evidence. When the Genesis record declares that God created the woman out of the material that he took from Adam, we require no other evidence to conclude that they shared DNA and that she was specially created. The fact that Scripture speaks only of a first man and first woman and that it presents them as the actual historical parents of the entire human race is evidence enough to believe those truths.

Contrary to how my young-earth view has been depicted (see p. 230), I do not believe that the Bible is a book of science—an accusation too often falsely leveled against young-earth creationists. The Bible presents theological and historical truths from God's viewpoint and in accord with his own wisdom and knowledge. The biblical writers' worldview is God's worldview, which he expects them to represent accurately. When the Bible says (on more than one occasion) that God created the heavens and the earth and all they contain in six actual days, that discloses God's view, not man's. God always speaks truth and always expects his servants to speak and write truth—especially those whom he chose to write the Bible.

---

119. Robert Dick Wilson, *A Scientific Investigation of the Old Testament*, rev. by Edward J. Young (1959; reprint, Birmingham, AL: Solid Ground Christian Books, 2007), 68, 71.

If the Bible were a book of science, it would present human scholars' interpretations of the evidences they themselves observe, just like books and journals of science. If the Bible were a science textbook, it would present theories and report the testing of theories. However, the Bible, in contrast to science books, dogmatically communicates the direct revelation that God himself has provided. Only God witnessed the six days of creation, so no man can claim to speak of that series of events unless he has received revelation directly from the Creator himself. No science book can or will do this.

Just to be clear: my view is not concordism, because no concord exists between evolutionary science and divine revelation. The cause for the lack of concord does not reside in the Bible's ancient understanding of science. The writers were not speaking of subjective science; they were passing on objective divine revelation (2 Peter 1:20–21). The written record that God superintended did not agree with the ancient pagan scientists nor with the ancient scholars' worldview. The Bible confronted and contradicted those ancient pagan and secular viewpoints—just as it confronts and contradicts the subjective interpretations and worldview of modern scientists and secular scholars. We can benefit from comparative analysis of biblical and ANE materials as long as we understand and preserve the unique revelatory and inerrant nature of the biblical record.

Old-earth viewpoints accept modern scientists' interpretations of observable physical data—that is, how they get to an old-earth viewpoint. Even if an old-earth proponent rejects evolutionary theory, he relies on human scientific authority to arrive at adherence to partial biblical inerrancy. That is our chief difference.

A PASTORAL
REFLECTION

WHETHER OR NOT THERE WAS A
HISTORICAL ADAM, OUR FAITH IS SECURE

GREGORY A. BOYD

As a result of reviewing arguments for and against Adam as a historical person over the last several years, I am currently inclined to the view that Adam was, in fact, a historical figure. At the same time, the fact that I say I am "inclined" toward this view indicates that I do *not* see this belief as central to the orthodox Christian faith. I would never say I am "inclined" toward believing in the Trinity, the deity of Christ, the final resurrection of the dead, or any other essential Christian teaching. Hence, while I would not want in any way to minimize the importance of this debate, I also do not believe we should construe it as a debate over an essential Christian doctrine.

In this essay I will not offer a comprehensive review of all the considerations that led me to my current position. Instead, since I have been asked to write a pastoral reflection on why I don't see belief in a historical Adam as essential to the Christian faith, I will focus on four considerations that pertain to my position as a pastor of a progressive evangelical/Anabaptist church.[1]

The Role of My Experience

Inasmuch as our personal experience always influences our theological perspectives as well as our understanding of what it means to be

---

1. The church I pastor (Woodland Hills Church in Maplewood, Minnesota) was founded as a Baptist General Conference Church and is currently exploring possible membership with the Mennonite Church U.S.A. and/or the Brethren in Christ. This point shall become relevant later on.

a pastor, I think it appropriate to begin by sharing an experience that has influenced my view of the nonessential nature of the debate over the historicity of Adam. I came to Christ at the age of seventeen in a fundamentalist Pentecostal church that not only assumed that Adam was a historical figure, but also taught that every aspect of the Genesis account of the creation of the world and the fall of humanity had to be interpreted literally. The church thus espoused young-earth creationism. "If the creation and fall are not literal accounts of the creation and fall of humanity," I recall our fiery pastor teaching us, "then the entire Bible might as well be a book of lies!"[2]

Although my new friends in this Pentecostal church tried to dissuade me, I entered the University of Minnesota a year after my conversion. For my first course, taken the summer before my freshman year, I chose a class entitled "An Introduction to Evolutionary Biology." I had read three books —yes, three entire books! —defending creationism against evolution, including *The Genesis Flood* by John Whitcomb and Henry Morris.[3] Since I had never read so much on a single topic in my life, this preparation made me naively overconfident that I could protect the vulnerable college students taking this class from the lie of evolution and possibly even convert the professor. Things did not unfold quite as I had planned.

Beginning with the very first class, I interjected objections to the professor's teaching whenever he made a point that was "refuted" in one of the books I had read. Much to my surprise as well as my chagrin, in every instance the professor responded by gently dismantling my argument, in some instances graciously going out of his way to not make me look silly before my peers. I clearly was not the first passionate young-earth creationist this professor had encountered!

While two fellow Christians in this class applauded my relentless objections, most of the class had grown weary of them by the second and third weeks of the summer semester. But this remarkable professor actually defended me against their complaints, pointing out that a truly scientific mindset is one that is willing to question assump-

---

2. I share a much fuller account of my conversion and early struggles with the Christian faith to illustrate an important theological dimension of biblical faith in Gregory A. Boyd, *The Benefit of the Doubt: Dismantling the Idol of Certainty* (Grand Rapids: Baker, 2013).

3. John C. Whitcomb Jr. and Henry M. Morris, *The Genesis Flood: The Biblical Record and Its Scientific Implications* (Phillipsburg, NJ: P & R Publishing, 1960).

tions that everyone else takes for granted. The kind and respectful way this professor treated me, even as he made mincemeat out of all my creationist arguments, made his refutations all the more forceful. His demeanor contradicted the caricature I had created in my mind of evolutionists as godless liberals who were doing Satan's bidding as they furthered the propaganda that humans are mere products of time and chance.

By mid-semester I had used up all the anti-evolution ammunition I had garnered from my three books. In desperation I combed through Christian bookstores and several libraries looking for more help. My professor dismantled the several new arguments I had managed to find as effortlessly as he had my previous material. So by the end of this summer class, my fundamentalist faith in a young earth and in a literal Adam and Eve had become extremely shaky. I simply could not deny that evidence for an old earth and for some sort of evolutionary process leading up to the human race was overwhelmingly strong. Nor could I deny that all the arguments I had marshaled in defense of young-earth creationism and against evolution had been convincingly refuted by this professor. The only lifeline my faith could continue to cling to was a number of undeniably profound spiritual experiences that I had enjoyed throughout the year following my conversion.

It wasn't long, however, before the weight of the intellectual challenges my education was presenting to my faith went beyond what this lifeline could sustain. Indeed, it took only one more course at the University of Minnesota — a course in "The Old Testament as Literature" — to completely destroy my newfound faith. I desperately *wanted* to believe in God, Jesus, and the Bible. I loved the profound sense of fulfillment, meaning, and purpose my faith had given me, and my experiences with Christ in the year following my conversion had on occasion been nothing short of rapturous. But I simply found I could no longer deny, with intellectual integrity, that the creation story, the story of the fall, and a number of other biblical narratives did not seem literally true. And within the fundamentalist framework that I, at this stage of my life, identified as the Christian faith, this meant I had no choice but to accept that "the entire Bible is a book of lies."

The year that followed my loss of faith was far and away the most miserable year of my life. I had already explored the possibility of finding "truth" through eastern mysticism, accessed through the use of LSD and other drugs, prior to my coming to Christ.[4] Once I concluded that Christianity is therefore not true, the only alternative that remained, so far as I could see, was existential nihilism. I thus immersed myself in the writings of Friedrich Nietzsche, Jean-Paul Sartre, Albert Camus, and others, bravely trying to embrace the meaningless absurdity of existence—but frankly, it drove me to utter despair.

I cannot in this essay enter into the multitude of considerations that allowed me gradually to find my way back into the Christian faith. I will only note that I was initially motivated to give Christianity a second look by the sheer intensity of my existential anguish. If nihilism is true, I began to wonder, how come it feels so exquisitely painful and so completely unnatural to accept it? How could natural processes evolve creatures that desperately long for things like ultimate meaning that are nonexistent in nature itself? I thus began to explore ways of embracing the Christian faith that didn't require me to conclude that "the entire Bible is a book of lies" if certain biblical stories, including the creation and fall, are not literal.

As is true for so many contemporary Christians, I am largely indebted to C. S. Lewis for helping me find my way back to faith. I recall the sense of hope that I, as an anguished sophomore, was given as I sat in a café reading Lewis's *The Problem of Pain*. I had somewhere read that Lewis was the most respected Christian apologist among American evangelicals, and yet I found in him a way to affirm the inspiration of Scripture that did not require me to reject evolution or to think that every story in Scripture has to be literal.

Lewis writes that while "[t]he story [of the fall] in Genesis is a story ... about a magic apple of knowledge in the developed doctrine" of the fall that we have in the early church, "the inherent magic apple has quite dropped out of sight, and the story is simply one of disobedience." Then, to my surprise, I found Lewis going on to confess:

> I have the deepest respect even for Pagan myths, *still more for myths in Holy Scripture*. I therefore do not doubt that the version which emphasizes the magic apple, and brings together the trees of life and knowledge, contains a deeper and subtler truth than the version

---

4. I discuss my spiritual journey at length in *Benefit of the Doubt*.

which makes the apple simply and solely a pledge of obedience. But I assume that the Holy Spirit would not have allowed the latter to grow up in the Church and win the assent of great doctors unless it also was true and useful so far as it went.[5]

Lewis then concludes by saying that his work in *The Problem of Pain* was going to focus on the church's doctrine of the fall rather than on the "primitive" and mythic story in the Bible, "though," he adds, "I suspect the primitive version to be far more profound." Indeed, it is so profound that Lewis admits that "I, at any rate, cannot penetrate its profundities."[6]

However, for Lewis, labeling the biblical story a "myth" did not mean that it does not express an actual historical event. To the contrary, Lewis was convinced that the biblical narrative is unintelligible without the acknowledgment that something, at some point in our primordial past, went terribly wrong. But "[w]hat exactly happened when Man fell," Lewis stated, "we do not know." We simply don't have access to the requisite historical information to form any reliable "idea" regarding what "particular act, or series of acts, the self-contradictory, impossible wish [to be our own masters] found expression." But this question, Lewis argued, "is of no consequence," as long as we accept that the *meaning* of this historical fall is expressed in the God-inspired myth found in Scripture.[7]

While there were a number of hurdles I had to cross on my way back to re-embracing the Christian faith, this was one of the most important. Had I not found a way of reconciling belief in the Bible as God's Word with acceptance of some form of evolutionary theory as well as with other things I had learned about the myths shared by Scripture and other ancient Near Eastern literature, I seriously doubt that I would have ever found my way back into an evangelical version of the Christian faith.

---

5. C. S. Lewis, *The Problem of Pain* (New York: Simon & Schuster, 1996), 63–64, emphasis added.

6. Ibid.

7. Ibid. Lewis elsewhere expresses a similar agnosticism when he writes, "We do not know how many of these creatures God made, nor how long they continued in the Paradisal state. But sooner or later they fell" (A. N. Wilson, *C. S. Lewis: A Biography* [New York: W. W. Norton, 1990], 210).

This experience informs the approach I take as an evangelical and Anabaptist pastor to the issue of the historicity of Adam. Because Lewis helped me embrace Scripture without needing to deny evolution or affirm a literal Adam, I was able forever to leave the despairing world of meaningless nihilism behind and once again embrace a life-giving relationship with Jesus Christ. Hence, even though I am now inclined to affirm Adam as a historical figure, I think it would have been an absolute tragedy if I had been barred from this life-giving relationship because I could not accept this historicity at this formative point in my life. I shudder to think that I might have been condemned to live an empty, meaningless life in an absurd and pointless world, to say nothing of what might have become of me after death, simply because I could not, with intellectual integrity, affirm a historical Adam!

This is one of the main reasons that I, as a pastor of an evangelical and Anabaptist church, think it vitally important that we *not* put forth the historicity of Adam as a matter that is essential to the Christian faith. To be clear, I am all in favor of debating this topic, and I don't even have a problem with those who are convinced that affirming this historicity is essential for biblical reasons and for maintaining the over-all coherence of the Christian message, as long as they allow space under the broad tent of "orthodoxy" for people to disagree. Even if they can't understand how another sister or brother in Christ can deny Adam's historicity while affirming the inspiration of Scripture or without thereby undermining the coherence of the Christian message, I implore them to refrain from becoming dogmatic on this point and simply to trust the genuineness of those who disagree. The fact is, dogmatism on this point would have tragically barred C. S. Lewis, myself, and a multitude of others from the life-giving kingdom.

Mere Christianity

Speaking of Lewis, a second reason why I, as a Christian pastor, encourage us to not make the historicity of Adam essential to the Christian faith is that I do not believe that affirming this point has ever been part of what Lewis famously termed "mere Christianity."[8] While the church's foundational ecumenical creeds all presuppose that human-

---

8. C. S. Lewis, *Mere Christianity* (1943; New York: Simon & Schuster, 1996).

ity and creation are in a fallen state, and while all thus bear witness to a historical fall, none of these creeds leverages these convictions on the affirmation of a historical Adam. Hence, when people today make affirming a historical Adam a test of orthodoxy, it seems to me they are unnecessarily and unwisely tightening the definition of "orthodoxy" beyond that of the historic-orthodox church. In this way they are placing an obstacle to people entering the kingdom that is not required by the historic definition of "orthodoxy."

This point is reinforced by the confessions of faith within the particular tradition of "mere Christianity" that I and my church identify with: namely, the Anabaptist tradition. Beginning with the *Schleitheim Confession* (1527) and *Reidemann's Rechenshaft* (1540) and continuing through the *Dordrecht Confession* (1632) and the more contemporary *Mennonite Confession of Faith* (1963) and *Confession of Faith in a Mennonite Perspective* (1995), we find a uniform affirmation that humanity is fallen and in need of redemption, but no necessary connection between this affirmation and the belief in a historical Adam.

Hence, both the broader ecumenical creeds and the more specific Anabaptist confessions to which I adhere drive home the point that we are unnecessarily placing an intellectual hurdle for people to cross to embrace orthodox Christianity when we make affirming a historical Adam an essential aspect of the orthodox Christian faith. And, as I said, this is a hurdle many today find they simply cannot cross with intellectual integrity.

The Battle of Faith and Science

A third factor that informs my pastoral perspective on the nonessential nature of the debate over the historicity of Adam concerns the history of the Western Church's battles with science. As a pastor with an evangelist's heart, I am deeply invested in presenting the gospel in an intellectually credible fashion to nonbelievers in our culture. For this reason, I think it is incredibly significant that, from Galileo's Inquisition to the Scope's Trial to the present evolution debates, whenever the church has assumed a rigid opposition to the consensus of the scientific community, it has eventually harmed the credibility of the church in the eyes of the broader culture. In light of this unfortunate history, it seems to me that we who are called to be leaders of Christ's church should learn the lesson that when we perceive potential conflicts between our faith and various claims that are being made by the scientific establishment, we ought to assume a humble position of *maximal flexibility*.

I am not claiming that Christian leaders should never push back on the claims of the scientific establishment. For example, when self-appointed spokespersons for the scientific establishment such as Richard Dawkins go beyond the bounds of science and draw metaphysical conclusions that conflict with core aspects of the Christian faith, we absolutely must push back and demonstrate the invalidity of these pseudo-scientific conclusions.[9] But when there is a consensus within the scientific community regarding a matter that affects merely how we interpret particular passages of Scripture, such as we have with the potential incongruity of evolutionary theory and the historicity of Adam, the history of the church's conflict with science teaches us that the wisest approach is humbly to assume a flexible posture that seeks for various ways of interpreting Scripture so that they do not conflict with the prevailing scientific theory. Indeed, not only should the previous battles between the church and the scientific establishment teach us this, but the wise manner in which Augustine, Calvin, and other church fathers handled perceived conflicts between Scripture and the science of their day should teach us this much.[10]

There are a number of ways one can reconcile evolutionary theory with the belief in the historical Adam, several of which were discussed in this book. Some will find one or more of these possible solutions plausible, but others will not. My only concern as a pastor is that I see no good reason why those who feel they must interpret Adam in a nonhistorical way in order to reconcile their faith with science should be barred from the kingdom, or at least from the orthodox Christian faith, because they do so. This is why I advocate a posture of *maximal* flexibility when it comes to reconciling Scripture with science.

---

9. See, e.g., Richard Dawkins, *The Selfish Gene* (Oxford: Oxford University Press, 2006); idem, *The God Delusion* (London: Bantam Press, 2006). For an excellent Christian response, see Alister McGrath, *Dawkins' God: Genes, Memes, and the Meaning of Life* (Oxford: Blackwell, 2005).

10. See Kenton L. Sparks, http://biologos.org/blog/scripture-evolution-and-the-problem-of-science-pt–1 (accessed June 10, 2013). For an introduction to Augustine's view, see Matt Rossano, "Augustine of Hippo: A Role Model for Intelligent Faith," http://www.huffington-post.com/matt-j-rossano/augustine-of-hippo-a-role_b_659195.html (accessed June 10, 2013).

My conviction is that it can only enhance both the credibility of the Christian faith and the overall perception of Christians as intellectually open-minded people when we refrain from leveraging the credibility of our faith on one single way of reconciling Scripture with science. The credibility of the gospel and of our overall witness to the world is better served when we demonstrate instead that, while we may personally prefer one solution over others, there are in fact a number of more or less plausible ways of embracing both Scripture and the consensus of the scientific establishment.

The Historical Adam and Biblical Authority

The fourth and final consideration that informs my pastoral perspective on this issue concerns the nature of biblical authority. Inasmuch as evangelicals place Scripture over experience, reason, and tradition, this consideration is by far and away the most important one for this audience. Indeed, the reason why this issue is the hot issue it is today is that many evangelicals believe that denying the historicity of Adam undermines biblical authority, as several essays in this book make clear. It is argued, for example, that if Adam is not historical, then we must judge Jesus and Paul to be in error when they referred to him. So, too, how can we affirm that Jesus, the second Adam, is historical if we don't also affirm that the first Adam is historical? Relative to this, how can we affirm a literal, historical redemption if we don't also affirm a literal, historical fall?

I am deeply sympathetic to this line of questioning. Indeed, it is considerations such as these that currently incline me toward the belief that Adam was a historical figure. At the same time, beyond the three considerations I have already mentioned, there are three specifically biblical considerations that I believe should caution us against being dogmatic about our conclusions, thereby explaining why I am merely *inclined* to the view that Adam was a historical figure.

First, as we saw was true of C. S. Lewis, and as can be illustrated throughout the early church, one can affirm a historical fall without thereby committing themselves to the view that this fall is captured in a literal, snapshot way in Genesis 3. Many in the early church interpreted the Genesis story to be, in whole or in part, an allegorical or mythic expression of humanity's primordial rebellion against God. For example, Origen reflects how widespread a nonliteral interpretation of this story was in the third century, at least in his locale, while expressing a certain disdain for a literal interpretation. He writes,

> ... who is so silly as to believe that God, after the manner of a farmer, "planted a paradise eastward in Eden," and set in it a visible and palpable "tree of life," of such a sort that anyone who tasted its fruit with his bodily teeth would gain life; and again that one could partake of "good and evil" by masticating the fruit taken from the tree of that name? And when God is said to "walk in the paradise in the cool of the day," and Adam to hide himself behind a tree, I do not think anyone will doubt that these are figurative expressions which indicate certain mysteries through a semblance of history and not through actual events.[11]

In this light, I honestly see no warrant for the dogmatic insistence that denying the historicity of Adam undermines the historicity of the fall or the historicity of our redemption.

On top of this, most Bible interpreters throughout history have acknowledged that much of what we find in Scripture reflects God *accommodating* his revelation to the limited and fallen minds of those he's revealing himself to, as both Denis Lamoureux and John Walton emphasize in their essays. Interpreters have therefore always been willing to interpret large portions of Scripture in nonliteral ways, even in sections where it's clear the original author intended his writing to be taken literally. In this light, it strikes me as somewhat arbitrary—and quite contrary to the church's dominant interpretive tradition—for anyone to dogmatically deny at least the *possibility* that the story of Adam in Eden is a myth that was inspired as a divine accommodation to help readers throughout history, and in the widest diversity of cultural settings, to apprehend the meaning of a historical rebellion, the literal details of which might be as difficult as they would be unhelpful to understand. And even if someone is personally persuaded that the story of the fall should be interpreted literally, in light the church's interpretive tradition, why should they be allowed to close the door on a sister

---

11. Origen, *On First Principles*, trans. G. W. Butterworth (New York: Harper & Row, 1966), Bk. IV.3.1, 288.

or brother in Christ—a brother such as C. S. Lewis!—who disagrees with them on this matter?

Second, and closely related to this, whether or not one views Adam as a historical figure, the way in which Jesus and Paul speak about him—and this is in keeping with the way Adam is depicted in Genesis 2 and 3—is paradigmatic or archetypal in nature. That is, as Walton effectively argues in his essay in this book, Adam is the representative human.[12] Now, of course, one may argue that Adam plays this literary role because he was in fact the first actual human, and I am inclined to agree. But it nevertheless remains true that one could in principle affirm *the message* of what Jesus and Paul say about Adam while yet *denying* that he was the first actual human.

If a person responds by insisting that Jesus and Paul believed in a historical Adam, as almost all Jews did in the first century, this could be addressed by the above-mentioned principle of divine accommodation. That is, one could argue that God was stooping to accommodate and work through the worldview of the people at the time, just as we find him doing throughout the Bible. In this sense, Jesus and Paul's references to Adam could be interpreted along the same lines as (say) Jesus' reference to the mustard seed being the least of all seeds or to his reference to the eye as the lamp of the body, referring to the widespread ancient belief that eyesight involved light coming out of the eye (Luke 11:34). The point of his God-inspired teaching is not affected by the fact that his statements assume a worldview that was not, in these respects, scientifically accurate.

My point, again, is not to defend these particular positions, but rather to express my conviction that we ought to embrace people whose intellectual integrity compels them to espouse positions along these lines as sisters and brothers in good standing within the fold of the orthodox, evangelical faith. Even if one can't see how a fellow Christian can deny the historical Adam and yet affirm with logical consistency the authority of Scripture and other essential aspects of the faith, the worst that can be said about them is that they are, from this person's

---

12. Peter Enns argues along these lines largely on the basis of the literary role that "Adam" played in literature that is roughly contemporary with Jesus and Paul. See *The Evolution of Adam: What the Bible Does and Doesn't Say about Human Origins* (Grand Rapids: Brazos Press, 2012).

perspective, logically inconsistent. But logical consistency has thankfully never served as a test of orthodoxy.

Conclusion

The debate over the historicity of Adam is a good and healthy debate for Christians to have. In this essay I have simply argued that this debate should be construed as a debate *among* orthodox Christians, not as a debate that determines *whether or not* one *is* an orthodox Christian. Had I believed that affirming a historical Adam was a precondition for embracing the orthodox Christian faith, it is likely I would not be a Christian today. The same holds true for C. S. Lewis and a multitude of other Christians. Not only this, but there is nothing in the earliest ecumenical creeds of the church that requires this affirmation.[13]

The history of the church's debates with science along with the precedent of Augustine, Calvin, and other church fathers as they interacted with the science of their day should caution us against assuming rigid stances that oppose the consensus of the scientific community.

Finally, it is possible for scholars to affirm all the essentials of the Christian faith, including the inspiration of Scripture, while yet denying the historicity of Adam.

Even if many Christians find the interpretations of those who deny the historicity of Adam to be implausible, if not logically incoherent, this should not constitute grounds for questioning their orthodoxy. Paul teaches us that love believes the best and hopes for the best in others (1 Cor. 13:7). Since we are called to be first and foremost a community that exhibits love for one another, I submit that we ought to affirm the sincerity and integrity of those who feel the need to deny the historicity of Adam and welcome them into the fold of orthodoxy—even if some might do so while hoping to eventually convince them otherwise.

---

13. I am referring to the Nicene Creed (AD 325), the Creed of Nicaea (Nicento-Constantinopolitan Creed, AD 381), and the Apostles' Creed (ca. AD 700).

A PASTORAL REFLECTION
WE CANNOT UNDERSTAND THE WORLD OR OUR FAITH WITHOUT A REAL, HISTORICAL ADAM

PHILIP G. RYKEN

It was a moment of rare honesty, in which the accumulated frustration of living in a sinful world spontaneously erupted in a display of personal hostility. The little girl stood in front of a painting of Adam and Eve, angrily shook her fist, and shouted, "You ruined everything!"

Perhaps it is not surprising that the girl was the daughter of a theologian — one of my colleagues on the faculty of Wheaton College. Obviously, the girl had learned a good deal of doctrine already. She knew that something was wrong with her world. Things were *not* the way they were supposed to be. She also knew who was responsible for this unfortunate state of affairs: Adam and Eve.

But that is not all. The little girl knew as well that the people in the picture were not mere storybook characters, but real people who lived in the real world. Why else would she speak to them in the manner of direct address? She was connected to these people in a deeply personal way. Their story was part of her story, and her story was part of theirs. In fact, her words were unwitting evidence of her solidarity with humanity's first parents. Like her father Adam before her, she wanted someone to blame for her depravity.

As this incident illustrates, the historicity of Adam and Eve has profound implications for daily life. Does anything have greater explanatory power than the creation of the first people and their subsequent fall into sin? The dignity and downfall of humanity—as well as our hope of redemption—begin with Adam's story.[1]

Adam in Scripture and Science

Adam's story explains so many things because it is much more than an illustration of the human condition, such as one might find in the tales of ancient mythology. Adam is a real person of history, and therefore the events of his life are causes that produce genuine effects in the world. His story explains what *happens* because it tells us what *happened*.

The quest for the historical Adam begins in Genesis 1–3, but it does not end there. It is also based on the historical narrative in Genesis 4 and 5, where Adam and Eve are presented as living, breathing human beings who do down-to-earth things such as having conversations, sharing sexual relations, giving birth, and naming their children. Their historicity is confirmed by the detailed genealogies in 1 Chronicles 1–9 and Luke 3:23–38—complex, careful records that begin at the dawn of humanity and run through many ages of recorded history. It is based, too, on the matter-of-fact references that Jesus makes to their story in the Gospels (Matt. 19:4–6; Mark 10:6–9) and on the closely reasoned arguments in which the apostle Paul grounds Christian faith and practice in the history of Adam and Eve (Rom. 5; 1 Cor. 15; 1 Tim. 2). Taken together, these passages serve as the hermeneutical norm for our interpretation of the narrative history in Genesis.

All of this is demonstrated in greater detail elsewhere in this book. My point here is that even if questions remain about the way in which God made Adam and Eve, or about their role as the historical parents of the human race, the compelling case for their historicity runs right through Scripture. To deny the historical Adam is to stand against the teaching of Moses, Luke, Jesus, and Paul.

This is not to say that Christians who do not believe that the historicity of Adam is essential to Christian orthodoxy are simply ignoring the Bible. Many are sincere in seeking to understand carefully what the Scriptures do—and do not—claim about human origins. Still, the

---

1. In writing this essay I am indebted to Robert Bishop, Darrell Bock, Don Carson, Bryan Chapell, Jeff Greenman, David Helm, Beth Jones, Tim Keller, Doug Moo, Josh Moody, John Piper, Jim Samra, Richard Schultz, Dan Treier, and John Walton for their suggestions and corrections.

starting point for most challenges to the special creation of Adam is science rather than Scripture. According to the mainstream scientific consensus (there are dissenting voices, of course), the human race did not begin with a single pair but must have started with some larger population. Some Christians think that this emerging consensus gives us the real facts and find it at odds with the Genesis account of human origins. Naturally, they seek ways of reconciling their faith in Christ with their unbelief in Adam, whom they regard as merely a model or metaphor.

Fortunately, we do not have to choose between biblical orthodoxy and scientific credibility. General revelation and special revelation both tell us the truth. As time goes on, we may hope to understand better how the truth claims of science and Scripture converge.

In the meantime, it is wise to acknowledge that in addition to giving us various facts, both science and theology require interpretation. New scientific discoveries are not brute facts, but involve the careful assessment of evidence—evidence that may be reassessed later. And sometimes—as is the case with Adam and Eve—the discoveries of science send us back to the Scriptures to make sure that we understand the Bible properly, without reading things into (or squeezing things out of) the text. As our faith seeks understanding, we are wise to exercise patience both in our study of Scripture and with the progress of science.

In a culture that sometimes gives science more deference than it deserves, it is important not to let provisional theories of science cast aspersions on the clear truths of Scripture. But insisting on traditional interpretations of Scripture and refusing to listen to the truths of science damages the credibility of Christianity and raises unnecessary obstacles in evangelism. So humility is needed on all sides.

Adam in Christian Life and Doctrine

In what follows, I hope to show the pivotal role that Adam plays in Christian faith and practice. Fortunately, we do not need to speculate as to how the life of this man connects to real-life issues. We can simply look at the places where the Bible mentions Adam—with either the assumption or the assertion that he is a real person who lived in the real past—in connection with central tenets of the Christian faith.

Given his recurring presence in the biblical narrative, the logical and long-term effect of denying the existence of Adam is to weaken the church's grip on central biblical truths that make a difference in daily life. This is not to say that denying the historical Adam is tantamount to denying the Christian faith. Christians who abandon a traditional commitment to the historical Adam do not necessarily (or immediately) deny the doctrine of original sin, for example, or divorce themselves from the biblical view of marriage, or diminish the righteousness of Christ as the basis for justification. But because the Bible connects the Adam of history to so many other doctrines, our view of Adam inevitably influences our whole theology.

For what doctrines does it make a difference to defend the Adam of history? While we do not have the scope here to lay out a complete case, we can at least begin to show the foundational role that Adam plays in understanding human identity, forming a Christian worldview, and telling the gospel story.

1. The historical Adam gives confidence that the Bible is the Word of God.

Admittedly, Adam's detractors also claim to have Scripture on their side. But a natural, straightforward reading of the opening chapters of Genesis takes the man to be an actual human being, not a legend or mere archetype. Adam's representative role for the human race flows from his reality as a historical person, as introduced in an historical narrative. Jewish scholars were reading the Bible this way around the time of Christ, when they wrote, "O Adam, what have you done? For though it was you who sinned, the fall was not yours alone, but ours also who are your descendants" (4 Ezra 7:118 RSV). When ordinary people read the Bible, they readily infer that Adam is a person from history — humanity's real representative.

It is difficult if not impossible to account for Scripture adequately without an authentic Adam. Efforts to explain his story in some other way usually seem contrived. For example, how would a parent answer a child who wanted to know if Adam and Eve were real people? If the answer is no, then what are we to make of Cain and Abel, or Seth and Noah — Adam's direct, lineal descendants? In the continuous narrative of the book of Genesis, where does mythology end and history begin?

In effect, to deny the historicity of Adam is to delete the first chapter in the macro-narrative of redemption. At every other point in the biblical story, God works in history, engaging with real people. But without a historical Adam, the origin of humanity is left unexplained, and redemption turns out not to be rooted history after all. This distorts the story line of Scripture and diminishes confidence in the clarity and reliability of the Bible. Treating Adam as a mere idea or symbol severs the historical-relational connection that makes humanity accountable to God and serves as the starting point for faith in the one true God. Affirming the historical Adam, on the other hand, keeps the story line intact and reassures the reader that the whole Bible can be trusted to be true. Human beings are what the Bible claims we are: sons of Adam and daughters of Eve (see Gen. 3:20; Ps. 11:4; Eccl. 1:13).

2. *The historical Adam explains humanity's sinful nature.*

It is not simply Adam's created existence that is crucial to the story line of Scripture, but more specifically his fall into sin. Do we know how our story begins, or not? According to Genesis, God told Adam not to eat from the tree of the knowledge of good and evil (Gen. 2:16–17). This was an ideal test of obedience, in which humanity's destiny turned entirely on submission to the word of God.

Sadly, Adam failed this test and chose instead to disobey God, with deadly consequences for the entire human race. "Sin came into the world through one man," Scripture says, "and death through sin, and so death spread to all men because all sinned" (Rom. 5:12). As a result of Adam's original sin, every member of the human race has fallen short of the glory of God (Rom. 3:22–23). We are all natural-born sinners. To make matters worse, our sinful nature makes us guilty before God. "The judgment following one trespass brought about condemnation," not just for Adam, but for everyone: "one man's trespass led to condemnation for all men" (Rom. 5:16, 18; cf. John 3:36).

But suppose that this is not what happened after all. Imagine that God did not say anything to Adam about eating or not eating from any tree because, in fact, there was no Adam. Take Adam out of human history, and with him the fateful choice that corrupted God's good creation. In that case, what accounts for humanity's universal depravity?

Presumably, in the absence of any historical fall, each of us would stand before God on the basis of our own obedience or disobedience. We would bear no guilt for anyone's sin but our own. Certainly we would bear no guilt for Adam's sin, because the man never existed. Thus the historical basis for the doctrine of original sin has disappeared. If we find ourselves in a sinful condition, it is not because of our solidarity with Adam's sin, but only because of our own choice to sin against God.

This takes us back to the question that divided Augustine from Pelagius in the fourth and fifth centuries. Do we sin because we are sinners, or are we sinners because we sin? Once Adam is out of the story, it is hard to avoid the conclusion that our depravity is coincidental. For Pelagius, we do not come into the world with a sin nature, but each of us has the ability to choose whether we will obey or disobey God. We live in sinless innocence until we first choose to sin.

The Augustinian view, by contrast, holds that the universality of sin has a point of origin in human history. We are all equally sinful because all of us bear the guilt of the first sin of the first man. In the words of the rhyme that New England schoolchildren used to recite when they learned their ABCS, "In Adam's fall, we sinned all." This tragic event from human history makes sense of the psalmist's claim that he was "brought forth in iniquity" (Ps. 51:5), legitimates the prophet's appeal to Adam as a covenant-breaker (Hos. 6:7), and justifies the apostle's assertion that we are "by nature children of wrath" (Eph. 2:3). We are not just people who happen to sin; we are sinners who sinned in Adam.

3. The historical Adam accounts for the presence of evil in the world.

Sin is not the only doctrine that suffers when we doubt or deny the historical Adam. Deleting his story from the biblical macro-narrative also problematizes the doctrine of evil.

To be sure, evil is a problem for any theology. Those who lay its blame at the feet of Adam (or Satan, for that matter) still have to explain why God would permit his creatures to divide his heavenly court or mar his creation by choosing what is bad instead of what is good. Furthermore, we will never resolve our questions about evil without wrestling with them at the foot of the cross, where God the Son suffered the very worst evils in order to secure our salvation.

Nevertheless, the historical Adam sets the presence of evil in its proper context. At a minimum, a real Adam accounts for the origin of *moral evil*—that is, the evil that arises from human sin. If our father had not eaten the forbidden fruit, the world would never have known human trafficking, sexual abuse, terrorism, or a thousand other heinous iniquities.

Then add the physical calamities that afflict humanity: tornadoes, earthquakes, tsunamis, and hurricanes, as well as pestilence and deadly disease. Are these natural disasters—the sufferings that some philosophers place under the category of *natural evil*—part of God's creative intent for his people? If so, then God would be open to the charge that he is the author of evil. To express the problem most provocatively, if Adam did not fall, then God did, by putting human beings into a world inimical to their survival.

Fortunately, the first sin of the first man opens up other avenues of explanation. Adam's fall had consequences for creation. Moral and natural evil do not originate in the heart of God but in the choice of the free, upright moral agent God created as the representative of our race (see Eccl. 7:29). As a result of that man's iniquity, God subjected creation to temporary corruption in the hope of final redemption (see Rom. 8:19–22). The historical Adam thus helps to explain human pain and suffering without attributing any failure to God. When we see "nature red in tooth and claw," as Alfred Tennyson described it,[2] we are not seeing the world as it was meant to be, but as it became in consequence of Adam's sin.

This gives us solid hope to share with people in distress. However tempting it is to blame God for the sufferings of a fallen world, the real cause of all our woe is Adam's sinful choice. As for God, he stands resolutely against sin and all its fatal consequences. When we go to God for help in times of trouble—and when we invite other people to do so—we can trust his goodness completely, knowing that he is the enemy of evil and has a plan to destroy it.

4. The historical Adam (with the historical Eve) clarifies the biblical position on sexual identity and family relationships.

We have already noted that Adam has a representative role for the human race. This is not somehow at odds with his historicity. Indeed, for the first man to serve as a proper representative, he must have some form of solidarity with the people he represents. Adam's influence on our destiny is grounded in the shared nature of our common humanity.

The connection between Adam's particularity and the universal implications of his person and actions for the rest of the human race

2. Alfred Lord Tennyson, *In Memoriam* LVI, line 15.

extend to sexuality, marriage, and our relationships in the home and in the church. The answer to the question "Who were Adam and Eve?" provides essential information for answering the question, "Who am I?" Our sex is not simply the product of evolutionary change, but is part of the Creator's deliberate ordering of humanity. God made the man and the woman equal, but not identical. From the beginning they were different and complementary. This opened up the possibility for them to marry, as God brought the two together to become "one flesh" (Gen. 2:24).

That Adam and Eve have archetypal significance is evident from their very names: "Man" and "Woman." But when the Bible refers back to Genesis in order to explain marriage and sexual relationships, it appeals to concrete details in the historical narrative. For example, in order to clarify his teaching on marriage and divorce, Jesus referenced the actions, words, and intentions of God in creating Adam and Eve as a single pair—one man united to one woman for life (Matt. 19:4–6). When Paul wanted to explain the divine order of husband-wife relationships in the home and male-female relationships in the church, he appealed to the way God made Adam and Eve in the first place (1 Cor. 11:8–10) and to the circumstances of their fall into sin (1 Tim. 2:12–14).

These passages are famously difficult to interpret, especially when it comes to disentangling what is culture-specific from what is universal in Paul's instructions. The point to make here is that with any interpretation, the apostolic argument is grounded in the history of Genesis—on such details as who was made first (Adam) or who was deceived by the serpent's lies (Eve). Paul regards Adam and Eve as persons, not mere symbols, and his appeal to history is part of what makes his instructions normative. Lose the historical Adam, with his wife Eve, and the biblical view of women and men also loses part of its basis.

5. *The historical Adam assures us that we are justified before God.*

In turning to the doctrine of justification, we come to perhaps the strongest biblical argument for the historical Adam, as well as to our most pressing place of personal need. It is not simply the doctrine of sin that depends on an authentic Adam, but also the doctrines of salvation.

In Romans 5:12–21 Paul sets up the problem of humanity and its solution. In doing so, he structures his entire argument around the connection between Adam and Christ. It is as if these are the only two men who ever lived—the two men whose lives determine our destiny. Our standing before God is decided by our connection to one or both of these two persons. The sin of the one man Adam condemns us, making us guilty before God and resulting in our death. By contrast, the obedience of the one man Christ grants us righteousness by faith, justifies us before God, and leads to eternal life. We are either perishing in Adam or being saved in Christ (cf. 1 Cor. 1:18).

The link between Adam and Christ is not merely analogical, but also historical. As Paul describes the actions of these two men, he refers to things that actually happened in time and space. Adam trespassed, and as a result of his disobedience, death spread to the entire human race. If Adam's fall were only a story used by way of illustration, it could hardly have this effect in the world. Similarly, Christ obeyed, and as a result of his righteousness, many are justified. The life that Christ secures is as real as the death that Adam unleashed. But for this to be the case, the righteousness of Christ must somehow address a problem that truly exists, as a result of something that Adam actually did.

Implied in the parallel between Adam and Christ is that both men serve as representatives for their people. How can a single trespass or one act of righteousness either condemn or justify an entire race? Only if the person who transgresses or obeys does so on behalf of others, in which case the guilt or grace of that action may properly be transferred to their moral account. Paul's teaching in Romans 5 is that just as Adam's sin was imputed to the rest of his race, so also Christ's righteousness was reckoned to many by faith.

This assumes, of course, that the transgression or the act of obedience actually took place. Genesis 3 and Matthew 4 must be more than stories told to make a moral point; they must serve as reliable accounts of true historical events. After all, no one is condemned by a fable or justified by a fiction. Paul develops the parallel between Adam and Christ as he does because he knows that our destiny depends on it. Our soteriological connection to Christ is grounded in our anthropological connection to Adam. If we remain in Adam, then the guilt of his sin and our sin will bring us under the wrath of God. But if we come to Christ, we will be rescued by his atoning work. Both men are real representatives, which makes our salvation as real as our sin.

6. The historical Adam advances the missionary work of the church.

Most Western Christians regard the biblical genealogies as among the least relevant, least interesting passages in Scripture. What value is there in reading long lists of difficult names?

In other parts of the world, however, the reaction is nearly the opposite. As some missionaries have discovered, genealogies that trace back to the beginning of human history have a way of confirming that the Bible is trustworthy and true. When some cultures learn that the family records in the Old and New Testaments go all the way back to the first man, Adam, they know that the Bible does not tell someone else's story, but their own. This, in turn, helps to confirm the credibility of the gospel. The story that tells the truth about our ancestry in Adam can also be trusted to tell the truth about our destiny in Christ. The Bible announces to every tribe its forefather and to every clan the Savior.

The instinct to find identity in a common patriarch at the root of humanity's family tree is not the only way that believing in Adam supports the missionary work of the church. As we have seen, Adam's historicity explains the commonality of human sin. Sin and guilt are not acquired by cultural conditioning. All of us have a shared ancestor who rebelled against our common Creator. This gives missionaries and evangelists the certainty that every person they meet has the same sinful nature and thus the same need for salvation. Knowing why we are all equally sinful gives clarity and confidence in communicating the gospel across cultures. Our common predicament is part of a shared history that provides a point of contact for every conversation in which we share the good news.

Our unity in Adam also affirms humanity's unique and equal dignity, which is another crucial premise for Christian witness. The historical Adam leaves no room for *polygenism*—for human beings coming from different lineages and thus potentially having inferior or superior blood lines. We all belong to one family, and our common creation in the image of God is part of the Bible's impregnable wall against racial prejudice. The *imago Dei* is not an abstraction, but has a concrete basis in history. The divine image was granted to Adam and Eve as the first man and the first woman to represent our race (Gen. 1:27), and therefore it is an identity and calling we all share.

God "made from one man every nation of mankind to live on all the face of the earth" (Acts 17:26). This kinship calls for charity. The Adamic unity of the human race is part of the basis for loving our neighbor—a love we show supremely by sharing the good news about Jesus. Our family connection through Adam does more than explain what is wrong with our world; it also calls us to act in the interests of our common destiny by proclaiming the gospel to all our cousins.

7. *The historical Adam secures our hope in the resurrection of the body and the life everlasting.*

Romans 5 is not the only place where Paul draws logical connections between Adam and Christ, nor is justification the only evangelical doctrine that the apostle grounds in the history of early Genesis. His argument for the bodily resurrection is based, similarly, on the parallel between the first and the last Adam.

Paul's purpose in 1 Corinthians 15 is to prove that believers in Christ will receive the same type of immortal body that the Holy Spirit gave to Jesus in his third-day triumph over the grave. To make his case, he compares the earthly body that God first gave to Adam in creation with the heavenly body that God gave to Jesus in his resurrection. He does not present Adam as a universal, but as a particular—not as a symbol, but as a named individual: "the first man Adam" (1 Cor. 15:45). Then, to describe the makeup of this man, the apostle appeals to a detail from the Genesis narrative: "The first man was from the earth, a man of dust" (1 Cor. 15:47).

The apostle is not giving a biology lesson here, of course, but he is making the point that we are made of the same stuff as the father of our race. This matters because the body we have in this life structures the body we will have in the life to come: "As was the man of dust, so are those who are of the dust; and as is the man of heaven, so are those who are of heaven. Just as we have borne the image of the man of dust, we shall also bear the image of the man of heaven" (1 Cor. 15:48–49). Because we are connected to Christ, the last Adam, our bodies will be raised on the last day, and we will bear the eternal image of the Son of God. But for this to be the case, we must first bear the dust-born image of the first Adam. To put on an immortal, imperishable body (1 Cor. 15:53), we must first have the mortal, perishable body that we inherited from "the man of dust." Thus the starting point for Paul's gospel of the resurrection is the historical Adam.

For Paul's analogy to hold true from beginning to end — and for us therefore to have confidence that God has promised us a real body in our resurrection — the reality of Adam's body must be maintained. Ontology is connected to eschatology. Did the first man have a real life or only a literary one? Was his body physical or merely fictional? Remove a material Adam from Paul's argument, and we have no bodies to be raised.

Earlier we noted that denying the historical Adam deletes the first chapter in the history of redemption. Here we see the effect this has on the last chapter. To deny the historicity of Adam is to take an essentially Gnostic view of early Genesis that severs creation from the consummation. The story line of Scripture forms an *inclusio* that begins with a bodily creation and ends with a bodily resurrection. If we conclude that the early chapters of the Bible are largely symbolic and that the Adam of Genesis is a literary figure rather than an historical person, then we adopt a hermeneutic that threatens to make the new heavens and the new earth promised in the last chapters of the Bible equally insubstantial.

Adam in Full

This brief outline of biblical doctrines that are closely connected to Adam is suggestive rather than conclusive. It may raise as many questions as it tries to answer.

What should be unmistakable, however, is that defending or denying the historical Adam has a direct bearing on many areas of faith and practice. His person serves an integrating function in Christian theology. Far from being readily isolable from the rest of biblical doctrine or peripheral to a thoroughly Christian view of the world, Adam's history and identity help us understand everything from creation to the consummation.

Just as importantly, believing in the historical Adam also helps us know how to tell the gospel story in the biblical way. Rather than excluding him from our defense of the Christian faith out of fear that he is an obstacle to conversion, we should let him retain his proper place in a full articulation of the gospel. The unity of humanity in Adam, wrote B. B. Warfield, is "the postulate of the entire body of the Bible's teaching—of its doctrine of Sin and Redemption alike: so that the whole structure of the Bible's teaching, including all that we know as its doctrine of salvation, rests on it and implicates it."[3] Adam should not be omitted from our apologetics and evangelism, therefore, but included the way Paul included him at Athens (Acts 17:26).

The goal of reaching skeptics for whom mainstream science casts doubt on the biblical account of creation is laudable. So is the wider goal of understanding humanity's story through both general and special revelation, through science as well as Scripture. Yet these goals must be pursued with theological integrity. Since at many points denying Adam's existence appears to be inconsistent with Christian orthodoxy, those who hold this view have the burden to prove how it strengthens rather than weakens an evangelical commitment to the universality of sin and guilt, the possibility of justification, the hope of resurrection, and other necessary doctrines of the Christian faith.

3. Benjamin Warfield, "On the Antiquity and the Unity of the Human Race," *Princeton Theological Review* 9.1 (1911): 19; also in *Biblical and Theological Studies*, ed. Samuel G. Craig (Philadelphia: Presbyterian and Reformed, 1968), 255.

NAME INDEX

SCRIPTURE INDEX